How to Achieve 27001 Certification

How to Achieve 27001 Certification

An Example of Applied Compliance Management

Sigurjon Thor Arnason · Keith D. Willett

Auerbach Publications
Taylor & Francis Group
New York   London

CRC Press is an imprint of the
Taylor & Francis Group, an **informa** business

Auerbach Publications
Taylor & Francis Group
6000 Broken Sound Parkway NW, Suite 300
Boca Raton, FL 33487-2742

International Standard Book Number-13: 978-0-8493-3648-5 (Hardcover)

Library of Congress Cataloging-in-Publication Data

Arnason, Sigurjon Thor.
How to achieve 27001 certification: an example of applied compliance management / Sigurjon Thor Arnason and Keith Willett.
p. cm.
Includes bibliographical references and index.
ISBN-13: 978-0-8493-3648-5 (alk. paper)
1. Electronic data processing personnel--Certification. 2. Computer security--Management--Examinations--Study guides. I. Willett, Keith. II. Title.

QA76.3.A77 2007
005.8--dc22
                                                                    2007015620

Visit the Taylor & Francis Web site at
http://www.taylorandfrancis.com

and the Auerbach Web site at
http://www.auerbach-publications.com

Contents

Preface

This book is primarily for the chief security officer (CSO), security management, and security professionals responsible for establishing and maintaining a security management program. The International Standards Organization (ISO) security standards provide an excellent foundation for identifying business risks and addressing those risks through a disciplined security management process. The intent of this text is to align security with organizational goals and generate *effective* security and compliance management programs. The primary goal is to assist the reader in developing an *information security management system* (ISMS) that enables the organization to obtain ISO 27001 certification.

Many security programs find foundation in the good experiences of the personnel working them. Although this is not bad, it is not always optimal. We, the authors, advocate a security management program with a foundation in industry security standards. Although no single industry security standard provides all the answers, a good industry standard does provide a widely accepted, proven framework within which to define a security program, and it provides a foundation from which to build that security program to satisfy the particular needs of the organization. This text uses the security standards ISO 27002 (formerly ISO 17799) and ISO 27001 as a foundation to develop a security management program as well as a compliance management program. The authors advocate supplementing the ISO standards with other organizational relevant standards like COBIT (Control Objectives for Information and Related Technology), National Institute of Standards and Technology (NIST), and Information Technology Infrastructure Library (ITIL); and organizational relevant compliance requirements like Sarbanes–Oxley (SOX) and the Health Insurance Portability and Accountability Act (HIPAA). Although there are many ways to "skin a cat," this is our way. We offer insights from our own experiences and provide a good starting point for the novice and some finer nuances for the seasoned security professional.

I thank my wife, Terri Meyer Willett, for her understanding and patience with the time commitment generating such a text requires. I welcome constructive feedback regarding the accuracy of the text as well as comments or ideas for potential future editions. Please provide feedback to Keith Willett at kwillett@ctntechnologies.com. Thank you for your purchase of this book and good luck in your endeavors to build an ISMS and achieve ISO 27001 certification.

Keith D. Willett, MScIA, CISSP, ISSAP

Implementing an information security management system can be demanding, as there is a need for resources from the business. Hopefully this book will help to reduce the workload, as it describes how information security can be implemented for audit and certification according to international standards. There are many ways to implement an information security management system as the organizational standard; because the system often tells what has to be done, but not how to do it, there is much leeway in interpretation. This book describes our view and our journey on the path to audit and certification according to the ISO 27001[1] standard. Other paths can be equal or better contingent on the business. I was inspired to write this book when I found that a book on this subject was missing. Writing a book on an international standard can be an endless task if you want to describe every view. This book illustrates our view, and we hope it will help those reading it get a better understanding on this issue.

I thank all the people who have helped me in writing the book. A special thanks to the following: Bjarnheidur Drofn Thrastardottir, my wife, for her help, understanding and support; Rich O'Hanley, my editor, without whom none of this would be possible; Keith Willett, my co-author; and Thomas R. Peltier, for his guidance. If you find inaccuracies or errors, or have any constructive comments, or ideas for potential future editions, please provide feedback to me at sigurjon.arnason@gmail.com or 27000@visir.is. I would be very grateful.

Sigurjon Thor Arnason

Introduction

The audience for this text is the chief security officer (CSO), security management, and security professionals, plus all others who have an interest in a disciplined approach to developing, implementing, and managing an information security program. The security practitioner who manages day-to-day security operations benefits from a clear alignment of security operations with management goals. Security management develops operational plans and performance goals with clear alignment to business risk management initiatives. Executives are able to incorporate into their governance process the ability to identify business risks and determine policy to address business risk with clear alignment to business drivers and business value. These three functions of security governance, management, and operations all work together to achieve optimal security measures to accomplish business goals.

Business challenges today include the need to identify and manage risk in an ever-changing environment of technical capability, technical complexity, and compliance complexity. ISO 27001 offers a disciplined approach that addresses business risk through assisting with legislative, regulatory, and other compliance management and passing compliance audits. Obtaining ISO 27001 certification is validation of good security management practices and offers proof of due diligence in addressing business risks, including risks to information and information technology.

There are many definitions of information security. For purposes of discussing ISO 27001 certification and compliance management, information security safeguards information and information technology to ensure confidentiality, integrity, and availability. Information security is sometimes abbreviated as *infosec*, and an alternate term of similar meaning is *information assurance* (IA). All these terms transcend a scope of merely data. Data resides on electronic media as well as on paper documents. Electronic media and paper documents reside within computers or file cabinets in offices within buildings. Data in transit may be across a network within the organizational boundaries or across the public network (Internet), cellular phones, laptops, in briefcases containing paper documents, or on magnetic tapes bound for off-site storage. The risks to data—to information—include risks inherent with personnel, organizational practices, physical aspects (e.g., buildings, offices, data centers), access control, communications, operations management, mobile computing, acquisition of hardware and software, and much more. Effective information security addresses risks in all these areas.

The root principle behind security is to ensure mission integrity, where the mission defines the reason for the existence of the organization. There are ever-present threats to mission integrity, including entities and events that may disclose sensitive information, modify information, disrupt the operating environment, and prohibit the timely use of information. Security is necessary to ensure *confidentiality, integrity,* and *availability* of key business functions, information, information technology, organizational resources, infrastructure, and relationships with partners, vendors, and customers; in short, security mitigates risks to mission integrity. Business areas exposed to risk do include the technical environment; however, there is much more than just information or information technology to consider for information security.

An emerging concern within the business environment with respect to information security is *compliance management*. Compliance management includes legislative and regulatory compliance as well as contractual obligations and other areas governing correct action on the part of personnel and automated entities performing business functions. Another set of security compliance requirements may be the security standards that the organization imposes on itself to ensure good security practices. Chapter 6, "Compliance Management," presents how to develop a compliance management program and incorporate the International Standards Organization (ISO) security standards as a basis for that program.

ISO Security Standards

This text uses the ISO security standards to assist in identifying relevant business risks and managing those business risks through the discipline of a formal information security management program. The details herein present a practical perspective on the ISO standards ISO 27002:2005, *Code of Practice for Information Security Management* (ISO 27002), and ISO 27001:2005, *Information Security Management Systems—Requirements* (ISO 27001). The reader will encounter guidance and tools on how to apply ISO 27002 and ISO 27001 to establish and manage what ISO 27001 calls an *information security management system* (ISMS), as well as a methodology to define internally imposed security requirements (e.g., ISO 27002) as part of a larger compliance management program. Chapter 1, "Introduction to International Standards Organization Security Standards," presents more detail on the ISO 27000 family and their interrelationships.

Important note: This text is not a replacement for obtaining the ISO standards, but a supplemental document that provides insight on getting the most out of the

ISO standards. To obtain the ISO standards, reference www.iso.org* or another reseller.

The use of the ISO security standards provides a broadly accepted foundation on which to build an organizational-specific security program or, as ISO refers to, an ISMS. In general, industry standards provide lessons learned from other organizations and promote consistency and comprehensiveness. "If I have seen further, it is by standing on the shoulders of giants"†; indeed, the executive, manager, and security practitioner will all benefit from using the ISO security standards as broad shoulders on which to stand, see the horizon, and progress in establishing and managing a quality security program.

The map of the territory is not the territory; the territory is your organization, your business environment, your operating environment. The ISO standards provide raw material to help map the security of your organization as well as the business and operating environment to which information security applies. ISO 27002, *Code of Practice for Information Security Management*, provides a technically agnostic perspective on establishing and managing information security controls. This text uses the details of ISO 27002 to establish a security management framework in which to define the organizational security program, assess the status of the security program, perform a gap analysis, and plan for gap closure, that is, increase compliance levels with ISO 27002. The details herein limit the perspective to ISO; however, no security standard is one size fits all. Expand the security management framework as befits your organization and your circumstances. The ISO-based framework and tools enable the claim that the organization is at least ISO 27002‡ consistent, hopefully compliant, and perhaps more, depending on the additional details to the framework.

ISO 27001§ provides requirements for an ISMS and describes a process on achieving such. The organization may even obtain ISO 27001 certification. Such a distinction shows a commitment to a disciplined management system in which to establish, implement, manage, and maintain an ISMS. The details herein provide guidance for executives, management, and security specialists to understand what a good information security management system is, how to plan for and implement an ISMS, and how to prepare for an audit of the ISMS to achieve ISO 27001 certification. Chapter 2, "Information Security Management System," presents more ISMS details.

---

* Last accessed November 2006.
† Sir Isaac Newton.
‡ All references to ISO 27002 herein refer specifically to the ISO 27002:2005 version unless otherwise noted.
§ All references to ISO 27001 herein refer specifically to the ISO 27001:2005 version unless otherwise noted.

ISO 27002 provides details on what to do and why (policy guidance), but not on how to do (procedures) or what mechanisms to use (standards). ISO 27001 provides details on how to establish a management system for information security. Interpretation of many aspects of these standards is organizational specific. As a starting point, Table 3.1 in Chapter 3, "Foundational Concepts and Tools for an Information Security Management System," provides an interpretation of the ISO 27002 standard. This interpretation is notional and is not comprehensive, but a good start toward defining an interpretation that fits your organizational needs.

ISO Security Standard Certification

The ISO is developing a new series of security standards, the first of which is ISO 27001, *Information Technology—Security Techniques— Information Security Management Systems—Requirements*. ISO 27001 replaces British Standard (BS) 7799, Part 2. BS 7799, Part 1 evolved into ISO 17799, *Information Technology—Security Techniques—Code of Practice for Information Security Management* and is now known as ISO 27002. Definitive plans are not yet available; however, tentative plans for additional ISO security standards in the 27000 numbering series include ISO 27003, covering security implementation guidance; ISO 27004, for metrics and measurements; and ISO 27005, covering risk management. For more detail, see www.iso.org.

Certification against these ISO standards is only defined for ISO 27001, that is, an organization may be certified ISO 27001 compliant. ISO 27001 describes how to build what ISO calls an ISMS. An ISMS is a process to create and maintain a management system for information security. ISO 27001 references details from ISO 27002 and describes how to apply the ISO 27002 security controls; however, the organization is not ISO 27002 certified. By virtue of using ISO 27002 and adhering closely to the guidelines therein, an organization may claim to be ISO 27002 compliant, but without official recognition of this claim via certification. Chapter 5, "Audit and Certification," contains more details on preparing for and obtaining ISO 27001 certification.

Why Certify against ISO 27001?

Certification finds no basis in legislative or regulatory requirement, so why bother? The best answer is to validate that investment in security controls meets business goals and provides business value. Business value is found in managing business risk, achieving high levels of legislative and regulatory compliance, and managing vulnerabilities and threats. The ISO security standards provide a disciplined approach to information security, business risk management, and compliance management. Certification provides an independent validation that the organization has applied that discipline effectively and proves due diligence on the part of executives and management, that they are addressing the information security needs of the organization.

The business value of certification includes a disciplined approach that promotes the development of security management processes, methodologies, tools, and templates that may be reused across the organization and through security planning, implementation, operations, monitoring, tracking, and reporting. With basis in an industry standard like ISO, the tracking and reporting tools promote easier audits; this implies less cost of the actual audit and higher likelihood of passing an audit.

Goals

The text sets out to increase reader awareness and understanding of the following:

- Foundation for creating a security management framework (SMF) and for establishing an ISMS
- ISMS and compliance management tools based on:
  - ISO 27002
  - ISO 27001
- Process to apply the tools in context of:
  - Planning for an ISMS
  - Implementation of an ISMS
- ISO 27001 certification:
  - Planning for certification
  - Obtaining certification

Details include defining what a security management framework is, the need for one, and the many uses of an SMF in establishing and maintaining an ISMS. There are many options in security standards on which to base the SMF. The reader will learn to evaluate and select security standards appropriate for an SMF specifically useful to his or her organization. The text focus is on the ISO 17001 and ISO 27002 standards as foundations for the SMF examples herein. A set of tools with basis in the SMF provides reusable resources to leverage across the organization. A common set of tools promotes consistency in assessments and tracking results. Application of the tools also supports ISMS planning and implementation. Moreover, a set of tools with foundation in the ISO security standards provides support achieving ISO 27001 certification.

Outline and Flow

The flow of this text uses the following outline:

- Introduction and overview of ISO security standards, the ISO 27000 family
- ISMS
- Security management framework
- Establish a starting point for developing an ISMS
- Developing the ISMS
- Audit and certification
- Compliance management

The ISO is developing a new set of standards dedicated to security, the ISO 27000 family. There is an introduction to this family with focus on the first official member, ISO 27001, and a soon-to-be-adopted member, ISO 27002. The ISO 27001 focus is on the ISMS, which is a discipline to establish, implement, manage, and maintain a security program. The ISMS uses a development, review, and revision cycle known as the Plan-Do-Check-Act (PDCA) model. The initial iteration of the PDCA model is slightly different from subsequent iterations. The initial iteration establishes from scratch or organizes existing practices under the discipline of a formal ISMS. There is a presentation of the initial development effort, then ongoing repetitions of the PDCA cycle for a disciplined maintenance of the ISMS; Chapter 4, "Implementing an Information Security Management System— Plan-Do-Check-Act," contains details of the PDCA process as the ongoing management cycle for information security.

Using the ISO security standards is an excellent step toward establishing good security practice to manage business risks effectively. Some organizations may desire official recognition of this good practice via certification. Material herein covers how to prepare for and achieve ISO 27001 certification. Moreover, there is an industry need for a compliance management discipline that transcends the ISO security standards and incorporates other compliance requirements, like legislative, regulatory, and contractual requirements. The compliance management methodology presents how to leverage the same ISMS processes and tools in a compliance management program; essentially, the ISMS becomes one instance of a broader compliance management capability.

Establishing a set of compliance management tools provides consistency, repeatability, and comprehensiveness. For larger organizations, such tools promote common language and understanding among what may be physically disperse organizations. Moreover, the tools and templates provide commonality such that multiple results produced by many different people may be compared apples-to-apples, and the analyst may produce an aggregate enterprise view from many disparate inputs.

The flow of the material presentation includes purpose, process, framework, tools, and application of each to identify and manage business risk. The purpose is the driving force behind security. The process is how to achieve an ISMS. The framework is a foundational construct that promotes consistency and comprehensiveness in defining, planning, assessing, implementing, tracking, and reporting on the ISMS. The tools provide assistance with defining the ISMS (the to-be state), assessing the current situation (the as-is state), performing a gap analysis (the difference between as-is and to-be), developing a transition plan (the process to move from as-is to to-be), prioritizing gap closure activities, tracking gap closure activities, implementing, reporting, and especially aligning all this with business* drivers.

Commentary

"Success in playing the game changes the game and tenacity in playing the old game converts success into failure."† This phrase is the root principle behind innovation. Security is vastly misunderstood and misrepresented in industry. Security professionals do a less than spectacular job in justifying security investments, quantifying expectations, measuring results, and proving business value. One result is an executive perspective that security is nice to have, but other aspects of the business take priority. Well, the game has changed. Security is no longer a "nice to have," but a legislative mandate. Examples include Sarbanes–Oxley (SOX)[16] in the United States and Basel II[17] in Europe. A formal methodology to define and execute an ISMS is essential to perform and prove due diligence in upholding stakeholder interests and legislative compliance.

Moreover, the concepts and legal requirements of due diligence and fiduciary responsibility require executives to address security and *prove* due diligence. If these reasons are not enough, there remains the principle of ensuring mission integrity in a new world-connected economy—this is just good business. While providing quality, effective security to ensure compliance and mission integrity, the security professional also needs to align security initiatives with business drivers and prove the business value of security. Our operating mantra should be, "If we cannot justify it in business terms, we should not be doing it." This text intends to provide guidance to define a security management program (an ISMS) in such a manner

---

* This text uses the terms *business* and *mission* interchangeably. ISO security standards have mainly a commercial focus; however, the concepts, methodology, and tools herein may apply to government as well, where the term *mission* may be more applicable than *business*.

† Jamshid Gharajedaghi.

that aligns with business goals and provides the ability to plan for, implement, track, and report on the business value of security.

At this point, the reader may wish to review the glossary for a brief introduction to terms, phrases, and definitions used in this text. A common lexicon and understanding of terms provide a foundation for understanding.

Chapter 1

Introduction to International Standards Organization Security Standards

This chapter begins by assuming the reader is generally familiar with information security, including what it is, and the potential application of information security within the organization. The assumption is that reader motivations are to apply a discipline to information security to be better at planning, implementing, and maintaining information security and achieving a highly effective information security program that is capable of receiving ISO 27001 certification. This chapter begins discussing such a discipline with an overview of security standards and with specific attention to existing and emerging International Standards Organization (ISO) security standards.

1.1   Objectives

Objectives for this chapter include presentation of the following:

- The cornerstones of information security
- A brief history of the ISO security standards
- A list of ISO security standards and the intent behind each
- An introduction to ISO 27001 and ISO 27002

- The relationship between ISO 27001 and ISO 27002
- The relationship of ISO 27001 and ISO 27002 to other ISO management standards
- An introduction to the Plan-Do-Check-Act (PDCA) model

This material provides the basis for an introduction of the information security management system (ISMS), which is the foundation of achieving ISO 27001 certification.

1.2 Cornerstones of Information Security

Traditional organizational assets are predominantly tangible in the form of property, equipment, buildings, desks, money, or other negotiable assets, like gold. Security concerns were mostly physical, in the form of guards, walls, vaults, and safes. Organizational assets today have added virtual assets like intellectual property in the form of electronic-based media (e.g., word processing files, spreadsheets, and databases). Moreover, negotiable assets are bits on a hard drive and transactions are executed via bit transfers on a network, wired or wireless. Organizational wealth is largely represented by cyber bits; hence, there is a need to protect these assets via information security controls. The traditional view of information security includes the three cornerstones of information security: confidentiality, integrity, and availability, also known as the CIA of information security. Confidentiality, integrity, and availability are security objectives where the intent of confidentiality is to ensure that only authorized personnel may access information or, to the contrary, ensure that information is not disclosed to unauthorized persons or entities (e.g., automated system or service). To ensure integrity is to guard against unauthorized modification or destruction of information, or that the information remains in the format the creator intended. A loss of integrity is the unauthorized modification or destruction of information. Availability ensures information is ready for use. A loss of availability is the disruption of access to or use of information or an information technology. Figure 1.1 illustrates the three cornerstones of confidentiality, integrity, and availability (CIA). FIPS PUB 199[3] contains more detail on the three cornerstones of information security.

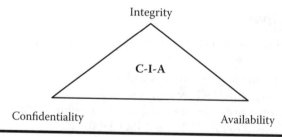

Figure 1.1 Security cornerstones.

How can an organization manage information security and the three corner-stones of security? One answer is to implement an ISMS and use the ISO standards as a guide to develop an effective ISMS. PDCA provides the methodology to implement an ISMS. ISO 27002 (formerly ISO 17799) provides the foundation for an effective ISMS, and ISO 27001 provides guidance on how to implement an ISMS via the PDCA process.

1.3 The History of ISO Information Security Standards

The U.K. Department of Trade and Industry (DTI) established a working group to produce a code of good security practice. The DTI published the *User Code of Practice* standard[4] in 1989. This standard was essentially a list of security controls that at the time were considered suitable, normal, and good practice, as well as applicable to the technology and environment of the time.

Figure 1.2 presents the development of ISO 27001[1] and the ISO 17799[2] (ISO 27002). The DTI user code of practice was published as a British Standard (BS) guidance document and later as a BS with the name BS 7799:1995, Part 1. Part 1 includes a list of controls that was a set of best practices for information security. A second part of the standard was added as BS 7799:1998, Part 2. The intent of Part 2 was an instrument to measure and monitor Part 1 and to provide a benchmark for certification. Following subsequent revision, Part 1 was published as

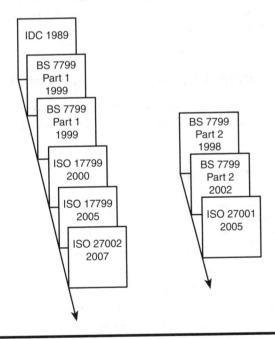

Figure 1.2   Development of the ISO 27001 and ISO 27002 standards.

BS 7799:1999, Part 1, proposed as an international standard (ISO), and published as ISO 17799:2000. Revision of Part 2 was released as BS 7799:2002, Part 2. The standard ISO 17799 was revised yet again and released as ISO 17799:2005, then a name change to ISO 27002:2005 in July 2007 BS 7799, Part 2 was then proposed as an international standard and was published as ISO 27001:2005. The next section presents the ISO road map for international information security standards in the new 27000 series.

1.4 Information Security Standards Road Map and Numbering

The ISO and the International Electrotechnical Commission (IEC) work jointly on international standards and guidelines. One joint objective is to produce security management standards. The collective effort for producing security standards includes Working Group 1 (WG1), Working Group 2 (WG2), and Working Group 3 (WG3). All these working groups are part of Subcommittee 27 (SC27), which is in turn part of Joint Technical Committee 1 (JTC1).[5] The scope of WG1 is security management standards including areas pertaining to new developments of standards in information security and development of ISMS standards. The aim of WG1 is to have a road map that identifies the requirements for a future set of international standards and guidelines to establish, implement, operate, monitor, and maintain ISMS. To support this road map, the ISO/IEC has decided on a new number series (27000) for international information security standards.

1.5 International Security Management Standards

Table 1.1 presents a list and brief description of some security standards that are or will be published in the ISO 27000 series. Anything marked "pending" is speculative at the time of this writing.

Table 1.1   ISO 27000 Family

ISO/IEC Standard	Description
(Pending) Vocabulary and definitions.	
27001	Information Security Management System requirements (specification)
27002	Code of practice for information security; management
27003	(Pending) Implementation guidance
27004	(Pending) Metric and measurement
27005	(Pending) Risk management

The ISO 27001 standard is discussed in detail throughout this text and is a new international security standard based on BS 7799, Part 2. Organizations that have been certified against BS 7799, Part 2 will have to renew their certification with the latest ISO 27001 standard. ISO 27002 is the new name for ISO 17799. ISO/IEC 27003 covers implementation guidance and is based on Annex B of BS 7799, Part 2; the date for publishing this standard is pending. The PDCA model, also covered in BS 7799, Part 2 (and ISO 27001), not only is used to implement information security standards, but is widely used to implement other management standards, including ISO 9001 and ISO 14001. ISO 27004 will address how to implement metrics to measures to gauge the performance and effectiveness of ISMS operations; again, the date of publishing is pending. ISO 27005 will likely cover risk management and will be comparable to BS 7799, Part 3, *Guideline for Information Security Risk Management.* Other planned standards at this time in the ISO 27000 series are ISO 27006, which is likely to cover the guide to the certification/registration process, and the ISO 27007 Guideline for auditing Information Security Management Systems.

1.6 Other Proposed Information Security Standards

ISO is considering a few other standards, all of which will be part of an international information security management standards road map, including standards that deal with:

■ ISMS monitoring and review guidelines
■ ISMS internal auditing
■ ISMS continual improvements

Other proposed guidelines are sector specific with a focus on healthcare, telecommunication, finance, and insurance. Under the premise that security is not a goal but a process, standards development and evolution will never stand still. As noted previously, the focus of this text is the ISO standards, and only information security standards from the ISO/IEC have been mapped for the near future. However, other national and international bodies have standards that can help to establish, implement, operate, monitor, and maintain an effective ISMS. These include but certainly are not limited to the National Institute of Standards and Technology (NIST) as well as many defense-related standards from the United States and across the globe.

1.7 Introduction to the ISO/IEC 27001 Standard

The ISO 27001 provides a common model for implementing and operating ISMS, and monitoring and improving ISMS operation. The intent of ISO is to harmonize ISO 27001 with other management system standards such as

ISO/IEC 9001:2000, which addresses quality management systems, and ISO/IEC 14001:2004, which addresses environmental management systems. The goal of ISO is to provide consistent and integrated implementation and operation of the ISMS with other management systems within the organization. The similarities among the standards imply similarities in the supporting tools and functions for implementation, managing, reviewing, auditing, and certification. This implies that if the organization has implemented other management standards or plans, too, there may be one audit and one management system where that management system applies to quality management, environmental management, security management, etc.

The 27001 standard provides guidance to implement an ISMS, as well as to obtain a third-party international certificate to prove that security controls exist and operate according to the requirements of the standard. The 27001 standard describes the ISMS as an overall management system from a business risk approach to establish, implement, operate, monitor, and maintain an ISMS. The ISMS should address all the aspects of the organizational structure, policies, planning activities, responsibilities, practices, procedures, processes, and resources. This text is a supplement to the ISO standards, not a replacement; therefore, the authors recommend obtaining the ISO standards relevant to the current organizational goals for a complete reference set.

With the ISMS in place, senior management now has the means to monitor and control security while reducing the residual business risk. After ISMS implementation, the organization may formally secure information and continue to fulfill the organization's customer, legal, regulatory, and stakeholder requirements. If certification is a goal, analyze the specifications in ISO 27001 Sections 4 to 8, as these clauses are mandatory for certification. Annex A in ISO 27001 presents a list of control objects and controls that are the same controls as in ISO 27002, but not the same level of detail. Annex B of ISO 27001 contains a table where the Organization for Economic Cooperation and Development (OECD) principles and corresponding ISMS procedures and PDCA phases show how the information security international standards fulfill the requirement of OECD. If the organization has already implemented ISO 9001 or ISO 14001, Annex C contains a table to correspond to ISO 9001, ISO 14001, and ISO 27001.

Figure 1.3 shows the ISO PDCA model used to implement the ISMS; the PDCA model is sometimes referred to as an ISMS cycle. Use this model to develop, maintain, and continually improve the ISMS. The objective of implementing ISMS is to have an overall management system built in consideration of business risk to implement, operate, monitor, maintain, and improve information security. Sections 4 to 8 in the ISO 27001 standard are mandatory reading, as they describe how the organization should implement and construct its ISMS. In these sections, there are general requirements for the ISMS, including how to establish, manage, monitor, and maintain the ISMS.

Figure 1.3 PDCA model.

1.8 Introduction to the ISO 27002 Standard

ISO 27002, *Code of Practice for Information Security*, is a commonly used international standard for information security throughout the world and provides insight to security controls to protect information and information technology. ISO 27002 does not address how to apply the controls. ISO 27001 provides direction on how to establish a management system that superimposes a discipline over how to select controls and how to establish good practices to apply the security controls. The procedures to actually implement the security controls are up to the organization and will vary according to the physical and technical environment.

What is information security and why is it important? Information security is the protection of an organizational asset (i.e., information) from unauthorized disclosure and unauthorized and unintended modification, and ensures the information is ready for use when needed. Legislation and other compliance requirements address privacy and accurate reporting of finances (e.g., Sarbanes–Oxley), and generally include the need for good security controls surrounding information. Traditionally, organizational asset space consisted mostly of tangible assets like equipment and buildings and negotiable assets like stocks, bonds, currency, or gold. The traditional valuation of an organization also included soft measures like goodwill, but relatively less valuation was given to knowledge, intellectual property, or information. The increase in organizational dependence on information, the value of information to the organization, and the value of the organization that finds root in information (e.g., intellectual property) result in the increased need to protect that information. Moreover, threats to the previous assets space were limited to physical proximity, that is, one needed access to the gold to steal it. Additionally, the thief needed the ability to transport the gold from vaults, through a building, past guards, and during escape, including the crossing of county, state, and national borders.

Information assets are mostly stored online as documents, database entries, or other forms of bits on media. Access to the organizational asset information is via a multitude of pathways, including inside the organization by using internal PCs and networks. If the organization connects to partners, the partners' entire networks offer potential pathways. If the organization connects to the Internet, the entire world has potential access. Access to information in the middle of Missouri in the United States is as close as the nearest computer in Malaysia. Access and ease of transport are well beyond the limits of tangible assets.

Additionally, theft and use of intellectual property may be from a country that does not consider such actions to be illegal, and if so, that country may not have extradition agreements with the United States, the United Kingdom, Iceland, or other countries. Moreover, such theft may be state sponsored to increase that country's ability to compete in the world market. The point is, there are a wide variety of motivations, means, and methodologies that support the threat space to the organizational asset of information. Thus, to remain viable, the organization must take information security seriously and implement an effective ISMS using a disciplined approach. To achieve an effective ISMS, the organization may choose to use the ISO standards as guidelines. ISO 27002 provides 12 chapters addressing security controls:

- Risk assessment and treatment
- Security policy
- Organization of information security
- Asset management
- Human resources security
- Physical and environmental security
- Communication and operations management
- Access control
- Information system acquisition, development, and maintenance
- Information security incident management
- Business continuity management
- Compliance

These 12 chapters cover approximately 39 key elements and 133 controls. Table 1.2 illustrates the structure and a short description of individual controls in

Table 1.2   ISO 27002 Security Control Structure

Control	Definition of security control with statement regarding necessary qualities to fulfill the control requirement
Implementation guidance	Includes information for implementing the control and guidance to fulfill the requirements of the control
Other information	In some controls there is a clause "Other Information," where there are references to information related to the specific control

ISO 27002. Use these guidelines to write policies and procedures, and refer to the objective of the clause to derive the intent. Then use details in the specific control to generate the details of the policies and procedures to satisfy the intent.

1.9 Relationship between ISO 27001 and ISO 27002

ISO 27001 presents a management system. That management system is for information security. ISO 27002 presents guidelines for security controls. ISO 27002 is more the *what* (i.e., a list of useful controls) and ISO 27001 is more the *how* (i.e., a procedure on how to set up a management system that guides how to establish and maintain the security controls). ISO 27001 is not a set of procedures that addresses each ISO 27002 security control; rather, it presents a management process to establish security awareness, set up an organizational infrastructure, and plan, implement, and maintain the security controls. An organization may not receive certification against ISO 27002; rather, the organization receives certification against the management system for information security; that management system is the ISMS in ISO 27001.

Annex A of ISO 27001 references the same controls as ISO 27002 with exactly the same numbering of those controls; however, there is only a short description of these controls in ISO 27001. Both standards along with the guidance in this text provide the ability to achieve ISO 27001 certification.

1.10 Relationship to Other Management Standards

ISO provides many standards for management systems; ISO 9000 is for quality management, ISO 14000 is for environmental management, and ISO 27000 is for security management. ISO 27001 provides an introduction to the relationship of the ISMS with other management standards. ISO 27001 intends to harmonize with other management system standards to provide consistent and integrated implementation and operation of an enterprise management system. Information security standards use the model of PDCA for implementing, monitoring, and improving the ISMS. Other management standards also use the PDCA model. Common features between management standards include:

- All founded on management commitment
- Responsibility definition
- Document control
- Record management
- Training
- Management review
- Internal audit
- Corrective and preventive actions
- Common PDCA model used for implementing and operation
- Audit processes

- Accredited assessment schema based on the common international standard ISO 19011:2002, *Guidelines on Quality and/or Environmental Management System Audit*[16]
- Requirements based on similar standards
- Certification body responsible for verifying auditor competence

If the opportunity presents, organizations that have more than one management standard to implement and manage may extend their ISMS to cover all management standards. The use of ISMS across many management standards and other essential compliance may be called a compliance management program (CMP). [See Chapter 6.] Benefits to one management system include leveraging investments in a single management system across the organization, a single point of focus for the auditors and certification, and ultimately less cost to the organization.

1.11 PDCA and Security Standards Cross-Reference

Any list of international, national, or other best practice standards in support of effective security management is destined to be incomplete. However, this section presents some of the more common standards in relation to the PDCA model (the numbers in brackets correspond to the references listed at the end of this book). Focus is on ISO, NIST, and British Standard Institute (BSI) standards.

1.11.1 Standards to Assist in the Plan Phase

ISO/IEC 27001, *Information Technology—Security Techniques—Information Security Management Systems—Requirements*, first edition, October 15, 2005, available from www.iso.org.

Control Objectives for Information and Related Technology (COBIT), available from www.isaca.org.

ISO/IEC 17799, *Information Technology—Security Techniques—Code of Practice for Information Security Management*, second edition, June 15, 2005, available from www.iso.org (now ISO 27002).

FIPS PUB 199, *Federal Information Processing Standards Publication—Standard for Federal Information and Information Systems*, February 2004, available from www.nist.gov.

SP 800-60, *Guide to Mapping Types of Information Systems to Security Categories*, available from www.nist.gov.

SP 800-30, *Risk Management Guide for Information Technology Systems from NIST* [National Institute of Standards and Technology], available from www.nist.gov.

ISO TR 13335-4:2000. Covers the selection of safeguards (meaning technical security controls). This standard is currently under revision and will be inserted into ISO 27005, available from www.iso.org.

SP 800-18, *Guide for Developing Security Plans for Information Technology Systems*, available from www.nist.gov. Guides the design and documentation of IT security controls.

SP 800-53A, *Guide for Assessing the Security Controls in Federal Information Systems*, draft available from www.nist.gov.

BS 7799-3:2006, *Guidelines for Information Security Risk Management*, available from http://www.bsonline.bsi-global.com/server/index.jsp.

ISO/IEC TR 13335-3, *Guidelines for the Management of IT Security: Techniques for the Management of IT Security from International Organization for Standardization*, available from www.iso.org.

1.11.2 Standards to Assist in the Do Phase

ISO/IEC 27001, *Information Technology—Security Techniques—Information Security Management Systems—Requirements*, first edition, October 15, 2005, available from www.iso.org.

ISO/IEC 17799, *Information Technology—Security Techniques—Code of Practice for Information Security Management*, second edition, June 15, 2005, available from www.iso.org (now ISO 27002).

SP 800-53, *Recommended Security Controls for Federal Information Systems*, available from www.nist.gov. In effect another ISMS standard; contains a handy cross-reference table comparing its control coverage to that of standards such as ISO 17799:2005.

SP 800-5, *Security Metrics Guide for Information Technology Systems*, available from www.nist.gov. Sounds more useful than it is (in my opinion), being little more than an enormous list of security things that could be measured.

FIPS 200, *Minimum Security Requirements for Federal Information and Information Systems*, available from www.nist.gov.

ISO TR 13335-4:2000. Covers the selection of safeguards (meaning technical security controls). This standard is currently under revision and will be inserted into ISO 27005, available from www.iso.org.

1.11.3 Standards to Assist in the Check Phase

SP 800-61, *Computer Security Incident Handling Guide*, available from www.nist.gov.

SP 800-37, *Guide for the Security Certification and Accreditation of Federal Information Systems*, available from www.nist.gov. Provides guidance on security certification, accreditation, and authorization of information systems.

SP 800-53, *Recommended Security Controls for Federal Information Systems*, available from www.nist.gov. In effect another ISMS standard; contains a handy cross-reference table comparing its control coverage to that of standards such as ISO 27002:2005.

SP800-26, *Government Audit Office Federal Information System Controls Audit Manual*, available from www.nist.gov.

1.11.4 Standards to Assist in the Act Phase

ISO/IEC 27001, *Information Technology—Security Techniques—Information Security Management Systems—Requirements*, first edition, October 15, 2005, available from www.iso.org.

ISO/IEC 17799, *Information Technology—Security Techniques—Code of Practice for Information Security Management*, second edition, June 15, 2005, available from www.iso.org (now ISO 27002).

SP 800-37, *Guide for the Security Certification and Accreditation of Federal Information Systems*, available from www.nist.gov. Provides guidance on security certification, accreditation, and authorization of information systems.

ISO 19011:2002, *Guideline on Quality and/or Environmental Management System Audit*, available from www.iso.org. Accredited assessment schema based on common international standard.

Chapter 2

Information Security Management System

Previous details herein describe the International Standards Organization (ISO) security standards, current state, future plans, and the relationship of the ISO standards to each other. ISO 27001 provides guidance for the creation of an information security management system (ISMS) and references the controls within ISO 27002 to establish and maintain an ISMS. This chapter defines and introduces the ISMS as a prerequisite to discussing foundational concepts and tools necessary to effectively build an ISMS.

2.1 Objectives

Objectives for this chapter are to:

- Define ISMS
- Clarify ISO intent for use of the term *ISMS*
- Provide the first glimpse at the business drivers behind an ISMS
- Introduce the following non-ISO concepts of ISMS and place them in perspective of ISMS:
  - Security management framework
  - To-be
  - As-is
  - Gap analysis
  - Transition plan
- Provide an understanding of common terms prior to using them in the context of the foundational concepts and tools that support implementing an ISMS

2.2   ISMS Introduction

ISO defines ISMS to be "that part of the overall management system, based on a business risk approach, to establish, implement, operate, monitor, review, maintain, and improve information security."* According to ISO, the "overall management system" within an organization includes much more than just security, and indeed, ISO offers many more management system standards. The ISO 9000 family is a series of quality management standards. The ISO 14000 family is a series of environmental management standards. The ISO 27000 family is a series of security management standards. Therefore, ISO introduces terms that are applicable to all management systems and uses them to guide actions with the intent to establish, maintain, and improve information security management.

Alternative names for ISMS are *security management program* (SMP) or *information assurance program* (IAP), and there are many potential others. The terms *SMP* and *IAP* are from the authors' experiences and not used by ISO. The intent of introducing these alternative names is to add clarity to the phrase *information security management system*. There may be confusion with many people trying to resolve the ISO use of the term *system*. The ISO intent of the term *system* in the phrase *ISMS* is to mean a process or methodology. Many people will interpret the term *system* to mean an actual device or application. With respect to applying for certification against ISO 27001, use the ISO term *ISMS*, or very clearly provide an alternative term with exactly the same meaning. The remainder of the text uses the term *ISMS* in keeping with the ISO definition; if an inadvertent use of *security program* appears, just substitute the phrase *ISMS*—they mean the same thing herein.

2.3   Security Management Framework Introduction

Whether defining an ISMS or an ISMS under a different name, the process, tools, templates, documents, and practices to achieve an effective ISMS are the same. Given the principle that one size fits all typically does not, there is need to customize a security program or ISMS for the organization at hand. A good starting point to achieve this is to develop an organization-specific security management framework (SMF).

An SMF provides an outline to define, discuss, plan, implement, track, and report on security issues relevant to the organization. A good SMF finds foundation in an industry standard for comprehensiveness, consistency, and generally promoting the use of industry best practices. The organization may add or detract from the security standard to define an SMF with specific relevance to that organization and its specific needs. There are many security standards from which to choose.

---

* ISO/IEC 27001:2005, *Information Security Management Systems—Requirements*, p. 2.

A brief list of sources for security standards includes the ISO standards, National Institute of Standards and Technology (NIST) Special Publications (SPs), Federal Information Processing Standards (FIPS), the U.S. Department of Defense 8500.x series including Security Technical Implementation Guides (STIGs), the European Network and Information Security Agency (ENISA), and many more.

The focus herein is on the ISO security standards as a set of international standards applicable to the commercial environment. The development of an SMF may also incorporate many other security compliance requirements, e.g., U.S. legislation like Sarbanes–Oxley and the Health Insurance Portability and Accountability Act (HIPAA). Many requirements in other compliance documents will overlap with the ISO standards. Therefore, an SMF based on ISO will cover by default at least some other compliance requirements. For example, creating a security working group (SWG) with cross-functional representation from many areas of the organization satisfies an ISO 27001 requirement. This same SWG also satisfies a requirement within HIPAA. By using a single SMF and creating traceability from that SMF to relevant compliance requirements, there is the ability to satisfy many requirements with one initiative. There is more on this capability in future sections.

2.4 ISMS Establishment Process: To-Be or PDCA

ISO advocates using a four-phase approach to establishing an ISMS in the Plan-Do-Check-Act (PDCA) model. ISO uses the PDCA model in many of its management standards and repeats it in ISO 27001 for consistency. Moreover, establishing good management practice by using PDCA provides the ability to reuse investments in such a practice in quality management, environment management, security management, and other organizational management areas. Therefore, PDCA is a fine choice and suits the tasks at hand to establish and maintain an ISMS. In paraphrase, the PDCA phases address how to establish policy, objectives, processes, and procedures relevant to managing risk (plan phase); implement and operate (do phase); assess and, where applicable, measure process performance against policy (check phase); and take corrective and preventative action (act phase). Supplemental concepts (not in the ISO standards) to help establish an ISMS include:

- To-be state
- As-is state
- Transition plan

In the context of managing business risk, the *to-be state* defines the target state of risk management. It includes management involvement, organizational structures, scope, policies, standards, procedures, and much more. The combination of ISO 27001 and ISO 27002 defines a reasonable to-be state for many organizations; that is, the security posture of the organization should adhere to the management system and controls in these standards. The SMF may start with ISO 27002 and incorporate other security standards to create an SMF specific to the organization; this SMF is then an outline of an organizational-specific to-be state.

In the context of risk management, the *as-is state* is a snapshot of the current security posture. Obtaining that snapshot uses a set of tools based on the SMF. The act of comparing the as-is state to the to-be state is a gap analysis. The gap analysis process and reports are also based on the SMF. Knowing the differences between *current* and *desired* provides details to develop a *transition plan* to move from as-is to to-be. The transition plan is also based on the SMF. The following sections elaborate on to-be, as-is, and the transition plan in the context of ISMS and managing business risk.

A quick but important side note: The introduction of to-be, as-is, and the transition plan at this point in the text is to make the reader generally familiar with the terms. To reiterate, these are not ISO terms. The final section of this text presents details on compliance management, and the to-be state, as-is state, and transition plan are integral to an abstract approach to compliance assessment (a part of compliance management). As Chapter 6, "Compliance Management," will explain in detail, the establishment and maintenance of an ISMS is an instance of a more abstract compliance management process. The primary intent of this text is to introduce the use and application of the ISO security standards and to achieve ISO 27001 certification. A secondary intent, but an incredibly useful intent, is to introduce an overall practice of compliance management, in which achieving ISO 27001 certification is but one aspect. By interweaving these concepts and pointing out the relationships, the reader will be able to create many compliance management tools for reuse and leverage investments in ISO 27001 certification across the business risk management landscape.

2.4.1 To-Be

This stage defines objectives for security in terms of business risk management and provides a framework within which to build an ISMS. The *business objectives* drive the contents of the ISMS. Becoming certified against ISO 27001 requires including Sections 4 to 8 of ISO 27001. Defining an SMF provides guidance for defining the ISMS. Chapter 3, "Foundational Concepts and Tools for an Information Security Management System," elaborates on the SMF.

The to-be stage produces an organizational-specific SMF enumerating security requirements that find foundation in industry standards and that is customized to address the business risk of the organization. The first use of this framework is to define an interpretation guide to provide a common list of terms, common definition of terms, and common understanding of concepts necessary to support the ISMS.

To-be efforts reside within the plan phase of the PDCA model. Note that the plan phase (determining the to-be state) is defining objectives for establishing the ISMS. Writing policy and procedures at this point is premature; such activity belongs in the do phase (or part of the transition plan that describes how to get from as-is to to-be).

2.4.2 As-Is

This stage determines the current security posture of the organization compared to the ISMS defined in the to-be stage. The as-is stage includes a discovery process, an analysis process (gap analysis), and a findings report. Chapter 3 provides details on discovery, analysis, and generating a findings report, including a baseline set of discovery questions and templates.

The as-is stage produces a discovery questionnaire customized to the SMF. Other products include project briefings, templates for discovery capture, analysis tools to review the results and generate useful findings, and ultimately a findings report that presents a snapshot of the organization's current security posture. The term *snapshot* implies that security is dynamic and may change quickly; therefore, any security finding is dated and has a limited useful lifetime during which the organization may make intelligent action decisions.

As-is activities apply to the plan and check phases of the PDCA model: initial ISMS planning in the plan phase and ongoing monitoring and review in the check phase. There is an opportunity to reuse the as-is tools in both phases. Moreover, there is motivation to reuse the same tools to provide the ability to easily compare results between initial planning and ongoing review of operations.

2.4.3 Transition Plan

The transition plan enumerates the details of how to go from the as-is state to to-be state. The actual transition process may take more than one budget cycle, depending on the extent of activity necessary to meet ISMS objectives. Given the lengthy and potentially expensive activities, the organization must prioritize, that is, intelligently allocate resources to first address the highest risks to the organization. Chapter 4, "Implementing an Information Security Management System—Plan-Do-Check-Act," provides details on developing a transition plan to achieve an ISO 27001-compliant ISMS.

The transition plan process produces a remediation analysis report and a transition plan document with at least a high level of detail. Depending on the depth of detail, the transition plan process may also produce a formal statement of objectives (i.e., formal project definition), cost model with a formal work breakdown structure (WBS), and project plan with milestones and deliverables. The transition plan may also prompt the creation of service level agreements (SLAs) either for external vendors or for internal operations. SLAs are formal enumeration of operational objectives, e.g., the up time objective is 98 percent of operational hours.

The creation of the transition plan applies under the do and act phases of the PDCA model. The transition between the initial as-is snapshot occurs during the do phase, and ongoing review and revision also produce transition plans in the act phase.

2.4.4 Operations and Maintenance

Operations and maintenance (O&M) provides ongoing support for the ISMS, including periodic review of the definition of the to-be state. Revisions to the to-be state may occur with new standards, i.e., revisions to the ISO 27001 or ISO 27002 standards. Other business drivers behind to-be revisions include new legislation, legislative reform, regulatory changes, contractual changes, and business environment changes that introduce new areas of vulnerability to mission integrity.

The O&M stage produces measures and metrics on performance as compared to SLAs. O&M will likely produce many reports relevant to security operations, including log reports, incident reports, root cause analyses, and many more. O&M applies in the check and act phases of the PDCA model.

Chapter 3

Foundational Concepts and Tools for an Information Security Management System

Chapter 1 introduced the International Standards Organization (ISO) security standards in general and focused on the differences and relationship between ISO 27001 and ISO 27002. Chapter 2 introduced the Information Security Management System (ISMS), the security management framework (SMF), and some terms that interrelate the establishment and maintenance of the ISMS to overall compliance management. This chapter expands on the SMF and introduces many concepts and tools to use during the establishment, implementation, operation, monitoring, review, maintenance, and improvement of information security and an ISMS.

3.1 Objectives

Objectives for this chapter include the following:

- Provide foundational concepts and tools for ISMS development.
- Expand details of the SMF.
- Use the SMF to define a sample interpretation guide based on ISO 27002.

- ■ Use the SMF and interpretation guide as a common perspective for the organization on:
  - Security framework
  - Security lexicon
  - To define scope and plan for ISMS
  - Business risk management consistency and comprehensiveness
  - Align ISMS initiatives with industry standards to promote:
    - Easier, faster, less expensive ISO 27001 audit experience
    - Easier, less expensive ISMS maintenance
- ■ Present the initial planning and implementation of the ISMS as a special case in the PDCA model.
- ■ Introduce templates for policy, standards, and procedure.
- ■ Present use of the SMF in planning, tracking, and reporting details on the creation and use of policy, standards, procedures, and other aspects of the ISMS.
- ■ Segue from these foundational concepts and tools into ISMS implementation.

The ISMS development process uses terms, concepts, templates, analysis tools, reporting tools, etc. with specific meaning and intent. Establishing a foundation of this meaning and intent at this point provides better understanding of how to use them in the ISMS development and maintenance process.

3.2 SMF Applications

There are many details that go into an effective ISMS. Risk management categories or security categories include organizational security, asset management, physical security, human resources, communications, operations, information technology acquisition or development, business continuity, access control, and others. Each of these security categories consists of many security subcategories and security elements. For example, access control subcategories include user access, network access, and operating system access. In turn, network access consists of security elements like network access policy, user authentication, remote diagnostics, network connection controls, and network routing controls. The volume and nuance of detail can get very confusing; hence, there is the need to provide an outline or a framework within which to define organizational concerns; that is, there is need to define an SMF.

The security management framework herein is quite extensive and uses the ISO 27002 as foundation. Note that this is an example of an SMF; it is not *the* SMF, as there is no such thing. The SMF may literally align with ISO 27001 and ISO 27002 and stop there, or there may be additions, detractions, or modifications to the SMF to fit the specific needs of the organization. The benefits of a comprehensive framework, at least comprehensive relative to the organizational need, include a single framework that describes all *addressable* security considerations. While each and every security element is addressable, this does not imply the organization should necessarily implement safeguards for each element. A valid addressing of an element is a statement to the effect of *business risk in this area is not sufficient for the organization to invest in safeguards at this time.* A bit more elaboration is helpful, especially when new security personnel are reviewing the ISMS or an auditor is attempting to certify the ISMS. The intent is to convey to management, security investment review board, or auditor that every conceivable security element of interest to the organization was considered for the ISMS and that empty spaces are omission by design in consideration of business risk and return on investment, not omission by oversight.

A dogmatic approach to the ISMS follows the ISO 27002 outline exactly. While the ISO security standards are very good, they are not security scripture, and the authors advocate a more flexible approach that permits or, more precisely, *promotes* additions, modifications, deletions, and reorganizations that best fit the organizational security (risk management) needs. The goal is to generate an organization-specific SMF that finds basis in industry standards and provides guidance to the development of an ISMS and compliance management program. One caveat is that if the organization desires certification against ISO 27001, the minimum requirements to follow are sections 4, 5, 6, 7, and 8 of ISO 27001.

The SMF is an outline of security categories, subcategories, and elements to promote consistency and comprehensiveness. There are many uses of this framework once created. Other uses for the SMF include tracking the development, dissemination, and effectiveness of policy, standards, and procedures applicable to each category. Additionally, the organization may track service providers by category and element; some services may be internal, others by managed security service, others by outsourcing, and others by partners or vendors. The framework provides an outline in which to develop ISMS documentation and compliance management tools. The compliance management tools will include discovery questionnaires, analysis tools to process the discovery data, reporting tools to convey discovery and analysis results, and progress-tracking tools to track remediation activity.

A very useful construct is to use the SMF as the basis for a traceability matrix that aligns the security management program with compliance requirements and ultimately to root business drivers behind the need for security initiatives. Benefits of this traceability include the ability to provide justification for security budget requests and to defend security operations during budget cuts. A security mechanism (e.g., an intrusion detection system [IDS]) or security operation (e.g., computer security incident response team [CSIRT]) that is traceable to a legislative or regulatory requirement is very difficult for executives to cut from the project request or from the operational budget. Moreover, such a formal alignment provides the ability to generate return on security investment (ROSI) details with a foundation in mitigating business risk, e.g., cost avoidance in the form of organizational and officer fines by establishing and maintaining acceptable levels of legislative compliance.

The SMF based on ISO 27002 contains the following categories:

- Security Policy
- Security Management Plan
- Asset Management
- Personnel Security
- Physical Security
- Operations Management
- Access Management
- Solution Quality Assurance (SQA)
- Incident Management
- Business Continuity (BC) and Disaster Recovery (DR) Management
- Compliance Management

Each category may contain subcategories and elements that represent individual security requirements. The need for such a granular framework is to reduce the complexity of discerning risk management needs, planning risk management efforts, tracking implementation, and reporting on the effectiveness of the risk management efforts in terms of the business drivers that prompt the need for risk management at all. As many of the security requirements are open to interpretation, there is great benefit for the organization to develop an interpretation guide to convey the meaning and intent behind the SMF contents. The following section provides an example of such an interpretation guide; the organization will, of course, define its own interpretations and relevancy of each security requirement.

3.2.1 Interpretation Guide

Table 3.1 provides a sample SMF and sample interpretation guide. The framework is quite extensive and provides the foundation to define the ISMS, requirements traceability matrix, discovery questionnaire, analysis tools, reporting tools, remediation- and mitigation-tracking tools, responsibility matrix, and other useful tools. The interpretation guide below is a notional interpretation. Actual interpretation may vary from organization to organization depending on business goals, business environment, or other compliance requirements influencing business operations; for example, a healthcare organization doing business in the United States may be subject to Health Insurance Portability and Accountability Act (HIPAA) Final Security Rule (FSR) legislation. If so, the interpretation guide may include an *ePHI* qualification to some security elements. HIPAA legislation defines ePHI as electronic protected health information and provides compliance requirements with specific intent to safeguard ePHI. ISO 27001 uses the term "normative references" to denote the presentation of common lexicon and definitions to ensure all parties use the terms appropriately to establish common understanding and meeting of the minds.

Table 3.1 Security Management Framework and Interpretation Guide

Category/Sub-Category/Element	Requirement	Interpretation/Commentary
Security Policy		*If necessary, the text provides an interpretation of a vague requirement or provides commentary to increase clarity.*
Information and Information Technology Security Policy		The organization needs security policy that reflects compliance requirements and supports the organizational mission.
Documentation	Management produces an overarching security policy that includes control of information security and clear implementation guidance.	A successful security program must have executive and management backing. Guidance for an effective security program begins with policy.
Dissemination	Disseminate policy into enterprise initiatives for security awareness.	To be successful, people have to know about it and how to apply it.
Policy review	Review security policy at regular intervals or in the event of significant changes (review trigger events) that affect the current policy; additionally, there should be a board (security working group) to review this policy and any changes to the policy.	Establish policy review trigger events: calendar, security incident, business change, etc. Establish a security working group (SWG) and/or security governance group to review policy in business terms.

(continued)

Table 3.1 Security Management Framework and Interpretation Guide (Continued)

Category/Sub-Category/Element	Requirement	Interpretation/Commentary
Security Management Plan		
Intra-Organization Management		
Executive and management backing	Executives are accountable to stakeholders and should be involved in risk management. Management identifies business risk drivers behind security, then implements and provides oversight to information security functions within the organization.	The ongoing success of a security program requires management involvement, including governance, adjudication, compliance management, and operations oversight.
Information security consistency	Ensure cross-functional representation in SWG and other activities relevant to security governance.	This requirement implies the need for an enterprise perspective of security, including business planners, business operations, legal, as well as technology. Security is far more than just an information technology issue.
Security roles and responsibilities	Management clearly defines roles and responsibilities in security governance and management; e.g., security professionals or other individuals with a broad knowledge of security practices are responsible for information security.	There is a responsibility to assign accountability for security as appropriate throughout the organization. Moreover, there is a responsibility to engage knowledgeable people in security activities, i.e., security professionals. This is a requirement contrary to assigning the network or system administrator security duties if and when he or she can find the time.

Table 3.1 Security Management Framework and Interpretation Guide (Continued)

Category/Sub-Category/Element	Requirement	Interpretation/Commentary
Authentication and authorization	Management has a policy or policies for activities that take place within the data processing facilities that include access and activity management that requires identity and privilege management	There is need for identity and privilege management that includes authentication and authorization, respectively. Apply to physical access as well as cyber access. These requirements specifically apply to information processing facilities including access and all modifications that take place within the facilities.
Confidentiality agreements	Non-disclosure agreements must be set up so that management has legal recourse in the event of a security breach.	The confidentiality agreement establishes mutual understanding between employer and employees. Employees are aware of responsibilities.
External authority relationships	Establish policies and practices that outline the proper authorities to contact in the event of emergencies; review and update contacts on a regular basis.	Prepare for emergencies, including whom to contact in the event of an emergency. Include review of contacts in periodic review of emergency preparedness plans (business continuity, disaster recovery, continuity of operations plan, etc.).
Professional organizations	Memberships with security professional organizations are encouraged to provide information about current security practices, to provide security alerts, and to share information on new threats and vulnerabilities.	Leverage lessons learned by many, both inside the organization and outside.
Independent assessments and audits	Management must initiate a regular independent review of the information security program as well as snapshots of the current security posture.	Despite good intentions, there is value in third-party review. There may also be legislative requirements for independent review of security practices.

(continued)

Table 3.1   Security Management Framework and Interpretation Guide (Continued)

Category/Sub-Category/Element	Requirement	Interpretation/Commentary
Second-Party Management		
Risk management	Before permitting second-party access to facilities, information, and information technology, an organization establishes rules that minimize risks with second-party access.	Establish agreements between the organization and vendors, partners, contractors, suppliers, customers, or any other external parties that have physical or cyber access to organizational assets.
Addressing security when dealing with customers	Establish policies with regard to what types of access each customer needs.	There is value in defining various roles (classifications) in which third parties may fit; subsequently, define role-based access according to need. A good security practice should not allow, at least not without good reason, global access to all parties.
Business agreements	Addition of appropriate risk management and security control clauses to business agreements that may include contracts, requests for proposal (RFPs), etc.	Include language in contracts or other agreements that address external party awareness, understanding, and compliance with organizational security practices. So many agreements get lost in the weeds of the letter-of-the-law; there is value in stating intent of the agreement to establish a spirit-of-the-law, explicitly listing what are permissible activities, and generally restricting all activities not explicitly permitted.

Table 3.1   Security Management Framework and Interpretation Guide (Continued)

Category/Sub-Category/Element	Requirement	Interpretation/Commentary
Asset Management		
Responsibility and Accountability for Assets		
Inventory	Identify and inventory all assets including their relative importance to the organization, ease of replacement, location of asset, and other applicable attributes to track asset lifecycle; align assets with the business functions they support.	Identify and enumerate corporate assets. Decide what metadata about the asset makes sense to track to establish tracking of physical location, use, lifecycle, end of life, discarding, etc. The alignment of assets with business functions begs the need to identify key business functions and determine which assets are critical to the successful fulfillment of these functions.
Ownership	Determine an asset owner for all assets; this is a point of accountability for implementing and enforcing standard policy and determining appropriate actions for discretionary policy.	If everyone is accountable, then no one is accountable. Establish an owner of the asset and designate responsibility for asset management to that owner. Such responsibility may include access or sharing of asset. *Note:* Assets may be intellectual property, documents, computers or other cyber-devices, and more.
Appropriate use	Establish policy, standard, and procedures for appropriate use of information and information technology.	Establish enterprise policy for appropriate use to provide guidance for owners to make intelligent decisions on asset management.

(continued)

Table 3.1 Security Management Framework and Interpretation Guide (Continued)

Category/Sub-Category/Element	Requirement	Interpretation/Commentary
Information and Information Technology Classification		
Classifications	The organization produces classification guidelines. The asset owner assigns and enforces appropriate classification to all information and information technology to protect these assets accordingly.	Determine information and information technology classifications with respect to effective management business risk. Risk features may include value to organization; potential harm to organization if disclosed, modified, or otherwise rendered unavailable; compliance requirements; etc.
Labeling and handling	Label and establish procedure for proper handling of all information and information technology appropriate to its classification level.	Provide guidance to personnel and authorized third parties on the appropriate handling of information and information technology.
Personnel Security		
Pre-Hire	.	
Security-related roles and responsibilities	Engage human resources (HR) to help outline all job candidates' security roles and responsibilities; this includes security professionals as well as non-security specific areas.	First, there is the implication to determine security roles and responsibilities. Second, involve HR to ensure job descriptions, hiring decisions, orientation, reminders, and termination procedures to reflect details of the roles and responsibilities.

Table 3.1 Security Management Framework and Interpretation Guide (Continued)

Category/Sub-Category/Element	Requirement	Interpretation/Commentary
Background checks	Acquire or perform a background check to the extent permissible and practicable; such checks may include criminal, financial, validity of claims on résumé (degrees, certifications, training, experience).	There is a responsibility to hire personnel appropriate to the position; additionally, there is a responsibility not to hire inappropriate personnel. For example, persons with a criminal background are likely not the best choice as security guards.
Agreements	Employees, partners, contractors, and other second parties having access to organizational assets sign appropriate agreements as terms for the association. These may include non-disclosure, confidentiality, non-compete, non-solicitation, and other agreements that minimize organizational risk with the association.	Engage legal advice when specifying conditions of employment to ensure compliance with local, regional, and national laws. Specify relevant terms and conditions in employee or third-party agreements.
Tenure		
Awareness	Upon initiation of the association, the organization provides an orientation describing security responsibilities.	Management is responsible for ensuring employee awareness, understanding, and compliance with security policies and procedures.

(continued)

**Table 3.1   Security Management Framework and Interpretation
Guide (Continued)**

Category/Sub-Category/Element	Requirement	Interpretation/Commentary
Security education, training, and awareness (SETA)	The organization provides initial and periodic (minimally annual) security awareness briefing and/or training to employees, additional awareness for managers, and additional training and education for security professionals.	Include tracking of employee awareness, understanding, and compliance. Example metrics, including tracking awareness, may be simply recording return receipts on e-mails or requiring a unique log-in to an awareness briefing. Tracking understanding may involve a quiz or test. Tracking compliance may include installation of anti-malware software or personal firewall, including appropriate settings according to organizational policy.
Sanctions	Establish sanction policies and procedures for non-compliance with security policy, standards, and procedures.	Stating a law with no enforcement of the law renders the law a paper tiger... no claws and no bite; the same with policy. Include wording to the effect that the organization has the right to enforce policy, but not the duty. Such wording permits leeway for varying circumstances, that is, a judgment call on the degree of the offense.

Table 3.1   Security Management Framework and Interpretation Guide (Continued)

Category/Sub-Category/Element	Requirement	Interpretation/Commentary
Change of Employment Status		
Termination	Establish policy and procedure for employee termination. Address both voluntary and involuntary termination. The procedures include termination of identity credentials and privilege credentials as befit the situation, including online accounts, restriction of access to facilities, etc.	Provision of a procedure ensures a systematic checklist to revoke identification and privilege credentials and to collect credentials like company identification cards, credit cards, and keys. Termination may be an emotional time for the parties involved; establishing procedure inserts a rational perspective.
New position	Establish policy and procedure to handle employee transition to a new position.	Provision of a procedure ensures a systematic checklist to review privileges; revoke old, grant new. Also, include a new position orientation that includes security awareness and responsibilities.
Asset accountability	As befits the circumstances surrounding change of employment status, review assets issued to employee in context of the new status.	Using a checklist that includes details from asset logs, collect information and information technology issued to the employee. These may include paper documents, identification cards, PCs, laptops, cell phones, etc.
Access management	As befits the circumstances surrounding change of employment status, review identity and privilege credentials; revise or revoke accordingly.	Let the circumstances guide the review, revision, or revocation of credentials. Policy should call for expedited revocation upon involuntary separation as a matter of good security practice.

(continued)

Table 3.1 Security Management Framework and Interpretation Guide (Continued)

Category/Sub-Category/Element	Requirement	Interpretation/Commentary
Physical Security		
Physical Proximity		
Perimeter	As befits the campus, building, floor, or room, establish policy, standards, and procedures to safeguard physical perimeters according to requirements for level of protection. Safeguards may include walls, fences, gates, lighting, card readers, entry gates, video, guards, manned reception desk, etc.	Consider the need to protect physical assets, but, more importantly, the information assets residing within physical buildings or on information technology. E.g., the cost of replacing a laptop is often far less than the implications surrounding the loss or exposure of information on the laptop.
Entry/exit	Limit the number of entry/exit points and protect entry/exit areas of an information facility so that only authorized individuals may gain access. Log entries/exits.	Limiting entry/exit points reduces costs of security measures. This also limits the areas to cover in the event of interdiction.
Rooms	Obfuscate, or at the least do not blatantly advertise, the presence of secure facilities; generally keep secure facilities away from public areas (e.g., loading docks).	Use a room numbering or naming convention that provides guidance for employees but otherwise does not convey the importance of the facility. E.g., a door sign of Room E91.426 is far less noticeable than one reading *Research & Development*.

Table 3.1 Security Management Framework and Interpretation Guide (Continued)

Category/Sub-Category/Element	Requirement	Interpretation/Commentary
External threats	Establish emergency procedures for natural, technical, and human risks. Natural threats to the area may include flood, hurricane, or ice storms. Technical threats include loss of utilities like electric or water. Human risks may include targeted attacks (e.g., terrorist) or incidental (e.g., riot or protest). With respect to availability of services, acquire, implement, and maintain uninterruptible power supplies (UPSs), emergency power-off switches, water supply, telecommunications equipment, and other supporting utilities.	A general set of procedures is often less useful than ones specific to the situation. Physical proximity of facilities to surrounding areas (e.g., close an airport and in a landing flight path, in a flood zone, or in an area prone to earthquakes) provides justification for special needs. Anticipate and plan contingencies for the practicably predictable. Plan for continued availability of utility services. Consider that continued operations depend on physical presence of people; i.e., loss of water may result in building closure by health department; moreover, loss of water may shut down air conditioning if only a water-cooled system is in use. The point is *power* is not the only concern.
Sensitive areas	Establish policy, standard, and procedure that address areas in which secure work is performed.	If work on strategic initiatives or tactically sensitive initiatives requires secure operations, ensure workers adhere to appropriate restrictions on where to perform the work. Strategic initiatives may include research and development. Tactical initiatives may include proposal work in response to a multi-million-dollar RFP or generally protecting the processing of financial data.

(continued)

Table 3.1 Security Management Framework and Interpretation Guide (Continued)

Category/Sub-Category/Element	Requirement	Interpretation/Commentary
Public areas	Monitor publicly accessible areas, e.g., lobbies, reception areas, loading docks. Place access controls between these public areas and the private areas in the organization.	Monitoring is one aspect and an important one. Additionally, restrict access between public areas and other organizational property. This may include card readers, cipher locks, passing by guards, etc.
Asset Security		
Asset safeguards	Implement safeguards for the physical protection of information technology from unauthorized access or incidental damage.	Physical access safeguards are one thing, and positioning of equipment to avoid unauthorized viewing is also important; e.g., it is not a good idea to place the CFO in a first-floor corner office with ceiling-to-floor windows and no blinds.
Wiring	Wiring is a critical support mechanism to continued operations and includes power, voice, and data services. Safeguard communications media to protect confidentiality (avoid disclosure) and availability (avoid denial of service). Introduce cabling security measures such as marking, segregation, conduits, and shielding.	This includes public service demarcation points from organizational facilities to public mediums (e.g., public switched telephone network [PSTN], cable, or Internet services). Also, consider cabling security for leased lines between facilities. If planning redundant paths for business continuity, leaving one side of the building and another, only to meet down the block at the same PSTN point of presence (POP), is not sufficient.
Maintenance	Perform proper preventive and corrective maintenance to ensure integrity of business operations.	Acquisition and implementation are the first steps; there is need for effective and secure operations and maintenance (O&M).

Table 3.1 Security Management Framework and Interpretation Guide (Continued)

Category/Sub-Category/Element	Requirement	Interpretation/Commentary
Asset reuse	Establish policy, standards, and procedures to destroy, overwrite, or delete sensitive data before reuse of the asset; verify these actions prior to reissuing.	Throwing the baby out with the bathwater is not good; neither is throwing intellectual property, customer data, or otherwise sensitive information out with the old equipment. Many legislative requirements address the need for secure disposal and reuse. With regard to reuse, e.g., if the VP of HR gets a new PC and his or her old one gets recycled to the mail room, ensure payroll information is deleted and cannot be revised by commonly available cyber-forensic tools.
Asset disposal	Establish policy, standards, and procedures to destroy, overwrite, or delete sensitive data before disposal of the asset; verify these actions prior to disposal. Disposal may include discarding to trash, resale to employees, donation to charity, etc.	Throwing the baby out with the bathwater is not good; neither is throwing intellectual property, customer data, or otherwise sensitive information out with the old equipment. Many legislative requirements address the need for secure disposal and reuse. With regard to reuse, e.g., if the VP of HR gets a new PC and his or her old one gets recycled to the mail room, ensure payroll information is deleted and cannot be revised by commonly available cyber-forensic tools.

(continued)

Table 3.1 Security Management Framework and Interpretation Guide (Continued)

Category/Sub-Category/Element	Requirement	Interpretation/Commentary
Off-site use of assets	Establish property management policy and procedures. At the least, include approval authority prior to asset removal and record the removal and return transaction.	Protecting the asset itself is good but often not nearly as important as the information on the asset (e.g., data or documents on a laptop). Accounting for the location of the asset assists in quickly identifying loss of that asset and assessing the full implications of the loss.
Operations Management		
Operational Procedures and Responsibilities		
Operations	For all information technology and supporting infrastructure, establish operating procedures for aspects like system start-up, shutdown, maintenance, backup, and recovery.	Mark Twain once said that "the graveyard is full of indispensable men!" True; however, the loss of a key person still hurts, especially if he takes key knowledge with him. Facilitate the learning organization by recording procedures for personnel transition as well as expedient recovery in the event of an incident.
Configuration management	To prevent the introduction of untested code and data into an operational environment, separate production, testing, and development environments.	Provide for staging areas that require formal check-in, testing, validation/ verification, acceptance, and rollback processes; separate the duties of each step such that one individual cannot introduce code from development to production.

Table 3.1 Security Management Framework and Interpretation Guide (Continued)

Category/Sub-Category/Element	Requirement	Interpretation/Commentary
Log management	Establish policy and procedure to manage and log all changes to information, information technology, and facilities.	Provide for accountability and, when possible, non-repudiation of activity. An effective change management program safeguards information and information technology assets as well as provides for forensic capability in the event of an incident.
Outsourcing and Managed Services		
Service delivery	Ensure business agreements address service definitions, security controls, and service level agreements.	Contracts engaging third-party services should obligate the third party to honor security requirements of the organization.
Monitor and audit	Monitor and audit service providers, facilities, services, security controls, and performance claims.	Trust but verify; this is good business practice as well as good security.
Change management	From service initiation through maintenance and operations, manage business risk via formal change management. Evaluate changes with respect to risk posture; e.g., changes to key information technology pose larger risk and thus deserve more careful planning.	Plan–Do–Check–Act; evaluate potential impact on operations and business flow; verify modifications; prepare to restore to original state in the event of difficulty. *Note:* Although the interpretation mentions business operations, consider all aspects of business risk relevant to the situation. This may include sensitive relationships, legislative or regulatory implications, contract considerations, and more.

(continued)

Table 3.1 Security Management Framework and Interpretation Guide (Continued)

Category/Sub-Category/Element	Requirement	Interpretation/Commentary
Capacity Planning		
Capacity management	Project and monitor the consumption of resources in context of those projections; adjust resources accordingly to provide expected levels of service.	A security management program considers at least confidentiality, integrity, and availability. The availability of a full disk to accept further transactions, logs, etc. is somewhat limited; likewise, going over a certain percentage full on many disks results in questionable integrity of existing data. Plan accordingly.
Acceptance Management		
System acceptance	Develop formal test plans that include validation of solution capability (business function), performance levels, and security posture; include verification of security features governed by legislative mandates.	Enumerate expectations of a new solution, or solution upgrade or modification. Define criteria for successful operation (that it works at all) and for efficient operation (that it works in accordance with service level agreements [SLAs]). Define criteria for secure operation (that it works securely). Validate each of those criteria. Align the security validation with business drivers in context of business risk management to show value up the management hierarchy.

Table 3.1 Security Management Framework and Interpretation Guide (Continued)

Category/Sub-Category/Element	Requirement	Interpretation/Commentary
Malware and Malware Carriers		
Malware	Anticipate, prevent, defend, and monitor the introduction of malware to the organization. Malware includes viruses, spam, spyware, Trojan horses, and many other varieties.	Approach anti-malware controls from a defense in-depth perspective. Implement safeguards at the perimeter (i.e., public facing devices and entry/exit points to the internal network). Move inward. Also, extend outward to third parties with connectivity or data feeds or message exchanges.
Malware carriers	Establish policy, standard, and procedure to provide configuration guidance that minimizes risks from malware carriers. Malware carriers include e-mail, mobile code (code downloaded and executed on the fly while Web browsing), file transfers, etc.	The increase in e-commerce and any pendulum swings back to thin clients increase the introduction of mobile code. E-mail continues to grow as a business communications tool. An effective security program promotes defining policy and implementing controls that raise awareness of malware carriers and how to address their safe use as a business tool.
Backup Management		
Backup	Establish policy, standards, and procedures for an effective backup strategy that includes information on mobile devices, remote devices, servers, etc. Integrate a backup management strategy as part of an overall business continuity/disaster recovery plan.	Ensure backup policy, standard, and procedure. Test the integrity of backups. Include tests of backup media to gauge integrity of backup. Also, test recovery procedures. Recovery times are significantly less when they are predictable and proceduralized.

(continued)

Table 3.1 Security Management Framework and Interpretation Guide (Continued)

Category/Sub-Category/Element	Requirement	Interpretation/Commentary
Network Security Management		
Data in transit	Employ security controls to minimize business risk to operations and operational efficiency. Safeguard applications using the network, safeguard data traversing the network, log activity and transactions, and monitor network performance.	Think defense in depth; define network boundaries, protect exterior perimeters with appropriate use of demilitarized zones (DMZs) for public facing devices, protect entry/exit points with VPNs, etc. Think data in-transit versus data at-rest. Implement and enforce an electronic messaging policy that addresses all forms of electronic communication, e.g., e-mail, instant messaging, wireless, PDAs, cell phones, and VoIP.
Network infrastructure	Identify all network infrastructure mechanisms (e.g., routers, switches). Implement appropriate safeguards for administration, configuration, and function. Monitor operations and performance levels; degrading performance may be early warning of a pending security event.	The network infrastructure provides the path for data in-transit to traverse. Safeguarding the data is one task; safeguarding the path is another.

Table 3.1 Security Management Framework and Interpretation Guide (Continued)

Category/Sub-Category/Element	Requirement	Interpretation/Commentary
Media Management		
Removable media	Develop and implement procedures for the management of removable media, including external hard drives, laptops, USB storage devices, CDs, DVDs, tapes, etc. Include appropriate use and enumerate restrictions.	Devise a policy with respect to removable media management and security. Follow with standards and procedures that enumerate the types of removable media and specify requirements for each.
Media disposal	Establish policy, standards, and procedures for media disposal. Specify criteria where erasing or degaussing is acceptable and when physical destruction is required.	An information and information technology classification scheme will provide direction on how to devise media disposal policy, standards, and procedures.
Media storage and transport	Establish policy, standards, and procedures for media transport and storage. Include labeling, transport method, storage place, storage method (e.g., climate controlled); also, include guidance for media retrieval, e.g., requesting media from archive site. Safeguard media containing information during physical transport. Use couriers to ensure confidentiality and integrity of media and the information therein.	Considerations here complement an information and information technology classification scheme. Safeguards may vary according to classification. Consider media sensitivity and transit methods when creating a physical media transit policy. Extend document classification to information classification and include this in media transit guidance. E.g., clear text on a USB via USPS is almost as much exposure as clear text across the Internet.

(continued)

Table 3.1 Security Management Framework and Interpretation Guide (Continued)

Category/Sub-Category/Element	Requirement	Interpretation/Commentary
Communications Management		
Information transfer	Establish policy, standards, and procedures for the transfer of information from the organization to second parties. Include appropriate clauses in business agreements to ensure effective and safe information transfer across any potential communication medium (voice, data, and paper).	Consider transfer of information at all; additionally, consider exchange of information between communities with need to know and communities of varying sensitivity or security levels. Such considerations enable drawing upon vetted principles of information exchange, e.g., read-up and write-down.
External connectivity	Develop and implement policies and procedures to establish, operate, and maintain secure connections to second-party networks.	A security chain is as strong as its weakest link. Who connects to your network? How secure are their systems and networks?
E-Commerce Management		
Electronic commerce	Safeguard information involved in electronic commerce (e-commerce) infrastructure. Consider legislative and other compliance requirements for transaction processing and privacy.	There is an implication for robust identity management that includes transaction non-repudiation as well as other non-repudiation on other communications. If organizational success depends on immediate action of customer request via e-mail, there is need to have non-repudiation should the customer later change his mind and attempt to withhold payment.

Table 3.1 Security Management Framework and Interpretation Guide (Continued)

Category/Sub-Category/Element	Requirement	Interpretation/Commentary
Transactions	Safeguard information involved in electronic commerce (e-commerce) transactions. Consider legislative and other compliance requirements for transaction processing and privacy.	Successful e-commerce depends on the effective transmission, receipt, and processing of valid online transactions. Receipt of partial or invalid transactions may delay processing and affect cash flow or, worse, cost the organization in time and materials.
Organizational information and image	Safeguard the integrity of information on the organizational Web site. This information portrays organizational information and image to the public.	Public perception often depends on what they see; and *good will* is a balance sheet line item. Conveying an accurate public presence and image is critical to maintaining good will.
Monitoring		
Audit logs	Capture appropriate details to logs, review logs individually for anomalous activity, and consolidate logs for an aggregate review. Store and archive according to organizational policy and legislative mandate. Add safeguards to defend the integrity of log files.	Define useful log information relevant to that system and in context of what activity to monitor; keeping an abundance of details on all activity results in voluminous amounts of data with reduction in ability to filter for anomalous activity. Activity logs provide insight into activity and support the re-creation of chronologies and investigation into anomalous events (i.e., cyber-forensics). For recreation or investigation to be valid or admissible in court, there is need to protect the integrity of the logs.

(continued)

Table 3.1 Security Management Framework and Interpretation Guide (Continued)

Category/Sub-Category/Element	Requirement	Interpretation/Commentary
Information technology activity	Establish procedures to monitor activity on information technology, including user activity (log-on/log-off), utility activity, application activity, etc. Review activity logs for anomalous activity.	Establish a baseline of *normal* activity—often organization, site, or even system specific. Monitor system use for activity outside the norm, that is, anomalous activity.
Administrator and power user logs	Log activity by administrators and other power users (users with high privilege accounts).	These user *id*s (let's distinguish *user* from *user id*) have higher privileges than most. Looking for anomalous behavior associated with these user ids is appropriate.
Error logging	Log system and application failures. These may offer a clue to anomalous activity that is interfering with operations.	Expectations versus exceptions; most business operations support *expected* events and transactions with the assumption that the majority of activity is valid with respect to organizational mission and goals. However, there is the need to define *exceptions* in events and transactions, record details of those exceptions, and review those details for potential investigation. Exceptions may point to a flaw in business process or may point to activities with more sinister intent.

Table 3.1 Security Management Framework and Interpretation Guide (Continued)

Category/Sub-Category/Element	Requirement	Interpretation/Commentary
Clock synchronization	Identify an appropriate time source and synchronize all clocks on relevant information processing systems within an organization or self-contained domain to that time source.	*A man with two watches never knows what time it is.* A network with multiple time sources produces logs with uncertain chronology. This interferes with both the ability to perform digital forensics effectively and may also interfere with prosecution by not providing adequate surety on the accuracy of event details. Security activity including activity baselining, anomaly detection, and forensics activity may depend heavily on accurate timelines. Synchronizing times across the organization, or at least within a security domain, increases accuracy and effectiveness.
Access Management		
Access Control Policy		
Access control policy	Establish an access control policy, document, and review with respect to access requirements.	Start with an access control policy that defines the organizational intent behind access control. Support the access control policy with access control standards and procedures. Standards may include the use of a particular set of mechanisms (e.g., secure token). Procedures address the issuance, revocation, and general management of access privileges.

(continued)

Table 3.1 Security Management Framework and Interpretation Guide (Continued)

Category/Sub-Category/Element	Requirement	Interpretation/Commentary
User Access		
Identity management	Establish a formal process for users to obtain unique identifications. Include procedures for requesting identification, adjudication of request, grant/deny, maintenance, and revocation. Also, include assessing claim of identity during use.	Include such processes for identity management (authentication) and privilege management (authorization). Identity management also includes a verification process that the identity credential belongs to the person or entity presenting the identity credential. Such verification may include PINs, passwords, biometrics, physical devices, tokens, etc. Passwords provide identity validation, and the possession of a valid password often authenticates the user identity credential. Formal password management that includes issuance, revocation, periodic changes, and enforcement of strong passwords is an essential part of an effective security program.

Table 3.1 Security Management Framework and Interpretation Guide (Continued)

Category/Sub-Category/Element	Requirement	Interpretation/Commentary
Privilege management	Establish a formal process for users to gain privileges for use of information technology and access to information. Include procedures for requesting privileges, adjudication of request, grant/deny, maintenance, and revocation. Also, include assessing claim of privilege during use.	An effective security program includes identity management as well as privilege management. Controls check and enforce privileges through an authorization process. To increase effectiveness and manageability of what can become an extremely labor-intensive process, consider defining roles and associating standard privileges with each role. Make special privilege assignments by exception. This promotes both manageability and highlights particularly sensitive privileges through a separate process.
Review of privileges	Often, once a privilege is granted, there is no taking it back. Good security practice is that if a user does not need a privilege, he or she should not have it. Review privileges on a regular basis for need and for actual use. If neither is evident, revoke the privilege.	Consider change of responsibilities, promotions, and movement between tasks in context of user access rights. The point is not to restrict unnecessarily, just to be aware of who has access to what and to make a conscious decision to maintain those access rights or modify.
Information access	Devise and implement information classification. Use these classifications to govern access to information as part of the overall privilege management scheme.	Acquire, implement, and use mechanisms to enforce access control.

(continued)

Table 3.1   Security Management Framework and Interpretation Guide (Continued)

Category/Sub-Category/Element	Requirement	Interpretation/Commentary
Segregation	Information technology housing or processing sensitive information (according to information classification) may require isolation from other parts of the organization network.	Such areas may include R&D, strategic planning, and other communities of interest (COIs) that operate on an ad hoc or ongoing basis.
User Responsibilities		
Password configuration	Require users to follow organizational standards for the generation and use of passwords of an appropriate strength.	Develop and enforce a password policy that includes the use of strong passwords and explicitly prohibits the use of simple passwords including company name, employee's name, and similar easily guessable configurations.
Unattended information technology	Ensure policy, standards, and procedures for safeguarding unattended information technology. This includes use of password-controlled screen savers, door locks, locking of laptops in desks, etc.	Policy may address the need for manual system lock upon exiting the area as well as an inactivity time-out system lock in event of distracted or forgetful employees.
Work area management	Secure documents and devices according to classification levels. Sensitive documents go in locked file cabinets. Be aware of office traffic when leaving work area unattended.	Even in a secure building, there is risk of unescorted personnel or authorized personnel after hours having access to information or information technology.

Table 3.1 Security Management Framework and Interpretation Guide (Continued)

Category/Sub-Category/Element	Requirement	Interpretation/Commentary
Network Services		
Entity identification	With the introduction of dynamic services on the network, these services and other devices need unique identifiers. A requesting service (not a person) presents a claim of identity that is validated like a user id. A service provider does the same.	This may assist in establishing connections to a specific device and not just a device or user with an id and password. Identification methods may be to validate the device's MAC address, serial number, or unique id assigned (similar to a user id).
Network communities	Group users and devices according to their classification levels. Particularly sensitive business functions may reside in separate areas on the network.	For example, separate finance from R&D. Although both depend on each other organizationally, systemically they may be separate.
Traffic management	Establish policy and procedures for network traffic management that address traffic segregation, traffic traversing various network segments (routing), and externally bound traffic.	Provide formal procedures and tracking to align technical controls with policy governing those controls.
Operating Systems		
User identification	Assign unique user id per user. Require each user to use his or her, and only his or her, user id. Provide all users with unique user ids for their personal use only, and implement an appropriate authentication technique for their claims of identity.	With the increase in e-commerce and other online transactions that become binding, there is an increased need for non-repudiation. Although this requirement does address non-repudiation, a unique identification is the first step. This requirement implies the need for formal identity management.

(continued)

Table 3.1   Security Management Framework and Interpretation Guide (Continued)

Category/Sub-Category/Element	Requirement	Interpretation/Commentary
Identity authentication	Assign unique user id per user. Require each user to use his or her, and only his or her, user id. Provide all users with unique user ids for their personal use only, and implement an appropriate authentication technique for their claims of identity.	With the increase in e-commerce and other online transactions that become binding, there is an increased need for non-repudiation. Although this requirement does address non-repudiation, a unique identification is the first step. This requirement implies the need for formal identity management.
User privileges	Explicitly assign privileges according to business need.	Access to operating system level introduces business risk. Only qualified personnel with a need for access should be granted this privilege. Moreover, effective privilege management permits only execution of the functions for which they require access.
Privilege authorization	Validate claim of privilege prior to allowing access or executing requested task, service, or application.	Privilege authorization is traditionally part of identity authentication in which a static set of privileges goes along with the user id. The introduction of attribute-based access control (ABAC) uses a more dynamic model in which user privileges associated with a user id come and go according to the business situation. Considering privilege management separate from identity management becomes a more important distinction.

Table 3.1 Security Management Framework and Interpretation Guide (Continued)

Category/Sub-Category/Element	Requirement	Interpretation/Commentary
Identity validation management	Establish policy and practice for identity validation; e.g., user provides a validation of his or her claim of identity. One method is a password. Use password management to ensure the use of appropriate password configurations and strength.	*Note:* The use of passwords exclusively is one-factor authentication; consider the appropriate use of multi-factor authentication in terms of what the user knows (e.g., password), has (e.g., secure token), is (e.g., fingerprint), or does (e.g., signature or other activity metric).
System utilities	Establish policy and procedure to control the existence and execution of utility programs.	Consider defense in depth with respect to protection of system utilities. OS access protection is one line of defense, and access to system utilities is another. Standard OS configurations that permit the existence and execution of utility programs are another.
Inactive sessions	Lock or shut down inactive sessions. Require a password to reaccess locked sessions.	Users may be distracted and forget to log out, or an endpoint may drop with an active session open to hijacking.
Connection time restrictions	Restrict connection times as part of a defense in-depth program. Anticipate expected operating hours, and restrict access to those dates/times. Provide for exception requests to accommodate business need.	Consider time of day, day of week, holidays, seasonal needs, etc.

(continued)

Table 3.1 Security Management Framework and Interpretation Guide (Continued)

Category/Sub-Category/Element	Requirement	Interpretation/Commentary
Remote Workers		
Mobile workers	Ensure policy, standards, and procedures to facilitate the effective and secure support for mobile workers, including the use of information technology outside the organization and connectivity to the organization.	Mobile computing is a great productivity enhancer; it also may mean that sensitive data travels between sites, nationally or internationally, where exposure to theft is greater. Mobile workers are, by definition, on the move more than teleworkers.
Teleworkers	Ensure policy, standards, and procedures to facilitate the effective and secure support for teleworkers, including the use of information technology outside the organization and connectivity to the organization.	Consider organizational compliance requirements and work flow with respect to teleworkers' activities. E.g., data entry or processing of medical data via telework has implications from HIPAA Final Security Rule. Teleworkers are less mobile than mobile workers; teleworkers may operate exclusively out of home offices. Equipment needs and operations are different between mobile workers and teleworkers.

Table 3.1 Security Management Framework and Interpretation Guide (Continued)

Category/Sub-Category/Element	Requirement	Interpretation/Commentary
Solution Quality Assurance	**Security as a Quality Attribute of Solution Development and Acquisition**	
Information Technology Security		
Compliance requirements	Compliance requirements are externally imposed (e.g., legislation) as well as internally imposed (e.g., security standards such as, ISO 27002). Include security controls that adhere to compliance requirements as part of solution acquisition and solution development.	Let business need drive the acquisition of security measures. Include the need for security measures in statements of business requirements; specifically, how the security measures help manage business risk.
Information Accuracy		
Input integrity	Ensure policy and standards to ensure correct data is accepted as input to applications. Moreover, ensure all applications enforce correct input.	Garbage in–garbage out; insecure data constructs in–integrity of security controls out. E.g., the latter means to guard against cleverly constructed data inputs that may include executable code embedded in HTML format.

(continued)

Table 3.1 Security Management Framework and Interpretation Guide (Continued)

Category/Sub-Category/Element	Requirement	Interpretation/Commentary
Internal integrity	Ensure policy and standards to review and validate data within applications, databases, etc. to detect corruption and to evaluate corruption as a warning signal for anomalous activity.	Malicious data may enter a system for lack of data input validation (check before writing). A second line of defense is for applications to check data prior to processing (check before reading). With the increase of e-commerce and the introduction of a new paradigm of need-to-share to supplement need-to-know, there is increasing dependence on messages and transactions. There will be an increase in the use of and dependence on metadata as well. The intent here is to discern the appropriate protection and enforce that protection for message integrity.
Output integrity	Validate data considered as output from a business function, service, or application to ensure form and content are in keeping with expectations. This includes checking for the potential dissemination of malware.	This is another line of organizational defense, or even a method to minimize liability for passing on malicious data outside the organization. There is culpability in initiating a malicious act as well as facilitating a malicious act, even if unwittingly.

Table 3.1 Security Management Framework and Interpretation Guide (Continued)

Category/Sub-Category/Element	Requirement	Interpretation/Commentary
Cryptography		
Cryptography policy	Ensure policy, standards, and procedures to establish the need for cryptography as well as the appropriate and effective use of cryptography.	Consider the practical use of cryptography within the organization.
Key management	Ensure policy, standards, and procedure for key management that include request for cryptographic keys, key issuance, key revocation, and key escrow.	The loss of a cryptographic key may render a device or data unusable; that is, the organization has lost the utility of that information or information technology. Effective key management will provide for secure key storage and recovery as well as additional organizational needs surrounding the use of cryptographic keys.
File Security		
Production applications	Establish policy, standards, and procedures to control the installation of software and file transfer to production systems.	This may include the standard desktop as well as production servers. The policy and procedures should balance operational effectiveness with business risk management. Considerations of the latter include legislative compliance requirements as well as a penchant of users to circumvent blocks to productivity.

(continued)

Table 3.1 Security Management Framework and Interpretation Guide (Continued)

Category/Sub-Category/Element	Requirement	Interpretation/Commentary
Test data	As a rule, test data should closely reflect production data. Many organizations transfer a snapshot of production data into the test environment with all its inherent safeguard requirements for privacy and as potential classified data.	Good test data reflects reality. Many times, test data is an excerpt of real data—real data that is subject to safeguards as prescribed under legislative or regulatory requirements.
Source code protection	Also part of configuration management, separate development, test, and production environments. The development environment contains actual or potential intellectual property and should be protected accordingly.	The multitude of reasons includes safeguarding the integrity of the code from an operational perspective as well as restricting the opportunity to introduce malware into the code.
Development Environment		
Change control	Establish and enforce policy for formal change control to manage application source code and test data.	Both well-meaning accidents and malicious intent may result in the loss of data or data integrity, including documents containing intellectual property or source code. A formal change control process includes version control as well as a chronology of modifications including what and by whom.

Table 3.1 Security Management Framework and Interpretation Guide (Continued)

Category/Sub-Category/Element	Requirement	Interpretation/Commentary
Operating system (OS) upgrades	Validate business functions, services, and applications on new OS versions prior to introducing to the production environment.	Look before you leap; and there is an implication to scout out a path backward just in case you land somewhere you did not expect.
Application upgrades	Validate business functions, services, and applications in the event of application upgrades prior to introducing to the production environment. A given application upgrade may affect more than just the application itself; therefore, the entire production environment needs to be tested.	Excessive modifications increase risk to operations. Strict controls include planning around operational need to minimize productivity impact; there is especially the need for determining back-out trigger events and a back-out process that restores the original operating conditions. Trigger events may include an unexpected operational emergency, detection that the new software modification negatively affects the operations, or the inability to install modifications.
Memory and other leaks	Acquisition of new applications, OS upgrades, and application upgrades introduce potential vulnerabilities. One category of vulnerabilities is memory and other leaks in which data may traverse to unexpected areas (e.g., buffer overflows).	Consider security flaws as software bugs and review the software quality assurance of the development process accordingly.

(continued)

Table 3.1 Security Management Framework and Interpretation Guide (Continued)

Category/Sub-Category/Element	Requirement	Interpretation/Commentary
Acquisition	Any security restrictions the organization may place on in-house development should also be imposed during solutions acquisition from sources outside the organization.	Impose security restrictions and monitor solution development to ensure appropriate personnel work on the code. Establish testing procedures that review not only operational integrity but also security issues in a source code review as well as functional testing.
Vulnerability Management		
Patch management	Establish and enforce policy, standards, and procedures to discover and treat vulnerabilities with operating systems, applications, utilities, etc. This includes production systems, user systems, technical infrastructure, and security infrastructure.	This includes at least a patch management process for all OSs, OS versions, applications, application versions, etc.
Incident Management		
Computer Security Incident Response Teams (CSIRT)		
CSIRT operations	Ensure policy to establish CSIRT operations as part of overall network management or operations management	A CSIRT service includes support for detection, notification, triage, escalation, response, treatment, root cause analysis, and organizational feedback with regard to security events.

Table 3.1 Security Management Framework and Interpretation Guide (Continued)

Category/Sub-Category/Element	Requirement	Interpretation/Commentary
Detection	Establish policy and procedure for the detection of security events. This includes automated monitoring as well as awareness training for employees to be on the lookout for potential incidents and how to report them.	Monitoring and detection are the first steps in an effective CSIRT operation.
Notification	Establish and enforce policy to report information security events through appropriate CSIRT services; i.e., primary employee initial notification point is the help desk.	Notification of a security event places the responsibility on the help desk to address the event as a routine occurrence or an exception that warrants escalation to a subject matter expert (SME).
Preemptive	Ensure a policy, standards, and procedure that add preemptive steps to security education, training, and awareness (SETA).	Preemptive steps include an awareness of early warning signals (e.g., degraded service levels) and knowledge of how to notify the appropriate internal service (e.g., help desk or CSIRT).
CSIRT Management		
Roles and responsibilities	Ensure policy, standards, and procedure to establish roles and responsibilities within the CSIRT service. These should address CSIRT alignment with strategic initiatives and compliance requirements as well as support of business functions that satisfy the core business mission.	There is need for management guidance as well as operational guidance; there may be greater and imminent need to stem the bleeding prior to discovering the root problem. A prepared management is ready to respond accordingly.

(continued)

Table 3.1 Security Management Framework and Interpretation Guide (Continued)

Category/Sub-Category/Element	Requirement	Interpretation/Commentary
Lessons learned	Establish and enforce policy for capturing and formalizing lessons learned from security incidents into organizational operations.	Security metrics are of growing importance to justify the implementation and ongoing operational effectiveness of security. Quantifying incident details assists in conveying the benefits of security and may provide input to a ROSI model.
Submissibility	Ensure policy, standards, and procedures to establish criteria for identifying and capturing evidence surrounding security incidents. Decision to pursue prosecution should be for good business reason, not merely lack of submissible evidence.	Requirements may vary according to jurisdiction. A single enterprise policy may apply in a multi-national organization; however, the standards and procedures will vary between jurisdictions.
Business Continuity (BC) and Disaster Recovery (DR) Management		
Information Security Aspects of Business Continuity Management		
BC/DR management process	Using a combination of threat analysis, risk analysis, vulnerability analysis, and business impact analysis (BIA), develop a plan for business continuity and disaster recovery.	Business continuity is the superset of disaster recovery. Consider organizational needs in terms of downtime tolerance or uptime objectives. Such considerations drive decisions toward real-time recovery (low downtime tolerance) and off-site recovery that may take hours or days longer.

Table 3.1 Security Management Framework and Interpretation Guide (Continued)

Category/Sub-Category/Element	Requirement	Interpretation/Commentary
Threat assessment	Identify events and entities that can cause interruptions to business processes.	Review the threat-space to the organization. Determine realistic probabilities of threat realization. The results give insight on where to allocate limited resources for business risk management. In general, mitigate high probability risk; accept low risk. Such a rule may not be preferable but may be the best economically viable option.
Risk assessment	Using the results of the threat assessment as input, identify events and entities that can cause interruptions. Heed the rule that possible does not necessarily mean probable.	This implies the need for a vulnerability assessment as well as a BIA that first identifies key business processes, key personnel supporting those processes, and key infrastructure supporting the personnel and processes. Given limited resources (and security resources are always limited), focusing on the subset of business activities that generate the most organizational benefit will provide the highest return on business continuity investments.

(continued)

Table 3.1 Security Management Framework and Interpretation Guide (Continued)

Category/Sub-Category/Element	Requirement	Interpretation/Commentary
BC/DR plan	Develop and enforce plans to maintain business operations at specified service levels. Include a plan to restore operations to acceptable service levels in the event they fall below acceptable levels. Address trigger events for invoking DR operations (e.g., X hours of unacceptable service level).	Implies the need to develop SLAs to determine a baseline measurement for acceptable operational efficiency. For each key business process, develop continuity and restoration plans. Walk through scenarios of loss of site (e.g., fire), extended loss of access to site (e.g., biohazard/quarantine), short loss of access to site (e.g., ice storm), loss of key personnel, and loss of key asset or infrastructure. Business continuity is an enterprise concern. Even in the event of a holding company with many discrete sub-organizations, there is need to establish and ensure the protection of organizational interests. Leveraging an enterprise approach to security in general, and specifically business continuity, will promote consistency across the enterprise.
BC/DR maintenance	Test, review, and update BC/DR plans regularly to ensure that they are current and meet organizational operating goals.	Review in context of changing business environment or technical drivers (e.g., end of life for key business continuity tools).

Table 3.1   Security Management Framework and Interpretation Guide (Continued)

Category/Sub-Category/Element	Requirement	Interpretation/Commentary
Compliance Management		
External Compliance Requirements		
Legislation, regulation, codes, and standards	Explicitly enumerate all relevant external compliance requirements, including legislation, regulation, codes, standards, etc. Decompose these documents into business requirements with meaning to organizational operations.	Formally address the need for compliance management. Devise processes and procedures to enumerate all applicable compliance requirements. A large part of this text addresses how to establish and manage compliance requirements. The scope of external requirements includes positive affirmations for organizational operations (i.e., thou shall) as well as negative restrictions (i.e., thou shall not). For example, this includes the appropriate use of software, music, documents, and all other artifacts that fall under legislative requirements. E.g., the music industry may go after ABC, Inc. as an unwitting facilitator of music sharing if there is no due diligence and preventive measures to discourage such activity. At the very least, instilling an ethics program and disseminating appropriate use policy will reduce, if not eliminate, culpability and organizational repercussions.

(continued)

Table 3.1   Security Management Framework and Interpretation Guide (Continued)

Category/Sub-Category/Element	Requirement	Interpretation/Commentary
Record retention	Ensure policy, standards, and procedures to capture, store, and retain appropriate records of the form, with the content, and for the duration specified by compliance requirements.	This includes tax records, organizational documentation, audit logs, and more. The scope of this effort is driven by legislative mandates as well as good business practice.
Privacy management	Ensure policy, standards, and procedures to implement and enforce appropriate privacy protections as specified by compliance requirements.	In addition to legislative mandates for privacy, customer good will becomes an issue as public awareness increases for the need to protect personal information.
Data protection	Ensure policy, standards, and procedures to implement and enforce the protection of data owned or under the custodianship of the organization. This includes the appropriate use of data (for business purposes) and access only by authorized personnel.	This implies the need for an appropriate use policy that states the intent of appropriate use as well as provides examples of inappropriate use. The goal is to provide a statement of appropriate use with a caveat that anything not in keeping with the intended use is inappropriate. A contrary method attempts to enumerate a list of inappropriate action with the implication that anything not on the list is therefore appropriate. The latter plays to the *letter-of-the-law*; the former establishes a *spirit-of-the-law*. Management needs training on how to discern inappropriate action and how to handle accordingly.

Table 3.1 Security Management Framework and Interpretation Guide (Continued)

Category/Sub-Category/Element	Requirement	Interpretation/Commentary
Internal Compliance Requirements		
Security policies, standards, and procedures	Ensure all personnel are aware of and incorporate security policies, standards, and procedures into the fulfillment of their duties as employees of the organization.	External compliance requirements are qualifications imposed on the organization from outside. Internal compliance requirements are self-imposed restrictions in the name of good business and to manage business risk. Consider "compliance" to address all compliance requirements, including external, internal, explicit, and implicit will-drive policy.
Security controls	Review and validate that the application of security controls on information and information technology is in keeping with accepted industry standards (e.g., ISO 27001, ISO 27002).	There are organizational and policy compliance assessments as well as auditing and validation of technical controls. Organizational policy drives the regularity and depth of verification and validation.

(continued)

Table 3.1 Security Management Framework and Interpretation Guide (Continued)

Category/Sub-Category/Element	Requirement	Interpretation/Commentary
Audit Management		
Security control audits	Security controls impose restrictions on business operations to manage business risk. An audit of security controls ensures they are present and are working as intended.	A security controls audit may be non-intrusive to information technology. An audit that includes validation of technical controls may include automated vulnerability scans or hands-on validation. Any activity that touches the device or traverses mediums that facilitate operations may interfere with operations. Careful planning will identify low-volume time of day or non-critical time of month (e.g., low accounting or finance activity). Such precautions will minimize the potential of impact during audits.
Security audit tools	Ensure policy and procedures for the appropriate use of audit tools. Explicitly deny access and use of audit tools to unauthorized personnel. Ensure authorized personnel are trained and competent in the use of security audit tools.	Security validation tools (e.g., vulnerability scanners) are subject to malicious use. Even with good intent, the novice user may cause great harm by disrupting organizational operations with audit tools.

As a matter of philosophy on security management, the authors promote the development of a sound security management program (ISMS) first. Second, add qualifications that address instances of other compliance requirements. These qualifications may be ePHI if HIPAA applies security controls called out in Sarbanes–Oxley (SOX) Section 404 or specifics within the Australian Security Industry Act 2003 or European Directive on Data Protection. Developing HIPAA security policies or SOX security policies is not a replacement for security policies and is, in actuality, a subordinate qualification to the broader security policies. Besides, a duplicate set of policies (one set for HIPAA, one set for SOX, one for security) adds administrative overhead to review and maintain these policies. It is better to start with a solid foundation of good security policies and add qualifications according to legislative, regulatory, or compliance requirements that may come and go.

The *Requirement* column in Table 3.1* closely follows the ISO 17799 outline and restates the ISO requirements in terms of positive affirmations, as in "establish and enforce" or "management implements." The interpretation and commentary are notional. As with all such statements, applicability and interpretation are organization specific.

Much confusion comes from misinterpretation of terms and phrases; an organizational glossary assists in normalizing understanding. There may still be disagreement on specific meanings; however, as long as everyone operates from the same basic understanding, the chances for a successful ISMS increase. Likewise, the enumeration of a security management framework using industry standards or legislative guidance (e.g., SOX) requires a common understanding of the components of that framework. Then all personnel act from that common understanding to increase consistency in planning for security controls, implementation of security controls, compliance assessments, preparing materials for auditors, etc.

3.3 ISMS Initial Planning and Implementation

The PDCA model is a cyclical model with intent of imposing an ongoing management system for information security. The initial preparation is similar to, but a special case of, the ongoing efforts. The initial planning and implementation set up in the ISMS and the subsequent iterations of Plan–Do–Check–Act (PDCA) begin with checking the status of the ISMS (Check Phase) and proceed with acting upon necessary revisions (Act Phase), planning how to act upon the revisions (Plan Phase), and implementing revisions (Do Phase), all in a continual cycle.

---

* *Note:* The table closely follows the outline of ISO 27002 standards and represents the intent; however, the details in this table, and generally in this text, are not a replacement for the ISO standards, and the authors recommend acquiring the relevant ISO security standards to use in conjunction with the information herein.

The objectives for initial planning and implementation include the following:

- Collect background details on the organization.
  - Business type
  - Mission
  - Site locations
  - Etc.
- Identify key players for the ISMS development process.
- Identify drivers (motivations) behind risk management and the need for an ISMS.
- Obtain a high-level snapshot of the organization's security posture, that is, current ability and practices to identify and address business risks.
- Collect details that will contribute to establishing the scope of the ISMS.
  - Sites, operations, business functions, information, information technology, infrastructure, etc.
- Define the objectives of an ISMS, e.g., good-enough practice? ISO 27001 certification?
- Begin to outline the contents of the prospective ISMS.
- Establish schedule for ISMS development.
- Begin to outline the processes to establish and maintain an ISMS.

The material below presents details on how to approach initial planning and implementation and achieve the objectives in the list above.

3.4 Establishing Current Status of Organizational Security Management (Assessment Process)

The discovery process to obtain these details takes place in two macro-phases: *background discovery* and *compliance level discovery*.

3.4.1 Background Discovery

The background discovery task begins by learning more about the organization, organizational goals, mission, operations, general background, role of security, and overall cultural perception of security. Background discovery gathers these details by way of questionnaire or survey. Many of the questions in background discovery are not traceable to the ISO standards; however, they still represent important information to assist in determining the current compliance level (the next discovery phase) and ultimately generate the documentation necessary for ISO 27001 certification.

3.4.1.1 Organization Background Information

Background information includes what the organization is; who the major players are, including executives, decision makers, authorizers, and deciders with respect to security; and why security is important to the organization. Additionally, background discovery discerns where security is important, including physical and cyber locations. Background discovery details include at least the following:

- Organization
  - Organization name with address of each facility and/or site
  - Organizational charts; management hierarchy
  - Legal structure; e.g., holding company with separate legal entities versus single legal entities
  - Mission
- Personnel
  - Name of the CxOs with contact information, including CEO, COO, CFO, CIO, CSO, etc.
  - Name of security management personnel with contact information, including relationship to CxOs, both formal and informal
  - Name of IT managers with contact information
  - Name of security managers with contact information
  - Name and contact information of emergency contact persons in all locations
  - Number of employees in each site
  - History of information security, including any problems and where they occurred
- Facilities
  - Main activity in each facility and/or site
  - Emergency telephone numbers for all facilities
  - Range of hours of operation for each site
  - Location of areas containing sensitive material
  - Location of areas containing the most valuable assets
  - Location of central computer systems and backup systems
  - Description of connectivity with other departments and partners
- Technology
  - Data center locations
  - Network maps
  - Entry/exit points to/from the network, e.g., Internet, virtual private networks (VPNs)
  - Relationship of external connector, e.g., ISP, partner, vendor, customer
  - Role of technology in operations
  - Voice communication details
    - PBX locations, voice services to the organization, role of voice communications in operations

This information will give a good background of the organization, organization mission and operations, key personnel, and general details from which to develop a custom compliance discovery process, or, generally, the following:

- Objectives of the organization
- Reasons the organization is in business
- Key business functions
- Roles and responsibilities, governance, management, planning, implementation, operations, and maintenance of:
  - Security
  - Business risk management
  - Vulnerability management
- Security objectives, e.g., policy
- How the organization accomplishes operational and security objectives, i.e., procedures and practices
- How results are conveyed to management and other areas of the organization, e.g., reporting

The final background discovery question set is organization specific and reflects organizational structure, physical locations, operations, operating goals, the role of security, and goals for security. The following sections contain a general question set as a foundation for an organization-specific questionnaire. This high-level questionnaire divides the questions into three categories: general information security posture, security arrangements, and information security infrastructure. Gather supporting documentation for the claims in addition to the questionnaire responses. Many organizations have good practice without documenting that practice. Part of the discovery process is to distinguish practice from procedure and to note what procedures are necessary to formally reflect practice. Record all answers in supporting documentation to assist in the compliance discovery process as well as in producing documentation for the ISMS creation and ISMS certification.

3.4.1.2 General Information Security Posture Questionnaire

The objective here is to discern the general information security posture of the organization, including existing policies, security activities to date, the formality of security policy and practice (e.g., formal documentation), and the presence of business continuity plans.

1. Has the organization implemented a policy for information security?
   a. The organization should have an information security policy document.
   b. The policy should document scope.

    c. The policy should document roles and responsibilities.

    d. The security policy should obtain approval at the board level.

    e. There should be security operating procedures for all users, platforms, data, networks, and applications.

2. Has the organization performed a risk assessment?

    a. The organization should have a documented risk assessment methodology.

    b. The risk assessment should identify all applicable risks.

    c. The risk assessment should assess the organizational impact of risks.

    d. There should be a list of options for the treatment of the risks.

3. Does the organization have a documented internal audit process for information security?

    a. The organization should conduct a regular compliance review undertaken by an internal or external auditor.

    b. Handling of personal data should comply with applicable data protection legislation.

    c. There is a commitment to review information security at a minimum annually.

4. Does the organization have a business continuity management plan?

    a. The plan should address business continuity and disaster recovery.

    b. The organization should have a managed process in place.

    c. The organization should test, review, and maintain the business continuity plan (BCP) and disaster recovery plan (DRP); testing is at least annual.

    d. The test of the process should be undertaken yearly at a minimum.

3.4.1.3 Security Arrangements

The security arrangements question set is in four categories:

- *General,* where the responsible persons have the responsibility that information operation is conducted according to the law and regulations
- Security arrangements regarding *employees and external workers*
- Security arrangements regarding *external security*
- Organizational and technical security arrangements

3.4.1.3.1 General

A1. Has the organization implemented a policy for information classification?

    a. There should be a formal classification for information.

    b. Classification should take into account business needs.

    c. Policy should be associated with information assets.

    d. Policy should be used to decide protection priorities in terms of its integrity and availability.

A2. Has the organization implemented a policy for handling and labeling documents?

    a. There should be a formal policy on how the organization assets are labeled.

    b. Policy should include documentation and physical equipment.

    c. Policy should include software and data.

    d. Personnel and automated systems should handle documents in accordance with information classification.

A3. Does the organization have a clear desk policy?

    a. Organization should have a policy for clear desks.

    b. There should be a regular review of the policies.

    c. There should be a rule on handling information on the desk.

    d. There should be an active screen saver on all PCs and portable computers.

3.4.1.3.2 Employees and External Workers

B1. Does the organization perform pre-employment screening?

    a. The organization should conduct a background check on prospective employees and external or contract workers.

    b. The security manager should clear background checks for new potential employees and contractors.

B2. Does the organization perform a new employ orientation for information and information technology security?

    a. The organization should make new employees aware of security policy, standards, procedures, and practices.

    b. Initial awareness should include a section on ethics and stress the importance of protecting organization and customer interests.

B3. Does the organization use a confidentiality agreement?

    a. The organization should have an appropriate legal contract that is signed by both staff and contractors who work in the building or who can be remotely connected to the organization's information system, where sensitive information access may occur.

    b. Among other things, the contract should include that all information is provided solely for use for the organization.

B4. Do all employees and visitors in the organization wear passes?

    a. Both employees and visitors should be required to wear identification passes at all times.

    b. The passes should be visible when within the organization.

3.4.1.3.3 External Security

C1. Does the organization have secure physical protection and storage?
    a. The organization should have physical protection in place with clear perimeters.
    b. There should be sufficient security lockers for all classified media to prevent unauthorized access to sensitive information and systems.
C2. Is there a clear physical protection plan in place?
    a. There should be a written policy for physical protection.
    b. The perimeter for an individual area should be clear.

3.4.1.3.4 Organizational and Technical Security Arrangements

D1. Has the organization implemented unique user passwords and accounts?
    a. The organization should have implemented a policy for the use of passwords.
    b. For all users of the information system, both employees and others that have access, there should be a unique password and account for each individual on specified systems and they should be security controlled.
    c. There should be a regular review of user access rights.
D2. Has the organization any policy on use of passwords?
    a. The organization should have a good security practice on selection and use of passwords.
    b. Passwords on specified systems should be eight characters or longer.
    c. The passwords should be combinations of numbers and letters or special characters.
    d. There should be a rule on how often the passwords are changed.
D3. Has the organization implemented a document access policy?
    a. The organization should have a policy that defines the granting of data access permissions.
    b. The policy should be defined as to which user may access each data item.
D4. How does the organization security team store and distribute information?
    a. The organization should have a policy as to how to store data in the information system.
    b. There should be a list on how the system locks users and group accounts.
    c. There should be accountability as to how data and software are stored in the organization.
    d. There should be documentation explaining the intent and procedures on how organizations exchange information (e.g., via encrypted link, VPN).
D5. Is there a policy for the security of electronic mail (e-mail)?
    a. The organization should have implemented a policy to reduce both business and security risks associated with using electronic mail.

      b. Each employee should have a copy of the policy.

      c. All employees should use and understand the policy.

D6. Is the organization using monitoring tools to trail records?

      a. The organization should have, at regular intervals, an internal review and audit.

      b. That review and audit should include log files.

      c. Monitoring and audits should be done specifically where there is sensitive information according to classification.

D7. Does the organization have a policy for testing security in applications and new systems before implementation?

      a. There should be a policy for testing new security applications.

      b. There should be a policy for testing new security systems.

      c. There should be security testing of new applications before implementation.

      d. There should be security testing of a new system before implementation.

      e. When the organization is developing new applications, a security testing requirement should be identified and approved prior to developing the application.

      f. The organization should test all systems, software, applications, and network software before implementation.

D8. Does the organization have a policy in place to prevent malicious software?

      a. The organization should have written detection procedures to detect and prevent all malicious code.

      b. Appropriate awareness procedures should be implemented.

      c. The organization should specify accountability obtaining recent information on threats and continually updating the anti-malware software.

D9. Has the organization implemented a policy for change control procedures?

      a. The organization should have a change control procedure in place covering all stages of management and development.

      b. The policy should include all hardware, system software, networks, documentation, and network software.

      c. The procedure should include approval of ownership.

      d. The work responsibilities should be included.

      e. There should be a fall-back plan.

      f. There should be an estimation of time.

D10. Does the organization have a written policy on Internet use and access?

      a. The organization should have a written policy on Internet use and access.

      b. The organization should have procedures on how to connect to the Internet.

      c. The organization should have a procedure to defend its network from the Internet.

D11. Has the organization implemented a policy for the testing of data backup and restoration?

      a. The organization should have a policy for regularly testing data backups.

      b. The organization should have procedures for regularly testing restoration.

    c. The organization should make copies of essential data and software regularly.

    d. The organization should remove backups and store off-site.

3.4.1.4 Information Security Infrastructure

1. Does the organization have a security manager?
    a. The organization should have a security manager.
    b. The security manager should hold an executive-level position.
    c. All levels of the organization should be security aware and act in keeping with the security policy using available security procedures and otherwise act in keeping with the policy.
    d. There should be an approved financial budget to implement information security and a written instruction of managerial duties.
2. Does the organization have regular training and education in information security?
    a. The organization should provide education and training in information security for all staff.
    b. The organization policies, procedures, and work rules should be part of the training.
3. Has the organization implemented a procedure for reporting an incident?
    a. The organization should have a procedure for reporting all incidents and problems.
    b. The organization should document and review all mishaps or problems in information security and use the findings to reinforce existing security measures or modify accordingly to strengthen the organization's security posture.

3.4.1.5 Findings and Report

The questions provide a high-level snapshot of the business environment and the organization's security posture. Obtaining answers to these questions is relatively quick (contrary to the comprehensive audit question set), and the process is relatively less expensive than an audit or more formal assessment. The benefit is a quick determination of the strengths and weaknesses in the organization's security program. It is possible to quantify this snapshot to provide a numeric baseline and subsequent data to compare against the baseline. Such quantification may provide insight into areas requiring immediate attention as well. The specifics of quantification and interpretation of the meaning are organization specific.

Table 3.2 shows example results for which general compliance levels are greater than 60 percent. This score would indicate that the organization has a good understanding of information security. General scores that are between 40 and 50 percent will show there is a need for more general arrangements. Any compliance that is

Table 3.2   Compliance Results in Percentage

	20% and under	21%–40%	41%–50%	51%–60%	61% and greater
Compliance Categories					
General					X
General Arrangements			X		
Employee Arrangements					
External Security Arrangements					
Technical Arrangements					
Infrastructure					

lower than 60 percent indicates the organization needs to do some work in that area to improve information security. General arrangements less than 60 percent imply the need for modifications to general arrangement security. The findings report conveys the results of the questionnaire as well as the analysis results and recommendations on subsequent actions.

3.4.2 Compliance Level Discovery

The discovery process derives the current security posture of the organization via interviews, document review, and perhaps verification and validation. Verification includes viewing that the actual controls are in place; validation ensures they actually work by hands-on testing or a demonstration of functionality. *Appendix A: ISMS Assessment Discovery Question Set* contains an extensive question set on which to base discovery interviews; Table 3.3 presents an excerpt from the full question set. There is a specific pattern of the questions. The first questions discern if X exists; e.g., does the organization have a password policy? If so, the next set questions discern the quality of X; that is, what are the features of the password policy? The latter assists in assessing the compliance level of the password policy as compared to the compliance requirement, in this case the ISO 27002 guidance. Add questions and features according to organizational need, and cover all the relevant compliance requirements. Note that cross-indexing compliance requirements (e.g., overlaps between ISO 27002 and NIST, or ISO 27002 and SOX) will provide the ability to ask a single question and establish a single set of features that may satisfy more than one compliance requirement. With a cleverly designed question set, the assessor may establish compliance levels as compared to multiple compliance requirements (hint!). The question set excerpt in Table 3.3 provides an example of

Table 3.3 Excerpt from Full Compliance Assessment Question Set

Category	Ref #	ISO 27002	Question
Risk Management	1	4	
Risk Mgmt	1.1	4.1	Does your organization have a policy that addresses the need for risk management?
Risk Mgmt	1.2	4.1	Does this policy require, specify, or otherwise address the following:
Risk Mgmt	1.2.1	4.1	Identification of an acceptable risk posture for the organization?
Risk Mgmt	1.2.2	4.1	Risk assessment?
Compliance Management	2	15	
Compliance Mgmt	2.1	15	Does your organization have a policy for compliance management?
Compliance Mgmt	2.2	15.1	Does this policy require, specify, or otherwise address the following:
Compliance Mgmt	2.2.1	15.1	The scope of compliance management: explicit business requirements, implicit risk management (therefore, security) requirements, and explicit security requirements?
Compliance Mgmt	2.2.2	15.1	The need to identify and enumerate relevant legislative, regulatory, and other requirements with which the organization must comply?
Etc.			

such cross-indexing by showing a cross-index between the questions and the ISO 27002 sections.

Experience shows that people have little tolerance for extensive question sets for either in-person questioning or by way of survey. A more successful approach is to develop an interview process for an assessor (e.g., security professional) to discuss security issues with the appropriate person with knowledge of that particular area. The interview process discerns all the details of the question set without necessarily asking each and every question. In support of this interview process, consider the following interview guide to engage people in discussions about security in a conversational manner. This conversational manner obtains better cooperation than clinically going through each individual question.

The interview guide aligns with the full discovery question set and permits the assessor to engage the interviewees in conversation. As key points are covered, the assessor may mark down cues to responses. The assessor may then complete the full question set on his or her own. This may seem somewhat labor intensive on the part of the assessor; however, this is a more certain way of obtaining complete and more accurate information. Feedback from assessors following this method in the process of recording detailed answers assists greatly with their confidence level in writing the gap analysis and remediation analysis reports and making recommendations for managing business risks. The discipline of a comprehensive question set forces the assessors (in a good and positive way) to complete the interview guide and the question set. If the assessor does not gather all the relevant answers during the initial interview, a follow-up phone conversation or e-mail to discern the missing data is far easier than handling the entire discovery process remotely.

In planning for discovery and the interview process, the assessor should map personnel contacts with each SMF category and element to ensure he or she is asking the right people the right questions. This is more expedient, as people familiar with the business practices will know the answers more readily; moreover, the accuracy of the information greatly increases when not gathering best guesses, simply because the interviewee feels the need to respond with something other than the more accurate "*I don't know*." The interview guide by nature is not comprehensive in wording but is comprehensive in detail and prompts the assessor with key words and concepts to engage in conversation.

The question set may be quite extensive and is specific to the compliance requirement set applicable to the organization. The question set in the interview guide below is a sample using the question set in *Appendix A: ISMS Assessment Discovery Question Set*. The questions are numbered 1, 2, 3, etc. The tables provide a series of key points for check marks or other notation according to the need of the assessor.

3.4.2.1 Sample Interview Guide

SECURITY POLICY

> *Remember*: Engage in conversation… ask open-ended questions and note responses… follow up with specific questions as necessary.

An organizational security management program includes:

- Information security policy
  - Information security policy document
    - Review of information security policy

Table 3.4 Security Management Policy Feature Checklist 1 (Sample)

✓	*Feature*	✓	*Feature*	✓	*Feature*
	Security goals		Align security goals with business goals		Align security goals with business operations
	Formal review process				
	Review Trigger Events				
	Business change		Calendar		Security incident
	Policy Features				
	Review of policy effectiveness		Formal process to define, write, review, and approve		Clear direction and visible management support
	Resource allocation for security		Specific security roles and responsibilities		Provisions for security awareness
	Require security working group (SWG) and enterprise coordination of security				
	Supplemental				
	Security procedures that align with policy		Sanction policy for non-compliance		
	Asset security				
	Etc.				

1. Do you have security policies within your organization?
2. Is there a policy that addresses executive sponsorship and management support of security?
3. Does this policy include the following? (Table 3.4)
4. Does your organization have a procedure that describes how to implement policy? (Table 3.5)
5. Does your organization have a policy for asset management? (Table 3.6)

Table 3.5   Security Procedure Feature Checklist 2 (Sample)

✓	Feature	✓	Feature	✓	Feature
	Assessment methodology/ procedure		ID significant threat changes and exposure		Assess adequacy of security controls
	Promote SETA		Monitoring and response		
	Etc.				

The pattern of the interview guide is the same as the full question set in *Appendix A: ISMS Assessment Discovery Question Set*; that is, does your organization have X? If so, does X contain features Y_1, Y_2, Y_n? As an assessor, ask open-ended questions to the effect of *does your organization have a security policy? Tell me about it.* As the conversation entails, prompt for additional detail not covered by the initial description. Check off key points as they are covered by noting a "Y" for yes, this feature is present, or, "N" for no, this feature is missing. Other useful notations may be "U" for unknown by this interviewee or "NA" for not applicable. Also, as an assessor, note a confidence level in the interviewee's response. If the interviewee conveys himself or herself as an unreliable source, by all means be polite and attentive, but note a low confidence in the details. Sometimes taking information at face value leads to false results.

3.5   Analysis of Discovery Results

Now that the assessor has all this discovery data, there is need to consider what to do with it. From the discovery details, review the compliance requirements for the organization and review the high-level risks of the organization. Discern if ISO 27002 and ISO 27001 play a valid role in assisting to manage business risks. (They likely will, but due diligence and critical considerations require reaffirmation.)

Table 3.6   Asset Management Policy Feature Checklist 3 (Sample)

✓	Feature	✓	Feature	✓	Feature
	Associate asset and security process(es)		Identify accountability and responsibilities		Authorization levels
	Etc.				

Review the SMF according to the discovery details and add, detract, or modify the SMF. At this point, there is a clear definition of requirements to address business risk. Compare the findings from discovery details with the requirements of the SMF and record the differences in a gap analysis report. Then consider options and recommendations for gap closure, that is, move from As-Is (discovery detail on current security posture) to To-Be (compliance requirements, now summarized in the SMF) and record the conclusions in a remediation analysis report. Subsequent prioritization of initiatives to mitigate risks by moving toward higher levels of compliance with the compliance requirements results in projects, tasks, or other initiatives. The details of these initiatives will likely reside in many documents, including ROI spreadsheets, project plans, formal definitions of project intent and necessary resources to accomplish the objectives, etc. However, record the status of the initiatives to increase compliance levels in the same SMF to enable easy comparison of findings, gaps, remediation recommendations, and actual projects to accomplish the remediation. The following section provides a look at reporting templates to assist with this effort.

3.5.1 Reporting Templates

Reporting templates includes reporting of findings, gap analysis, remediation analysis, tracking remediation progress, developing action plans with responsibility and due dates, and other such activities necessary to plan, develop, implement, track, and maintain an effective security management program. Table 3.7 presents a variety of report samples. Each header (i.e., *Finding, Gap Analysis, Remediation Analysis,* and *Remediation Progress*) may be in separate files, or the organization may choose to put all detail in a single file. The benefit of using the SMF is each report will use exactly the same categories, subcategories, and elements to promote easy comparison of details between reports.

The efforts to this point provide for the identification of compliance requirements (e.g., ISO 27001 and ISO 27002), discovery process to understand business motivations for identifying and addressing risk, discovery of the current organization's security posture, analysis of gaps between As-Is and To-Be, and enumeration of a number of initiatives to increase compliance levels; one of those initiatives may be (and hopefully *will* be) to formally define an ISMS. More details on the ISMS definition and development occur in many of the following sections.

3.6 An Initial View of Developing an ISMS

The initial development of the ISMS provides a basis for the PDCA cycle to manage. The objectives of this section are to present the following with respect to developing an ISMS:

Table 3.7 Report Template Sample

Category/Element	Requirement	Finding	Gap Analysis	Remediation Analysis	Remediation Progress
Security Policy					
Information and Information Technology Security Policy					
Documentation	Management produces an overarching security policy that includes control of information security and clear implementation guidance	Describe the results of interviews regarding information security policy	Describe the differences between the existing policy and the desired policy (the requirement statement)	Describe steps to achieve the requirement	Enter details of project plans or less formal initiatives to achieve the requirement
Dissemination	Disseminate policy into enterprise initiatives for security awareness				
Etc.					

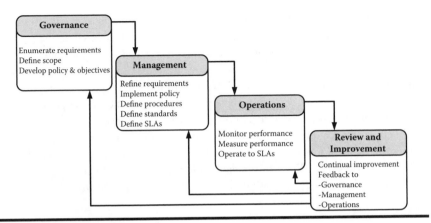

Figure 3.1 ISMS process development approach.

- Establish governance
- Establish plan for management
- Establish framework for operations
- Institute a methodology for continual review and improvement

Figure 3.1 shows the relationship between *governance, management, operations,* and *review and improvement.* Each provides input to the next, with review and improvement providing feedback to the first three. Note that ISO standards do not use the terms governance, management, operations, and review and improvement. Rather, these terms summarize many of the ISO concepts in a flow that represents executive and senior management involvement (governance), senior and middle management involvement (management), and security professionals who perform day-to-day tactical tasks (operations).

The following sections elaborate on the details of governance, management, operations, and review and implementation, followed by sections providing useful constructs for governance, namely:

- SMF baseline
- ISMS—policy, standard, and procedure development and maintenance tracking

3.6.1 Establish Governance

Security governance provides decision-making authority over issues relevant to the business need for information security and establishing an ISMS. Consider an alternative name to security governance as risk governance, as managing business risk is the root driver behind all security initiatives. There is need to define a governance board and a governance process for the organization. The governance board consists of executives and senior management; business line representatives able to represent business interests; legal advisors able to interpret legislation, regulation, and contracts; and security professionals able to represent the full scope of compliance requirements, security needs, and industry best practices.

The governance process results in enumeration of business requirements, defines the scope of risk management, and develops policies and objectives driving the entire ISMS establishment, implementation, and maintenance process. Governance establishes strategy and aligns strategy with business objectives.

3.6.2 Plan for Management

Management develops tactics to implement the strategy. Security management refines the requirements at the strategic level to the point of defining action items to meet strategic objectives. Management defines plans for and oversees the implementation of policy, and it helps guide this implementation through the definition of standards (what to use to implement policy) and procedures (how to implement policy). Management is also responsible for selecting the appropriate security controls and determining metrics and measures to gauge the presence and effectiveness of the security controls.

3.6.3 Framework for Operations

The framework for operations outlines and defines how to operate the security controls and how to monitor performance. Operations manage service level objectives or service level agreements. Management defines the metrics and goals; operations personnel measure the performance and report on effectiveness against the performance goals.

3.6.4 Institute a Methodology for Continual Review and Improvement

The entire purpose behind ISO 27001 and ISMS is a methodology for continual review and improvement of the security management system as well as the overall security posture of the organization. Review and analysis of existing security controls, changes to business environment, changes to the threat space, asset space, importance of key business functions, new vulnerabilities, and ever-changing stakeholder interests all provide feedback to governance, management, and operations.

3.6.5 SMF Baseline — An ISO 27002 Foundation

The SMF baseline is the security framework previously defined. The column headers in Table 3.8 are TBD_1 through TBD_n to represent any category useful to the organization. Many tools and templates herein will explain various categories and business uses of the SMF. Using this common SMF promotes consistency across many tools, templates, interpretations, discussions, planning, implementing, tracking, and reporting. The entire goal of such a common framework is to reduce complexity and increase manageability of organizational security. For the sake of space considerations, subsequent examples that use the SMF will list only the Security Policy section as an example; however, the implication is to use the entire framework.

The columns in the table may contain a number of details. There can be a single very detailed report or many reports isolating various findings, plans, or requirements. Using the same framework between documents enables an easy comparison because all points align to the same category or element in the framework.

Table 3.8   Security Management Framework Baseline

Category/Sub-Category/ Element	TBD_1	TBD_2	TBD_n
Security Policy			
Information and Information Technology Security Policy			
Documentation			
Dissemination			
Policy review			
Security Management Plan			
Intra-Organization Management			
Executive and management backing			
Information security consistency			
Security roles and responsibilities			

(continued)

Table 3.8   Security Management Framework Baseline (Continued)

Category/Sub-Category/ Element	TBD_1	TBD_2	TBD_n
Authentication and authorization			
Confidentiality agreements			
External authority relationships			
Professional organizations			
Independent assessments and audits			
Second-Party Management			
Risk management			
Addressing security when dealing with customers			
Business agreements			
Asset Management			
Responsibility and Accountability for Assets			
Inventory			
Ownership			
Appropriate use			
Information and Information Technology Classification			
Classifications			
Labeling and handling			
Personnel Security			
Pre-Hire			
Security-related roles and responsibilities			

Table 3.8   Security Management Framework Baseline (Continued)

Category/Sub-Category/ Element	TBD_1	TBD_2	TBD_n
Background checks			
Agreements			
Tenure			
Awareness			
Security education, training, and awareness (SETA)			
Sanctions			
Change of Employment Status			
Termination			
New position			
Asset accountability			
Access management			
Physical Security			
Physical Proximity			
Perimeter			
Entry/exit			
Rooms			
External threats			
Sensitive areas			
Public areas			
Asset Security			
Asset safeguards			
Wiring			
Maintenance			
Asset reuse			
Asset disposal			
Off-site use of assets			

(continued)

Table 3.8 Security Management Framework Baseline (Continued)

Category/Sub-Category/Element	TBD_1	TBD_2	TBD_n
Operations Management			
Operational Procedures and Responsibilities			
Operations			
Configuration management			
Log management			
Outsourcing and Managed Services			
Service delivery			
Monitor and audit			
Change management			
Capacity Planning			
Capacity management			
Acceptance Management			
System acceptance			
Malware and Malware Carriers			
Malware			
Malware carriers			
Backup Management			
Backup			
Network Security Management			
Data in-transit			
Network infrastructure			
Media Management			
Removable media			
Media disposal			

Table 3.8　Security Management Framework Baseline (Continued)

Category/Sub-Category/ Element	TBD_1	TBD_2	TBD_n
Media storage and transport			
Communications Management			
Information transfer			
External connectivity			
E-Commerce Management			
Electronic commerce			
Transactions			
Organization information and image			
Monitoring			
Audit logs			
Information technology activity			
Administrator and power user logs			
Error logging			
Clock synchronization			
Access Management			
Access Control Policy			
Access control policy			
User Access			
Identity management			
Privilege management			
Review of privileges			
Information access			
Segregation			
User Responsibilities			
Password configuration			

(continued)

Table 3.8   Security Management Framework Baseline (Continued)

Category/Sub-Category/ Element	TBD_1	TBD_2	TBD_n
Unattended information technology			
Work area management			
Network Services			
Entity identification			
Network communities			
Traffic management			
Operating Systems			
User identification			
Identity authentication			
User privileges			
Privilege authorization			
Identity validation management			
System utilities			
Inactive sessions			
Connection time restrictions			
Remote Workers			
Mobile workers			
Teleworkers			
Solution Quality Assurance (SQA)			
Information Technology Security			
Compliance requirements			
Information Accuracy			
Input integrity			
Internal integrity			
Output integrity			

Table 3.8   Security Management Framework Baseline (Continued)

Category/Sub-Category/ Element	TBD_1	TBD_2	TBD_n
Cryptography			
Cryptography policy			
Key management			
File Security			
Production applications			
Test data			
Source code protection			
Development Environment			
Change control			
OS upgrades			
Application upgrades			
Memory and other leaks			
Acquisition			
Vulnerability Management			
Patch management			
Incident Management			
Computer Security Incident Response Teams (CSIRT)			
CSIRT operations			
Detection			
Notification			
Preemptive			
CSIRT Management			
Roles and responsibilities			
Lessons learned			
Submissibility			

(continued)

Table 3.8   Security Management Framework Baseline (Continued)

Category/Sub-Category/Element	TBD_1	TBD_2	TBD_n
Business Continuity (BC) and Disaster Recovery (DR) Management			
Information Security Aspects of Business Continuity Management			
BC/DR management process			
Threat assessment			
Risk assessment			
BC/DR plan			
BC/DR maintenance			
Compliance Management			
External Compliance Requirements			
Legislation, regulation, codes, and standards			
Record retention			
Privacy management			
Data protection			
Internal Compliance Requirements			
Security policies, standards, and procedures			
Security controls			
Audit Management			
Security control audits			
Security audit tools			

3.6.6 ISMS — Policy, Standard, and Procedure Development and Maintenance Tracking

Using the SMF, a security professional may complete a development plan matrix to generate appropriate policy, standards, and procedures. The same matrix provides a place to track where each element fits in security policy, assignments to complete the documents, progress tracking, initial publications, and periodic reviews and modifications. Table 3.9 contains only sample entries; the final matrix is the complete framework. If the organization does not need a policy for a particular category or element, the framework provides the ability to note that conclusion. Such a record of consideration shows due diligence and a conscious omission; this is preferable to justifying an omission by oversight after an incident.

Appendix D: Policy, Standard, and Procedure Sample Templates contains sample templates for policy, standards, and procedures. These templates are for the security management level to revise and complete. Security governance may use the ISMS policy template in *Appendix E: ISMS Policy and Risk Treatment Templates*. Likewise, the security governance board may review and approve the details of the statement of applicability (SoA); a template is found in *Appendix B: Sample Statement of Applicability*. Security professionals should develop and provide the security governance board with the following:

- A first draft of the SMF
- References for best practices that justify the SMF as satisfying organizational needs
- A working draft of the ISMS policy, including appropriate sections for enterprise security policy
- A draft ISMS plan that includes preliminary outlines and details on:
  - Work flow
  - Milestones and deliverables
  - ISMS scope
    - Scope justification
      - Risk management plan
      - Risk assessment methodology
        - SoA
      - Security control selection
      - Metrics and measures
      - Communications plan
        - Awareness, training, and education
        - Internal dissemination
        - Feedback
      - Security working group (SWG)
      - Personnel skills assessment

Table 3.9   Sample Entry in Policy, Standard, and Procedure Development Plan

Category/ Element	Requirement	Policy	Standard	Procedure
Security Policy				
Information and Information Technology Security Policy				
Documentation	Management produces an overarching security policy that includes control of information security and clear implementation guidance	Policy Name: Owner: Initial Publication: Last reviewed:	Standard Name: Owner: Initial Publication: Last reviewed:	Procedure Name: Owner: Initial Publication: Last reviewed:
Dissemination	Disseminate policy into enterprise initiatives for security awareness	Addressed in <policy name>	Addressed in <standard name>	Addressed in <procedure name>
Etc.				

As a security professional, do not expect to arrive at to the first governance board meeting or SWG with a comprehensive solution. However, experience shows that a single champion providing an initial working draft for others to comment on, add to, or otherwise modify accelerates the development process tremendously. Include in the initial draft documents a series of checklists to convey the scope of the effort and provide participants with a metric of progress. Useful checklists include the following:

- ISMS inputs checklist
  - E.g., ISO 27001 and ISO 27002

- Compliance requirements
- Business drivers
- Risk analysis results

■ Activity checklist; formulate around the PDCA model
- Plan
  - ○ Define ISMS scope
  - ○ Define ISMS policy
  - ○ Define information security policy (likely within the ISMS policy)
  - ○ Define a risk assessment approach
  - ○ Identify risks
  - ○ Analyze risks in context of business objectives and stakeholder interests
  - ○ Enumerate risk treatment options
  - ○ Select control objectives
  - ○ Generate SoA
  - ○ Define metrics and measures to gauge performance of security controls
- Do
  - ○ Define and implement a risk treatment plan
  - ○ Implement security controls from the Plan phase
  - ○ Implement security awareness programs
  - ○ Establish ISMS operations
  - ○ Implement incident response infrastructure
  - ○ Define how to measure performance
- Check
  - ○ Monitor and review policy, standards, procedures, and practices
  - ○ Review effectiveness of security operations using metrics and measures (objective determination of effectiveness)
  - ○ Identify improvements for the ISMS
- Act
  - ○ Implement ISMS improvements
  - ○ Initiate PDCA cycle to accommodate improvements

■ ISMS output checklist
- Documents
  - ○ ISMS policy
  - ○ Information security policy
  - ○ Risk assessment management process
  - ○ SoA
- Services
  - ○ Business continuity management
  - ○ Incident response
  - ○ Etc.
- Organizational changes
  - ○ Enumerate each business unit and business function, and summarize necessary actions to accommodate effective risk management

- Communications
  - Establish a communications protocol such that directives come from those with authority

Note the last point above on establishing communications protocol. Experience shows that personnel receiving lateral requests from persons not familiar to the recipient are more likely to ignore those requests; that is, an assessor requesting a peer to schedule an interview regarding security issues with no prior notice is highly likely to be ignored. There may be no negative intent; overworked individuals are not looking for additional action items and most people have quite enough requests from their direct manager. Receiving communications with regard to an ISMS from their direct manager and the ability to establish task priorities result in a greater likelihood of cooperation and participation. Spending time on establishing a communications protocol and engaging management is time well spent.

Chapter 4

Implementing an Information Security Management System— Plan-Do-Check-Act

This chapter presents direction on how to implement an information security management system (ISMS). The ISMS development is a systematic process, and the material herein provides a description of the process, supporting tools, templates, and document outlines. In brief, the ISMS development process follows the Plan-Do-Check-Act (PDCA) model and uses security control detail from ISO 27002. The level of detail and documentation depends first on the security goals of the organization and second on the desire to obtain ISO 27001 certification. Certification often requires a more strict set of documents, process, and controls—more on this in Chapter 5, "Audit and Certification."

4.1 Objectives

After reading this material, the reader should understand the PDCA process and its purpose in the development and maintenance of an ISMS. The following is an outline of chapter objectives:

- PDCA model:
  - Accountability

- Plan phase:
  - Process and products of the plan phase
  - Scope definition
  - Assessment of current security posture (baseline)
  - Risk assessment process
  - Statement of applicability (SoA)
  - Documentation summary of the plan phase
- Do phase:
  - Process and products of the do phase
  - Risk treatment plan
  - Identify and allocate resources
  - Write policies and procedures
  - Metrics and measurements
  - Write and implement a business continuity management plan (BCMP)
  - Implement controls
  - Implement training
  - Manage operation and resources
  - Implementation procedure for information security incident
  - Documentation summary of the do phase
- Check phase:
  - Process and products of the check phase
  - Execute operational plan
  - Compliance assessment
  - Review of the effectiveness of the ISMS
  - Review the level of residual riskv
  - Conduct an internal ISMS audit
  - Regular management review of the ISMS
  - Record action and events that impact the ISMS
  - Documentation summary of check phase
- Act phase:
  - Process and products of the act phase
  - Implement identified improvements
  - Corrective and preventive action
  - Apply lesson learned
  - Communicate the results
  - Ensure the objective
  - Continue the process
  - Documentation summary of the act phase

4.2 ISMS Definition

The International Standards Organization (ISO) defines the ISMS as "that part of an overall management system based on a business risk approach to establish, implement, operate, monitor, maintain, and improve information security"* within the organization. The organization obtains certification against its ability to work within and maintain its ISMS. Clauses 4 to 8 of ISO 27001 are mandatory to achieve certification and together define the requirements for an ISMS. ISO requires the implementation and operation of an ISMS to be the same approach as other ISO management systems, that is, the PDCA model.

4.3 PDCA Model

The PDCA model has been part of manufacturing businesses for more than 50 years. The PDCA model is a cycle of activities designed to drive continuous improvement. First developed and discussed by Walter Shewarks in his book *Statistical Method for the Viewpoint of Quality Control*,[9] this model was made more popular by Edward Deming when he encouraged the four-step PDCA model for continual improvements. The organization may use the PDCA model as specified in ISO 27001 to implement an ISMS.

Table 4.1 provides an outline of the PDCA model and a short description of each phase. Within the PDCA process, the organization defines the scope of the ISMS, collects details on in-scope assets, performs risk assessment on in-scope business functions and assets, and assesses the applicability of security controls from ISO 27002. The organization then selects the appropriate safeguards (security controls) and captures the relevant decision process and rationale in a statement of applicability. Implementing the security controls is the next step and follows with the development of monitoring, review, and improvement procedures. Using

Table 4.1 PDCA Model

Phase	Descriptions
Plan phase	Define the ISMS scope and policy. Identify and assess the risks. Select control objectives and controls for the treatment of risk. Formulate a risk treatment plan. Prepare an SoA.
Do phase	Implement the risk treatment plan. Implement controls selected to meet the control objectives in terms of business risk management.
Check phase	Execute monitoring procedures. Undertake reviews. Conduct an internal audit.
Act phase	Implement ISMS improvements.

---

* ISO 27001, p. 2.

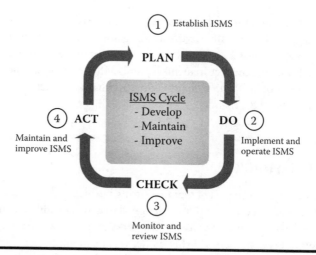

Figure 4.1 PDCA model.

management review input, the final aspect of the PDCA is to implement improvements in a continual cycle of diligence to balance risk management with operational objectives.

Figure 4.1 shows the PDCA model. The aim is to have the ISMS as part of an overall management system based on a business risk approach to implement, operate, monitor, maintain, and improve information security. Before beginning ISMS implementation, ensure the following critical success factors are in place:

- Senior management involvement; preferably a representative from the board of directors
- Visible senior management support, e.g., written memo or e-mail expressing ISO compliance as a strategic initiative
- Security governance policy
- Clearly articulated security requirements that find root in business drivers
- Security policies that align with business mission and objectives
- Management agreement on the implementation process
- Establishment of accountability for the ISMS and ISO 27001 certification, e.g., assign an information security manager
- Establishnment of a cross-functional forum (security working group)
- Provision of appropriate awareness, training, and education
- Establishment of metrics and measurements to evaluate ISMS performance and generate management reports in terms of business value

ISO 27001 specifies that management commitment includes providing "evidence of its commitment to the establishment, implementation, operation, monitoring, review, maintenance, and improvement of the ISMS."* Documentation requirements for ISO 27001 certification include "records of management decisions, and [proof] that [risk management] actions are traceable to management decisions and policies."† To this end, senior management involvement includes developing policy that drives ISMS efforts. Part of that policy includes a disciplined approach to developing the ISMS. ISO 27001 describes such a discipline in the PDCA model.

The PDCA model consists of four phases: plan, do, check, and act. The plan phase is the definition of the ISMS, a definition that finds foundation in ISO 27002 and aligns with clearly articulated business drivers behind security initiatives. The do phase implements the ISMS. The check phase monitors and reviews the ISMS, an operational perspective. The act phase maintains and improves the ISMS according to evolving business drivers. The following sections discuss each phase in more detail.

4.3.1 Accountability

Management support and involvement are critical to the success of the ISMS and maintaining an appropriate security posture that balances risk management with operational need and available resources and budget. A cross-functional forum with representation from management, legal, business lines (operations), information technology, and security performs most of the planning and provides governance and adjudication for the ISMS. Many organizations know the cross-functional forum as a security working group (SWG). *Governance* establishes policy, establishes the scope for the ISMS, and determines the constraints on the security initiatives, that is, available resources and budget. *Adjudication* resolves conflict. Conflict may result in operational demands versus secure operations. Moreover, there may be conflicting demands in a national law versus a local or regional law. The legal representation in the cross-functional forum provides a legal opinion of which takes precedent.

For day-to-day ISMS operations, a single point of accountability is best and can be an information security manager or ISMS manager. Whatever hierarchy the organization selects, there should be clear definitions of roles and responsibilities to ensure the meeting of business objectives, including operational goals, risk management, legislative and regulatory compliance management, budgetary constraints, and schedule constraints.

4.4 Plan Phase

The purpose of the plan phase is to prepare for the implementation of the ISMS. Preparations include defining the scope of the ISMS and defining the ISMS policy. Scope and policy will bound the subsequent risk assessment activity and ensure

---

* ISO 27001, p. 9.
† ISO 27001, p. 7.

focus on the appropriate assets, personnel, and business processes. The risk assessment will identify and analyze risks relevant to those aspects of the organization within scope of the ISMS. Determining how to address risk provides direction to the actual implementation of the ISMS.

The first step is to create a framework within which to define the specifics of the ISMS. Chapter 3, "Foundational Concepts and Tools for an Information Security Management System," covers such a framework, the security management framework (SMF), in detail. The SMF provides an outline to ensure that the organization addresses all relevant areas; therefore, consider all aspects of the SMF as *addressable*, meaning that the organization must understand the intent behind each requirement and specify its stance on that requirement. The organization may express each stance in terms of business risk management: *accept, ignore, transfer, share*, or *mitigate*. ISO 27001 defines an SoA as an articulation of the security control objectives and specific controls that are relevant to the organization's ISMS. The process of addressing all requirements in the framework provides focus on those areas where an SoA applies.

4.4.1 Process and Products of the Plan Phase

Each phase results in a series of products or deliverables. These are in the form of planning documents, implementation documents, operational documents like policies, procedures, standards, tracking documents, etc. The deliverables from the plan phase include documents that provide an ISMS framework, an ISMS scope, information security policy, risk management, security controls, risk treatment, and statement of applicability. Figure 4.2 shows the plan phase and the documentation of each process. If an organization is planning to apply for certification, this documentation will be part of the preaudit review, which is prior to the on-site audit.

The first process in the plan phase is to define the ISMS scope. The second process is to produce an information security policy document written in layperson's terms for easy reading and understanding of risk management. The information security policy document is for management, and all who take part in implementing

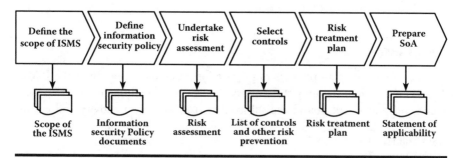

Figure 4.2 Plan phase documentation.

the ISMS, and should strongly reflect management's beliefs that if information is not secure, the business and the organization can suffer. The document should be short, one to two pages, and open for all employees and associates to review.

Risk management consists of three processes: *risk assessment, selecting controls,* and *risk treatment plan.* The risk assessment derives focus from the ISMS scope. The organization assesses risks to business functions and assets (e.g., information and information technology), with the primary focus being business functions. Business functions are those activities that the organization performs for customers (revenue generating) and for keeping itself operational (administrative). Key business functions are those activities that provide services core to the reason for the organization's existence. All other functions are supporting functions to varying degrees of criticality. The judgment of key and criticality is not to say that not all business functions are important; indeed, one hopes the very existence of a business function implies some important role. The distinction of key and degrees of criticality are relative terms to determine which business functions warrant higher levels of security controls.

If primary focus for risk assessment goes to business functions, a close second is to the personnel that perform those functions, followed by the information, information technology, and infrastructure supporting those personnel in delivering those functions. An assessment process that begins with key business functions naturally leads to identifying key personnel performing those functions and the assets they use. By rule of exclusion, any process, person, or technology not key plays a supporting role. The higher levels of criticality go to those directly supporting processes, personnel, technology, or infrastructure necessary to sustain the key business functions. An unpleasant analogy perhaps, but accurate, is the body can live without a hand sooner than without a head; therefore, the head is a key asset and the hand a supporting one—that is, of course, assuming the main goal is survival.

Having distinguished key aspects and supporting ones, there remains the need to identify risk management options (e.g., share risk, transfer risk, mitigate risk), select security controls, and proceed to implementation. The formal recording of how to address risk is in the SoA document. The following sections expand on these tasks within the plan phase of the PDCA cycle.

4.4.1.1 Defining the Scope

The scope of the ISMS describes the boundaries for ISMS in terms of organizational characteristics like location(s), assets, and technology. Business risk management helps define the scope with respect to information and information technology. The scope also finds influence in legislative, regulatory, or other external authoritative compliance requirements. Large organizations may find that a more manageable approach is to define multiple boundaries based on business function, geographical location, or security domains.

The ISMS scope is a formal document included in the ISMS package for potential audit, review, and maintenance. **Caveat**: Do not take the easy way out and generate a single-page scope statement to the effect of "All the organization is in scope." Be specific, enumerate the sites by address, describe the operations at each site even if by category or classification (e.g., sales office, customer service, distribution, headquarters, etc.), elaborate on the hierarchy of the organization and its structure, and describe relevant relationships within the organization between major parts. Although the desirable detail length is somewhat short of a sequel to *War and Peace*, the more detail, the more accurate are risk management decisions.

4.4.1.2 Information Security Policy

Characteristics of good security policies include conciseness, readability, actionability, enforceability, and flexibility. Policies are short and to the point in conveying principles that guide activity within the organization. Policies contain a minimum of specialized vernacular and acronyms; clearly explain any industry-specific terms. Employees at all levels will read the security policies to discern how they should act in the best interest of the organization; therefore, the policy should be actionable at every level of executive strategic planning, management of operations, and actual performance of tasks. The policy must allow for determination of compliance with the policy and enforcement of noncompliance. Moreover, policies should potentially apply to the organization for years and not become outdated with the end of life of any product supporting the policy. Any mention of a specific product use is in a standard, not a policy. Explanations on how to use products are in procedures, not in policy.

ISO 27001 defines two parts for information security policy: the *ISMS policy* and the *information security policy*. The ISMS policy is a high-level document that addresses the need for a *management system* for information security. The ISMS is the management system; the information security controls are specifics directed by the management system. The information security policy is a high-level document that addresses the need for information security. ISO views the ISMS policy as a superset of the information security policy; both may be in the same document under the name of ISMS policy.

The ISMS policy and the information security policy are part of the overall management system framework, a management framework that may include quality management (ISO 9000 family), environmental management (ISO 14000 family), and others. The point is, information security and the management of information security are but two of many aspects of the organization. The chances of success of each of these aspects and the overall cumulative success of the organization are much greater given coordination between each of these aspects. The ISO management systems offer good insight into how to achieve a large part of that coordination.

There are also many other policies and procedures for information security; these are topic specific and reflect the intent of the security controls taken from the ISO

27002 standard. The ISMS policy states the overall security vision and establishes the vision, setting the direction, aim, and objectives of information security. The ISMS policy states what to include in the security program and what to exclude; for purposes of audit, the policy must advocate explicit consideration of all ISO 27002; moreover, the policy must advocate the provision of explicit rationale for all security control exclusions. The ISMS policy demonstrates the intent of management and commitment for information security within the organization. These documents are organizational specific and incorporate a thorough understanding of the organization's business goals as well as its dependence on information and information security.

Appendix E, "ISMS Policy and Risk Treatment Templates," presents a template for the ISMS policy. This is a notional template, and the contents will vary according to the organization's risk environment, operating environment, and overall goals for the security management program. The ISMS policy contains details about the policy itself and attempts to convey the *who, what, why, when, where,* and *how* surrounding the intent of the ISMS policy. The details include creation of the policy, review, and approval, including the effective date of the policy. A policy statement conveys what the policy is (what), and a statement of purpose conveys the reason for the policy (why). Including a statement of scope conveys where and who fall under the guidelines of the policy.

Some individual or group within the organization may require an exception to the ISMS policy, albeit in rare cases and only for reasons that benefit the business more so than compliance. Include a statement regarding policy exceptions and how to seek dispensation from the policy (how). The policy calls out and explains any specialized terms or acronyms. The policy may include a section on roles and responsibilities (who) for policy creation, implementation, management, review, and revision. **Note:** Rather than include this specific information in each policy, a separate document of ISMS roles and responsibilities may be more appropriate, along with a reference to that document in each security policy. When individual responsibilities change, only one document changes, and the remainder of the policies still point to the one, now up-to-date, ISMS roles and responsibilities document. The template presents more details for consideration. The organization will likely not use the template as is; rather, pick and choose the sections most appropriate to capture the detail relevant to the circumstances at hand.

Review ISMS policy and other information security policies on a regular basis, with no more than 12 months from last review. Define trigger events for policy review. The first trigger event is last review plus 12 months. Other trigger events may include a change in business environment, like a merger, acquisition, or new business venture. Certainly, new legislation or regulatory reform will prompt policy review. Include a statement of review/revision trigger events in the information security policy.

A key question is why capture all this detail in written documentation. Just like a contract, written documentation ensures a meeting of the minds. The organization is working off a common understanding of the expectations (e.g., the SMF interpretation guide) and a common understanding of terms (e.g., organization-specific security glossary or risk management glossary). Moreover, the key point is for the organization to capture the policy, standards, procedures, interpretations, and definitions that ensure these details are not just in the minds of a few individuals. The authors have run across many excellent security practices in organizations that do not have a single written procedure. Although the practice is good, it is only as good and as enduring as the individual that practices it. The loss of that individual through retirement, resignation, or being hit by the proverbial bus implies a loss (or at least a degradation) of that excellent practice to the organization. Documentation captures knowledge and promotes the learning organization, where proven good practice by one becomes good practice available to all.

4.4.1.3 Organization of the Information Security Policy

The information security policy may include the following attributes:

1. Scope of the ISMS
2. ISMS policy
3. Importance of security for the organization
4. Explanation of how the organization will maintain information security and information security systems
5. Comment on a management framework that needs to be established to initiate, implement, and control information security within the organization
6. Procedures for approval, including information security, assigning of the security roles, and coordination of security across the organization
7. Responsibility of information security
8. Business continuity processes, management, and testing
9. Security awareness and training
10. Explanation of how reporting is done for a security breach and the consequence of a security violation
11. Virus control
12. Organization information classification
13. Safeguarding of organization's records
14. Data protection
15. Compliance with the ISMS policy
16. Security forum
17. Access control

The following sections provide additional detail for each of the attributes in the list above.

4.4.1.3.1 Scope of the ISMS

The scope of the ISMS may be the entire enterprise, regional, or business line (i.e., a holding company may comprise many separate business lines). Describe the locations and relationships with respect to operations, technical connectivity, interdependences, key assets, and key business functions. The scope provides focus for the remainder of the ISMS, security policy, and security controls.

4.4.1.3.2 ISMS Policy Document

ISO provides an integrated set of organizational standards that include ISO 9001: 2000, ISO 14001:2004, and now ISO 27001:2005. One effective management system may apply to many standards; ISO intends the ISO ISMS to integrate with other standards to create a single management system applicable to many aspects of the organization. To this effect, the ISMS policy is part of the management framework as well as part of the information security policy.

The ISMS policy is a high-level document where the organization prescribes the driving principles and overall sense of direction for actions regarding information security. An effective length is no more than a few pages. These pages should strongly reflect management's commitment to securing information and information technology. The ISMS policy document includes the need to preserve confidentiality, integrity, and availability of information, information technology and associated business functions, personnel, infrastructure, etc. The policy may also state the use of ISMS to support a compliance management program, that is, adhere to regulations, legislation, and other compliance requirements. Include a statement of management involvement, accountability to management, and the need for management review of the ISMS. Also, include a statement that conveys management commitment to invest money and labor to uphold information security.

4.4.1.3.3 Information Security Statement of Importance

Expressly state the importance of security to the organization and generally align the need for security with organizational mission and viability. The policy may include a statement to the effect of specific controls being contingent on the scope of applicability to provide focus to security initiatives with the goal of adding business value.

4.4.1.3.4 Maintaining Information Security and Information Security Systems

Describe the information security processes; note, this is different from actually stating the processes (much longer). Describe how to operate the ISMS and the intent of activities like monitoring, internal audit, and management review. Other parts of this ISMS document include mention of the need for business continuity plans (BCPs), disaster recovery plans (DRPs), and virus control (generally anti-malware). Describe the need for internal audit, management review, and security manager and how they will help the ISMS operation.

4.4.1.3.5   Comment on a Management Framework

Discuss the overall management framework of organizational activities (presumes a formal management framework similar to or in adherence with the ISO management standards). In context of the overall management framework, discuss the integration of ISMS to establish, initiate, implement, and control information security within the organization. Details of ISMS with respect to the management framework include how to implement and maintain the ISMS.

4.4.1.3.6   Approval Procedures for Information Security

Approval procedures for information security involve the assigning of security roles, responsibilities, accountability, and coordination of security across the organization. Describe this process for the organization. Often individual judgments rule the outcome of security and result in inconsistent, incomplete security controls that conflict with operational goals rather than complement or support them. The implementation of a cross-functional group for security governance promotes generation of security controls with representative input from many areas of the organization. Moreover, there is need for security adjudication, that is, resolving conflicts in various legislative, regulatory, standard-based, and other compliance requirements. For example, given a conflict between a national regulation and a provincial law, which takes precedent? This begs the need for involving legal representation in the security governance board that approves procedures for information security.

4.4.1.3.7   Information Security Responsibility

Define security responsibilities, accountability, and proof of performance (e.g., measures and metrics). Establish a single point of responsibility/accountability for any given security area; this is contrary to just using the blanket statement of "Security is the responsibility of human resources or information technology"; individual accountability promotes one-on-one conversations that take on the form of "What have you done and what are you going to do?" This is much more effective in producing results than hoping some member of a larger group decides to take ownership.

4.4.1.3.8   Business Continuity Process, Management, and Testing

Describe the need for business continuity management, including a BCP and DRP and other relevant preventive/recovery measures; include statements regarding management, accountability, and regular testing.

4.4.1.3.9 Security Awareness, Training, and Education

There is a clear progression in learning and a clear distinction between what various classifications of personnel require. An abstract learning progression is *awareness* → *understanding* → *use* → *effective use* → *secure use*. *All* employees must be aware of security issues and the need for security. All employees need to understand at least some security issues; however, the reality is that most will not. Most will comply, but out of following a directive that they may not understand completely—thus the need for safeguards that are transparent to user activity. For example, the admitting clerk in a publicly owned healthcare organization is aware of the need to lock her terminal upon leaving it unattended. She or he may understand that this is to protect patient information and patient privacy; however, he or she is likely not to understand at the level where such requirements trace to Sarbanes–Oxley (SOX) and Health Insurance Portability and Accountability Act (HIPAA) legislation. He or she is not concerned with the time-out parameters, standard configuration of the screen saver, or that this is part of the organization's standard image; it is enough that he or she activates the screen saver upon leaving the terminal unattended. This is one level of understanding.

Information technology professionals may not understand the level of traceability between the organization's standard image and the compliance drivers behind the standard configuration. They may generally understand that security policy requires X. This is a deeper level of understanding than that of the admitting clerk. Security professionals understand, indeed create, the traceability between compliance requirements and policy and between policy and procedures—yet again, a deeper level of understanding. The point is to devise awareness, training, and a program that spans the requirements of various levels and responsibilities.

4.4.1.3.10 Reporting on Security Incidents

Describe the need for an incident response infrastructure to accommodate monitoring, detection, notification, triage, escalation, isolation, treatment, restoration, root cause analysis, and organizational feedback to capture lessons learned. Include the need for standardization in incident reports, how to report security incidents, and defining consequences of security violations.

4.4.1.3.11 Virus Control

Describe the method used to control viruses and attacks on networks. This will include spam, spyware, and other attacks or cyber-nasties found. Describe how the organization maintains the anti-malware process as well as anti-malware mechanisms (e.g., software).

4.4.1.3.12 Organization Information Classification

Describe the method used for the classification of information. A simple classification system includes three classification distinctions: (1) *confidential* information, only for specific groups of employees; (2) *nonconfidential* information, for all employees; and (3) *public* information, authorized for viewing by all persons, including nonemployees. Overcomplicating the classification creates confusion and inconsistency. Be aware of the need to balance overprotection (classifying too much too high) and the manual efforts to handle exception requests and underprotection, where there is a greater potential to release sensitive information. Too much security will lead to many ignoring the policy; too little security may expose the organization to liabilities in releasing sensitive information (e.g., client data or intellectual property). Security is a balancing game between protecting organizational interests and empowering personnel to perform business functions.

4.4.1.3.13 Safeguarding of Organization's Records

Describe how the organization will safeguard important records. Include a section to address labeling and handling as well as enforcement. Align these details with information classification.

4.4.1.3.14 Data Protection

Describe the need for data protection within the organization. Address data in transit as well as data at rest. Data protection begs the need for identity and privilege management; identity authentication permits general access to a resource (e.g., allowed on the network at all), and privilege authorization permits a specific activity or access to specific resources (e.g., access to servers relevant to a role within the organization).

4.4.1.3.15 Compliance with the Security Policy Document

Describe how the organization will comply with the ISMS policy. More information can be found in Chapter 13 of ISO 27002[2] and Chapter 15, "Compliance."

4.4.1.3.16 Security Working Group

Describe the need for a security working group, or a security forum. Moreover, describe the tasks of the security forum. Information on the cross-functional forum can be found in ISO 27002[2] in "Control," Section 6.1.2, "Information Security Coordination."

4.4.1.3.17 Access Control

Describe the need for access control and granting, reviewing, revoking, and auditing access control. More information on access control is in ISO 27002, Chapter 11.

All 17 elements are part of the information security policy document and expressed in common, everyday layman language to promote easy reading and easy comprehension. The security policy document is proprietary in nature, as this expresses strategic direction and perhaps some specifics about the organization not intended for public consumption. The security policy may be part of the ISMS policy document.

4.4.1.4 ISMS Policy

The highlights of the information security policy document provide input to the ISMS policy. Note that policy is typically a high-level statement that establishes the direction for selecting standards and developing procedures. These latter two documents contain far more detail than the policies. Below is a notional ISMS policy in the form of a statement of objective and then the statement of policy.

4.4.1.4.1 ISMS Policy Example

The "Objective" section is a statement of intent. The benefit of stating the intent is, should an individual run across a situation not specifically enumerated in policy, procedure, standard, or other experience, a judgment guideline on how to proceed is provided. The policy provides specifics that accommodate the best knowledge available at the time of writing. If faced with uncertainty, act in keeping with the intent of the policy.

Objective

All employees of [name of organization] follow the ISMS policy that is part of the overall ISMS. The purpose of the policy is to safeguard the confidentiality, integrity, and availability of organizational information and information technology. Confidentiality is that information only accessible to those who have access permission. Integrity is that the quality of the information is secure and correct, and nothing is missing. Availability is that the information or information technology is ready for use upon demand.

Policy

[Name of organization's] information assets are protected appropriately, irrespective of the value, threat, and vulnerability that can arise. To follow this aim, the chief executive will see to it that sufficient investment and human resources are in place for this task. [Name of organization] will follow regulatory and legislation requirements to uphold confidentiality, integrity, and availability of information and information systems. [Name of organization's] aim with this policy statement is to establish an ISMS by using the standard ISO/IEC 27001 that will hinder unauthorized access, transfer, change, damage, and theft of information assets. All employees of [name of organization] are obligated to familiarize themselves with the policy and go by it. [Name of organization] emphasizes that employees must follow this policy and other objectives, controls, and guidelines. Any breach of the security policy will be taken seriously and investigated by the information security manager. Information security training will be offered to all employees. Periodically, [name of organization] will conduct a risk assessment to determine if further action is needed. The information security manager has the role to administer the process and maintain the ISMS for the organization and provide advice and guidance on implementation.

All managers of the organization are responsible for implementing the policy in their business area, and seeing that their staff act on it. [Name of organization] will prepare a business continuity plan that will be maintained and tested. Periodically, but not more than once per year, the ISMS policy will be reviewed for potential revision. Procedures will enumerate additional trigger events for policy review.

4.4.1.5 Risk Management

Risk management consists of defining a risk assessment approach, identifying risks, analyzing risks, and devising treatments for risks. The implementation of an ISMS relies on effective risk management; moreover, ISMS documentation includes how the organization will manage risk. This section covers risk management according to ISO 27001, Section 4.2.1, which includes direction to:

- Define the risk assessment approach for the organization
- Identify the risks to the organization
- Analyze and evaluate the risks
- Enumerate risk options and evaluate each according to organizational goals
- Enumerate organizational objectives for risk treatment
- Select appropriate controls for risk treatment
- Develop an SoA for each risk

There are many risk assessment methodologies. Some concentrate on asset space like equipment, buildings, PCs, servers, etc. The *asset space risk assessment* identifies vulnerabilities for each asset and enumerates a value of the asset to the organization should a threat exploit that vulnerability and affect confidentiality, integrity, or availability. Another approach to risk assessment focuses on threat space. The *threat space risk assessment* leads to an evaluation of those assets with the highest probability of attack or otherwise succumbing to a natural threat (e.g., hurricane). Yet another approach is to focus on business functions, specifically those business functions seen as key to the mission of the organization. The *business function risk assessment* leads to identification of key personnel, assets, and infrastructure that support performance of the key business functions. A business function approach narrows the focus to a subset of overall asset space and threat space. Prioritizing activities to address this narrower focus is an exercise in intelligent resource allocation, where the potential worst effects on the organization receive security treatments.

The objectives for a risk assessment are to identify risks, vulnerabilities, and potential threats, and determine the likely realization of a threat exploiting a vulnerability, and the resulting impact to the business. In context of ISO security standards, risk management should include at least the requirements from ISO 27001,[1] Section 4.2.1, including:

- Definitions of risk assessment approach and methodology
- Formal risk assessment plan
- When risk assessment should be performed, e.g., time-of-year restrictions
- How often it should be performed, e.g., not more than 12 months between assessments
- Risk assessment approach and methodology review and update
- Risk assessment performance
- Update of statements of applicability
- Update of initiatives driven by risk assessment results, e.g., business continuity

Outsourcing a risk assessment is always an option and often a good one to bring objectivity to the assessment. An outsider stepping on political toes is often more palatable to security management than their own staff stepping on those same toes. Risk assessments may be passive with respect to operational effects, meaning that risk assessment activities will not (should not) actively disrupt operations from a technical perspective. However, the assessment activities do take time and make demands on managers, administrators, operators, and other personnel. Publishing a schedule of risk assessment activities and seeking both input and active participation in creating the schedule lead to better overall cooperation. The authors recommend dividing risk assessment activities into sections, where each section focuses on a particular aspect of the organization (e.g., location, business line, business function [e.g., accounting]). In this manner, the auditor is focused, the participants are focused, and each section may be completed while awaiting scheduling for another section.

ISO 27001 does not include a thorough description of a security assessment methodology. Some other standards that may assist in developing an organization-specific risk assessment methodology include National Institute of Standards and Technology (NIST) documents SP 800-30,[11] SP 800-60,[10] and FIPS PUB 199,[3] as well as BS 7799-3.[20] One potential risk methodology is the 12-step methodology for risk management (Table 4.2); this is an asset space risk assessment approach.

Table 4.2   Risk Management Process

1	Information assets list	The risk assessment starts by producing a list of important information assets that support key business functions of the organization.
2	Categorization	Categorization prioritizes the assets according to criticality; further risk and vulnerability analysis is necessary for highly critical assets.
3	Vulnerability	Identify asset vulnerabilities using information from asset owners and prior risk assessments.
4	Threat	Identify threats. Identify prior incidents where the threat was realized. What is the probability of recurrence? Review industry experiences, e.g., CSI/FBI Computer Crime Survey found at www.gocsi.com.
5	Valuate threat	Valuate the likelihood that the threat will result in a security breach.
6	Valuate vulnerability	Valuate if a specific threat can take advantage of the vulnerability.
7	Valuate protections and policies	Valuate the protections and policies that have been implemented or will be implemented.
8	Probability	Determine the probability of a threat. Look at other businesses in the same industry. What is the status of information security in their organizations? Look at the result from the chapter analysis the status of information security.
9	Impact	Assess the impact of a successful exploitation. The value of impact will give a scale of the seriousness of a given risk, i.e., Threat $\times$ Vulnerability = Impact.
10	Risk factor	Risk is the likelihood of the threat exploitations and the magnitude of the impact, i.e., Probability $\times$ Impact = Risk.
11	Risk treatment plan	The risk that is left or operation that is necessary to lower the risk factor as implementing controls. This document is part of ISMS.
12	Select controls	Select controls from the standard and other preventions to lower the risk factor.

The first step is to produce a list of key assets at every location within scope. Asset criticality is according to the business function that uses the asset. Assets of high criticality are part of the risk assessment. Identify these assets by category; low-value assets may not be part of the risk assessment. The determination of low value is not by purchase price or resale value, but by *criticality categorization*. Steps 3 to 10 define the performance of the risk assessment, where every asset is analyzed. Step 3 finds all vulnerabilities for all in-scope assets. Step 4 identifies threats that may take advantage of those vulnerabilities, and so on according to the table descriptions.

The 12-step risk management process in Table 4.2 repeats periodically as part of the continuous improvement of the ISMS. The following sections cover each of the 12 steps in more detail; however, the risk assessment details here are but an overview. Three useful resources that offer additional insight into risk assessment are BS 7799-3, *Guidelines for Information Security Risk Management*[20]; SP 800-30, *Risk Management Guide for Information Technology Systems*[11]; and ISO/IEC TR 13335-3, *Guidelines for the Management of IT Security.*[12] One excellent reference on the topic of risk assessment is *Information Security Risk Analysis* by Thomas Peltier.[13]

4.4.1.5.1 Information Assets List (Step 1)

Table 4.2 presents an asset-centric approach to risk assessment. Expand the concept of assets to include business functions, people, information, information technology, and physical assets. Determining which assets to focus on first requires identifying critical business functions. Key business functions are those that define the reason for the existence of the organization. For example, to a customer, the key reason for insurance is to process claims; therefore, claims processing to an insurance organization are a key business function and a potential competitive differentiator. In that same insurance organization, processing accounts receivable (cash flow) is also a key business function, and one of importance to investors in that company. The systems that support actuarial calculations are important; however, the organization can survive without those systems longer than systems supporting billing and claims. Key personnel are those who directly carry out the key business functions. Key assets are those used by key personnel during the execution of key business functions. In the example, claims processing personnel and billing personnel are a higher priority in a business continuity scheme than actuaries.

The first step of the 12-step risk management process begins by assigning managers and information owners to select and list all assets important to the organization within the boundary of the ISMS scope. The focus is on key assets, or those assets critical to core operations of the organization. Security resources do not allow 100 percent protection of 100 percent of the assets 100 percent of the time; therefore, identifying key assets provides focus for limited security resources. One benchmark to identify an asset as key is to determine if the loss of confidentiality, integrity, or availability would harm the fulfillment of the core purpose of the organization or otherwise jeopardize organizational viability. If yes, that is a key asset. If no, the asset may still be important, just less important than key assets.

A data classification schema may assist in identifying key information assets. Legislative mandates covering certain data types and record retention will also drive risk assessment conclusions. The following is a notional list of risk assessment focus:

- Key business functions—those functions that comprise the core reason for the existence of the organization
- Key personnel delivering key business functions—key knowledge areas
- Key infrastructure supporting key personnel:
  - Information technology
  - Buildings
  - Property
  - Software
  - Equipment
- Information of value to the organization
- Organization brand and reputation—goodwill

Draw on information from the high-level or detailed discovery questionnaire to assist with generating an asset list. Additional investigations may be necessary. Management reviews and approves the final inventory list; the SWG also reviews and, at the least, recommends, if not adds, their own approval.

Table 4.3 presents the notional contents of an information and information technology asset list. The contents vary according to the organization and scope of the effort. A reference number provides unique identification for the asset. Asset details include an asset description, specification of owner, beneficiaries and users of the asset, asset location, criticality, and risk factor associated with the asset.

4.4.1.5.2 Categorization of Information Assets (Step 2)

Categorizing assets provides insight to the criticality of the asset to operations. Categorization starts with prescreening that first determines if the asset warrants additional analysis. Such prescreening includes the inherent value of the asset as well as the business function value of the asset; that is, does it support or provide a key service? Asset categorization assists in risk analysis as well as provides input to

Table 4.3   Asset Details

Reference Number	Asset	Asset owner
Asset users	Description	Location
Criticality	Risk factor	

Table 4.4   Asset Categorization Guide

C1	*Great effect:* Harm or loss of the asset confidentiality, integrity, or availability has great effect on normal operation. Longest tolerable outage is 24 hours or less. The critical factor is very high with the value C1.
C2	*Legal effect:* Harm or loss of the asset confidentiality, integrity, or availability has legal effect. The asset is relevant for legal requirements and important to the organization. Longest tolerable outage is 24 to 72 hours. The critical factor is high with the value C2.
C3	*Little effect:* Harm or loss of the asset confidentiality, integrity, or availability has little effect on normal operation. Longest tolerable outage is 73 hours up to six days. The critical factor is low with the value C3.
C4	*No effect:* Harm or loss of the asset confidentiality, integrity, or availability has no effect on normal operation. Longest tolerable outage is 7 days or more. The critical factor is very low with the value C4.

business continuity and disaster recovery planning. Table 4.4 presents a sample asset categorization scheme.

Table 4.4 shows four criticality categories: C1, C2, C3, and C4, with C1 representing the most critical assets to the organization. Assets with criticality of C1 and C2 receive more in-depth analysis regarding risk, preservation, monitoring, defending, and recovery, that is, an in-depth risk assessment. These are the most likely assets to receive risk mitigation. Asset categorization is one of many pieces of documentation that the ISO 27001 compliance auditor will review.

The guidelines here are samples only. The organization needs to provide its own interpretation of *great adverse effect* etc. If the organization does not have its own methodology for security categorization, the publications FIPS PUB 199[3] and SP 800-60, *Guide to Mapping Types of Information Systems to Security Categories*,[10] offer guidance.

4.4.1.5.2.1   Prerisk Assessment—Table 4.5 provides a template for risk valuation. Risk valuation is a collective recording of asset information, business functions the asset supports, vulnerabilities, threats, and relevant valuations. Each asset receives a valuation for threat, probability of threat occurrence, vulnerability level, protection, probability, impact, and risk factor.

4.4.1.5.3   Vulnerability (Step 3)

The risk assessors can now focus on the vulnerabilities of key assets. Vulnerability classifications include *technical* (e.g., software, hardware, electric), *natural phenomenon* (e.g., hurricane, flood), *external events* (e.g., major application vendor goes out of business), and *personnel* (e.g., key knowledge with only one person and unrecorded).

Table 4.5   Risk Valuation

Reference number		Asset:			
Asset owner:			Criticality value:		
Asset user(s):					
Asset description (name, physical location, type, network, communication, security categories):					
Business function(s) supported:					
Threats list			**Vulnerabilities list**		
Threat value		Vulnerability value		Protection value	
Probability value		Impact value		Risk factor	
Other information as action that has to be taken					

Table 4.6 shows a list of example vulnerabilities. The assessors record all vulnerabilities on the evaluation form illustrated in Table 4.5. The details should be specific on what the asset is and where it is located, as well as the business function(s) it supports, and the owner or person responsible for the asset.

Table 4.6   Example of Vulnerability

Stress	*Unstable electricity*	*No change; management control in place*
Lack of physical protection	Unprotected communications lines	Lack of documentations
External worker without supervision	Employee absence	No BCP in place
Lack of training	Unprotected storage	Wrong settings

To assist in identifying vulnerabilities, consider the following vulnerability categories:

- Information
- Equipment
  - Information technology
  - Infrastructure
  - Core business related (e.g., manufacturing equipment)
- Procedure
  - Management
  - Operations
  - Administrative
  - Support
- Personnel
- External dependencies

Review the above list in context of organizational operations and objectives. There may be additional categories, but at least these will apply. Information includes any data in any format that represents organizational intellectual property, falls under the guidance of legislative mandates (e.g., customer privacy), or otherwise provides value to the organization such that the loss of confidentiality, integrity, or availability of that data would hurt performance or jeopardize organizational viability. Consider the vulnerabilities of that information in its various forms, that is, what may happen to the information that may cause a loss of confidentiality, integrity, or availability. Similar considerations apply to equipment, personnel, etc. External dependencies represent any inputs to the organization critical for the organization to produce expected results. If the organization manufactures widgets, an interruption in raw materials flow will prohibit the production of widgets; therefore, a receiving raw material is an external dependency. Associated vulnerabilities may include network connectivity, software application performance that supports raw material inventory and kicks off automatic orders, cost or availability of fuel for materials transport, labor strikes, emerging environmental issues that reclassify a raw material as a hazardous material, and so on. Not all vulnerabilities will relate to information security; however, all vulnerabilities do relate to business risk and require risk management.

4.4.1.5.4 Threats (Step 4)

Vulnerabilities provide insight into the in-scope threat space. An organization in Colorado has little worry about flooding due to hurricane; however, loss of power due to storms is a vulnerability. Therefore, snowstorms and thunderstorms are a valid threat to prepare for. Table 4.7 provides a list of example threats.

Table 4.7 Threat Examples

Staff error	Malfunction	Water
Fire	Maintenance error	Weather
Dust	Software flaw	Earthquake
Sabotage	Forced entry	Circuit breaker

Table 4.8 Asset name: <name>

Threat	Vulnerability
Forced entry	Lack of physical protection
Maintenance error	Stress and lack of documentations
Sabotage	Unprotected communication lines

The assessors record all threats in the evaluation form illustrated in Table 4.5 for individual assets. Map threats to vulnerabilities prior to valuation; Table 4.8 shows an example of how to map threats to vulnerabilities. In the example, forced entry can happen because of lack of physical protection. Maintenance error can happen because of stressed and overworked employees or the lack of documentations as guidelines and procedures. After mapping threats to vulnerability and recording the result in the evaluation form illustrated in Table 4.5, start the valuation.

4.4.1.5.5 Valuate Threat (Step 5)

Step 5 in the 12-step risk assessment process is to valuate threats. The key question is, Is there any probability that the threat will result in security breach? The assessor may determine this using the information from the evaluation form (Table 4.5), details of prior organizational history, and experiences from other organizations.

Are there prior occurrences of the current threat within the organization? Is there a frequency to occurrence? Likewise, are there similar external organizations that have experience with this threat? Are there frequencies of occurrence available? Are these external organizations similar to this organization, e.g., physical proximity (e.g., natural threats)? Table 4.9 offers assistance in valuating threats.

When valuating the threat, consider how realistic it is for the threat to harm or cause loss of confidentiality, integrity, or availability. This potential reality may have many scales to record the likelihood; one such scale is as follows: U (unlikely), S (seldom), or L (likely). The assessor records the result of the valuation in the evaluation form illustrated in Table 4.5 for every asset. Note that different threat valuation methods use different measurement values. An alternative valuation is the mathematical formula illustrated in Table 4.5, where Threat × Vulnerability = Impact and Probability × Impact = Risk. This alternative method requires numeric values versus the scale herein that uses the letters U, S, and L.

Table 4.9   Guideline for How Realistic Threats Are and Will Result in Actual Harm to the Organization

U	*History:* This threat has not been involved in a security breach for the last year, and it is unlikely it will be. Probability: The surroundings or the knowledge and frame of mind have not been prerequisite that the threat has accord in security breach, and it is unlikely it will.
S	*History:* This threat has not been involved in a security breach for the last three months. Probability: The surroundings or the knowledge and frame of mind have in small part or seldom been prerequisite that the threat has accord in security breach.
L	*History:* This threat has been involved in a security breach for the last three months, and it is likely it will happen again. Probability: The surroundings or the knowledge and frame of mind have been prerequisite that the threat has accord in security breach, and it is likely it will happen again.

4.4.1.5.6   Valuate Vulnerability (Step 6)

Step 6 valuates vulnerabilities of key assets. When valuating the vulnerability, use the mapping between threats and vulnerabilities recorded in the evaluation form illustrated in Table 4.5.

For every asset, valuate how realistic it is for the threat to use specific vulnerability to harm or cause loss of confidentiality, integrity, or availability. Measure the value in this case as L (low), M (moderate), or H (high) (Table 4.10). Record the result from the evaluation in the evaluation form illustrated in Table 4.5 for every asset. Again, an alternative scale is possible and may include more granular subjective measurements (e.g., medium-low or medium-high) or numeric values to use in calculating a risk probability.

Table 4.10   Guideline for How Realistic Threats Will Exploit the Vulnerability to Harm the Organization

L	The vulnerability is small and it is hard for the threat to use the vulnerability to harm or achieve loss of confidentiality, integrity, or availability of the asset.
M	The vulnerability is there for the finding and the threat can use it to harm or achieve loss of confidentiality, integrity, or availability of the asset.
H	The vulnerability is great and it is easy for the threat to use it to harm or achieve loss of confidentiality, integrity, or availability of the asset.

4.4.1.5.7   Valuate Protections and Installed Policies (Step 7)

Step 7 reviews the policies and protections for each asset to determine if the protection is sufficient such that threats cannot use a vulnerability to cause loss of

Table 4.11 Physical Protection

External barriers	Controls to property entrance	Fences
Gates	Guards	Surveillance cameras
Building doors	Keys, cipher locks, pass cards, biometrics for entrance	Office and data center doors
Fire detection	Flood detection	Bomb-proof walls
Security guards	Burglar alarm	Backup power supply

confidentiality, integrity, or availability of the asset. Asset protection categories include physical, technical, personal, and procedures. Table 4.11 presents a list of example physical protections.

Table 4.12 presents a list of technical protections. The intent of technical protections is to safeguard information technology; this includes servers, network infrastructure (routers, switches, cables), media (hard drives, CDs, USBs, archive tapes), etc. The list in the table is hardly exhaustive and only presents a few common examples of technical protections.

The next type of protection on our list is personnel protection; Table 4.13 offers some examples. The intent is to hire low-security-risk people or at least avoid hiring high-risk people. At times there is a due diligence to specifically not hire a certain classification of people, e.g., convicted robbery felons in a position of trust that handles money transfers. Additionally, the intent is to make personnel aware of their security responsibilities and offer training and education to people directly involved with security issues.

Table 4.14 contains examples of procedural protections. Procedures offer enterprise direction on good security practice. Without procedures, the security posture is as good as the individual's awareness, training, self-initiative, and personal skill. Procedures capture lessons learned from many aspects of the enterprise and promote consistency and comprehensiveness. A good practice by one should be part of a good procedure practiced by all.

Table 4.12 Technical Protection

Disaster recovery plan	Malicious software (malware) detection
Security testing	Audit trails and logs
Passwords and authentications	Firewalls
Intrusion detection systems	Security incident response teams
Encryption	Virtual private networks (VPNs)
Operating system hardening	Insider threat management

Table 4.13 Personnel Protection

Pre-employment background check	Confidentiality agreements
Employee security awareness	Employment job description
Personnel security policies (e.g., forced vacation)	Ethics program

Table 4.14 Procedures Protection

Business continuity (BC) planning	Security working groups; security governance structure, security adjudication structure
Compliance assessments	Security feature policies and procedures (e.g., passwords, encryption for data at rest and in transit)
Malicious software protection plan	Incidents reporting and control
Information security policy	ISMS policy

Table 4.15 Implemented Protection

Low	If the evaluation is that the overall protection is under 60% of possible protection, it is customary to say that it is not acceptable.
Medium	If the overall protection is between 60 and 70% of possible protection, it is customary to say that it is acceptable but may need review of some aspects.
High	If overall protection is higher than 70% of possible protection, it is customary to say that it is good.

Table 4.15 offers guidance on how to respond to low, medium, and high valuations for protection methods. The determination of the quality of the protection methods provides insight to the need for subsequent corrective actions.

4.4.1.5.8 Probability (Step 8)

Step 8 determines the probability of a threat exploiting a vulnerability. The expression of probability may be in terms of a mathematical value or in more subjective terms. The former is more time consuming and often difficult to assign hard values to with rational justification. The latter is in softer, more subjective terms. Subjective categorizations are easier to define and are often good enough for the task. The examples here use a subjective valuation for threat in terms of unlikely, seldom, or likely; a subjective valuation for the vulnerability in terms of low, medium, or high; and a protection valuation of low, medium, or high. The combination of these valuations results in a *probability factor*.

Table 4.16 provides guidance for determining the probability factor. Find the threat valuation in the top row: unlikely, seldom, or likely. Then find the valuation for vulnerability in the second row. Finally, find the valuation for the protection in

Table 4.16 Guidelines to Valuate Probability

Threat		Unlikely		Seldom			Likely			
Vulnerability		L	M	H	L	M	H	L	M	H
Protection	H	G	F	E	F	E	D	E	D	C
	M	F	E	D	E	D	C	D	C	B
	L	E	D	C	D	C	B	C	B	A

the left column. Where these three values cross is a risk probability factor designated as a letter between A and G; A has the most risk probability for the asset and G the least. An interpretation of these probability factors is as follows:

- A—Regularly or often   6
- B—Frequent   5
- C—Likely   4
- D—Occasional   3
- E—Seldom   2
- F—Unlikely   1
- G—Very unlikely   0

4.4.1.5.9 Impact (Step 9)

Step 9 considers the potential result of a threat exploiting a vulnerability, that is, the business impact upon the loss of confidentiality, integrity, or availability of the asset. Note that intrinsic value of the asset is not as important as the value of the business function that depends on it. The intrinsic value of the screw that holds the flap controls to the wing of an airplane is not nearly as important as the function of controlling the airplane for in-flight safe maneuvering. Moreover, consider the relationship and connectivity between the asset and other assets; the current asset may be once removed from support of a key business function, but still be a critical dependency.

Table 4.17 provides a guideline to determine the impact as low, medium, or high. Record the result in the form presented in Table 4.5. The impact is in terms of

Table 4.17 Guideline to Determine Impact

	Impact: If threat would use the vulnerability to harm or achieve loss of confidentiality, integrity, or availability of the asset.
L	The impact is minimal for both harm and loss of confidentiality, integrity, or availability of the asset or organization image or brand.
M	The impact is not considered costly for both harm and loss of confidentiality, integrity, or availability of the asset or organization image or brand.
H	The impact is considered very costly for both harm and loss of confidentiality, integrity, or availability of the asset or organization image or brand.

asset value and potential loss of business operations due to loss of business function that the asset supports. Loss of flight control in an airplane is definitely high. Loss of coffee service is low (albeit many caffeine addicts would argue for high).

4.4.1.5.10 Risk Factor (Step 10)

Step 10 assigns a risk factor to each asset. Table 4.18 provides guidance on determining the risk factor. Find the impact valuation value from Step 9 in the top row (low, medium, or high). Next, find the probability value from the evaluation form (Table 4.5) for that asset (A through G as determined in Step 8). Insert the values from the Impact Table 4.17 and values for Probabilities from Table 4.16 in Table 4.18, and note the numeric value where the line cross is the value for the risk factor.

If the risk factor is 4 or more, the recommendation is to remediate to lower a risk factor. Consideration of the asset in and of itself (a discrete consideration) is one thing. Of extended interest is the business function that the asset supports; the greater value is in the business function. One risk assessment philosophy is to focus on the asset space (an internal focus). Another is to focus on the threat space (an external as well as internal focus, e.g., insider threat). Yet another risk assessment philosophy focuses on the business function with the presumption that the business function and its results are what deliver value to the customers and stakeholders. A focus on key business functions narrows focus to assets supporting those functions. Vulnerabilities of those assets narrow focus to the threat space that may take advantage of those vulnerabilities.

Table 4.18 Security Management Framework and Interpretation Guide

Impact		Low	Moderate	High
Probability	G	0	1	2
	F	1	2	3
	E	2	3	4
	D	3	4	5
	C	4	5	6
	B	5	6	7
	A	6	7	8

4.4.1.5.11 Risk Treatment Plan (Step 11)

Step 11 of the 12-step process produces a risk treatment plan. The risk treatment plan provides direction on how the organization will *address* each risk. Addressing may include ignoring, accepting, sharing, transferring, or mitigating each risk. The point is to produce a plan that specifies the action and provides a rationale behind each action. Those aspects that require action provide input to the ISMS and affect the security posture of the organization. Each action in the risk treatment plan

Table 4.19   Risk Treatment Plan Content Outline

Action list	Priority list of assets, risks, and how to address each risk
Select control	If applicable, select appropriate control from the ISO 27002 standard
SoC	Summary of selected controls(SoC)
BCM	Business continuity management (BCM) describes both BCP and DRP and details of each
SoA	Statement of applicability is a list of controls selected and list of controls not selected and the purpose of the selection
Writing policies and procedures	Description of how to write policies and procedures
Implementation	Description of how the plan will be implemented to build the ISMS

provides input to a project plan for execution. If sharing a risk (e.g., insurance) is more appropriate than risk mitigation, then noting an appropriate action to follow up with insurers, acquire quotes, determine the best business value, and acquire the coverage is part of the overall ISMS implementation.

The risk treatment plan should align with policy and show each risk, the method selected for the treatment of the risk, and how such treatment traces to policy and is in keeping with that policy. At times, part of the risk is that no policy exists; in this case, writing the policy becomes the first step in addressing the risk.

Table 4.19 contains a risk treatment plan content outline. Appendix E contains a risk treatment plan template.

The risk treatment plan document begins with an SoA. This may be a separate document from the risk treatment plan. If so, reference, document link, or hotlink the master SoA document in the risk treatment plan rather than copy it there. Maintaining a single SoA is difficult enough. Maintaining multiple copies quickly results in synchronization issues, adds confusion to which copy is most current, and adds maintenance costs to keep all copies up to date. The action list is a priority list of how to address organizational risks to each asset. The risk treatment plan allocates necessary controls to each asset and describes the actions that will address the risk as well as the priority in which to perform the actions. The risk treatment plan template shows many items in a single table. Multiple tables may be necessary for readability and to ensure that duplicate information does not appear. Again, avoid redundant details to avoid the confusion of multiple instances of the same information.

The risk treatment plan template also contains areas to provide guidance on the development process for policies, standards, and procedures, as well as a section to describe guidance for security control implementation. Note that neither of these sections in the template is for policy detail or implementation detail; rather, these describe

Table 4.20   Risk Treatment Plan

Location:							Department:		
Executed by:							Date:		
Management review:							Date:		
Asset Name	*Reference Number*	*Priority*	*Possible Treatment*	*Options*	*Risk Factor after Treatment*	*A/R*	*Initial Responsibility*	*Timetable*

the processes to accomplish each. The process details may include organizational details of policy proposal, review process, approval process, contact information, etc.

Table 4.20 presents an alternative outline for the risk treatment plan. The final outline and contents are organizational specific. This alternative outline is in the interest of presenting multiple views for consideration.

Risk treatment details in this variation include the location and department in which to perform the risk treatment. Other details include the name of the person to execute the risk treatment plan and due date, plus management review/sign-off and date. The columns present details to track the asset, priority, risk treatment, risk factor after treatment, accountability, and due date for treatment.

Any risk not in the risk treatment plan is by default a residual risk. Maintain a list of residual risks, or at least note residual risks in the SoA, to perform periodic reviews. Establish trigger events for review of residual risks. These trigger events may include calendar time (not more than 12 months from previous review), business environment change, threat environment change, or new vulnerability awareness.

4.4.1.5.12 Select Controls (Step 12)

Controls are the safeguards to mitigate risks. Selecting the right controls is essential to the protection of the asset and to lower the risk factor. For purposes of ISO 27001 certification, select controls from the ISO 27002[2] standard applicable to the organization. Note that some security controls necessary to the organization may not be in ISO 27002. If legislation or regulation specifies the need to protect a certain kind of data in a certain way, the organization must accommodate this

Table 4.21 Example Summary of Selected Controls

Reference Number	Description	Risk Factor	Criticality	Other Prevention	Reference to Selected Controls
Nr	Backup system	Value	Value		

legislative or regulatory mandate. This is the reason to compile a security management framework specifically applicable to the organization. Using ISO 27002 as a foundation for this framework is fine; however, add or modify details according to all applicable compliance requirements. Showing a certifier that the organization is at a minimum compliant with ISO 27002 and ISO 27001 obtains certification; showing the certifier that the organization's security posture is much more than that is icing on the cake, plus the a la mode* and the cherry.

When selecting controls according to the results from the risk assessment, the aim is to reduce or remove the vulnerability and therefore reduce risk. Select controls that can reduce the impact and help with the recovery if a threat occurs. At this point, there is a list of assets with associated controls, referred to as the *summary of selected controls*, and it is part of the risk treatment plan and the ISMS.

Table 4.21 shows an example of what one item in the SoC could look like. The first column represents the asset reference number, then a description of the asset. The third column identifies the risk factor. The next column is the criticality of the asset. Next is a placeholder for other preventative measurements that have been implemented, and finally there is the list of selected controls from the ISO 27001[1] standard. Though the table shows only one control as an example, there may be many controls for each asset. The same controls may repeat for many assets requiring similar protection.

When selecting controls to lower the risk value, there are some basic rules. First, select controls driven by legislation or regulation. Second, select controls specific to the organization's business environment. Lastly, select controls that find foundation in industry best practices like the ISO 27001 standard. After selecting all relevant controls, review and plan for implementation of each. Implementing each control incurs cost. The key question is, Do the benefits outweigh these costs? Moreover, there are potential costs (risk of loss) for not implementing each control. This cost–benefit analysis drives control implementation planning and prioritization and is the final decision for mitigating risks or accepting risks. Note that obtaining ISO 27001 certification does not require implementation of all controls. It does require full knowledge and awareness of all risk and justification for actions or postures toward risk. The SoA provides details of the organizational posture toward all risk in terms of ignore, accept, share, transfer, or mitigate.

---

* Meaning the American interpretation of a la mode, which is ice cream on top.

Table 4.22 Asset Description

Provide description and information about the asset here.						
Reference Number	Task List after the Risk Assessment	Responsibility	Risk Factor	Start Date	End Date	Status
1	List of actions to perform					
2						
Selection of prevention: Create action plan to lower risk factor as listed above. Included should be responsibility risk factor, start date, end date, and status. Here can be listed controls selected from the ISO 2700[1] standard divided into: • Controls because of legal assumption • Controls because of good practice and the business • Controls selected to lower the risk factor						

Table 4.22 is a form to capture asset details and selected control details. Most of the information in this form is available in other forms as part of the ISMS establishment process. The many variations of forms and reports are a good argument for creating a database of security details. The discovery process of interviews, surveys, or hands-on provides input to the database. Then back-end reporting may consolidate the details in a variety of formats useful at various technical and managerial levels. Creating and maintaining this database is an extra expense; however, the idea has potential in reducing ongoing maintenance costs of security documentation.

The process of writing policy is outside the scope of this text; however, using a standard format for policy, standard, and procedure promotes consistency, comprehensiveness, and ease of use/readability. Appendix D, "Policy, Standard, and Procedure Sample Templates," contains sample templates for security policy, standard, and procedure. Table 4.23 presents a brief overview of a policy outline.

4.4.1.6 Prepare the Statement of Applicability

The last task in the plan phase is to produce a document called *statement of applicability*. The SoA addresses each security element in ISO 27002; see Appendix B, "Sample Statement of Applicability," for an outline of SoA contents and notional samples of SoA contents. The purpose of addressing each element is to ensure the organization considers each and provides a rationale for risk remediation, risk transference, or ignoring the risk. The framework provides a checklist approach to ensure that any omissions are conscious and not by oversight. Appendix B's sample SoA contains notional SoA with categories for control reference, control name, statement of applicability, and control summary. Table 4.24 provides potential additional columns for the SoA.

Table 4.23   Policy Outline Overview

Policy and Procedure Content Outline	Description
Goal	Select the controls to lower the risk factor of specific information assets.
Objective	Specify the objective of the policy and procedure.
Responsibility	Specify responsibility for policy and procedure, usually the owner of the information assets.
Purpose	Expand on the details generally to heighten the quality and security of the process included in the control.
Who, what, when, where, how	What are the objectives? How do we reach the objectives? When do we perform tasks? Who performs them? Where are they applicable?
Reporting	Define reporting goals and develop report templates to promote comprehensive and consistency.
Metric	Identify a metric and implement a measure to discern the effectiveness of the policy or procedure.

In Table 4.24, the first column is a reference to the control in the ISO 27001 standard. The second describes required actions and includes the risk treatment plan. The third describes if the policy for that selected control has been implemented fully, partially, or not at all. The fourth describes the control that has not been

Table 4.24   Example of a Statement of Applicability

Control Reference	Description	Implement	Justify	Procedure Approach	Comment
A.10.7.2	A paper shredder has been added. New process for secure disposal of media has been implemented.	Fully		Please refer to the control and policy document.	To reduce the risk of unauthorized access to sensitive information. See the result from the risk treatment plan.

selected or implemented and why. The fifth describes the procedure approach (method). The last column is for additional comments, e.g., justification for a particular control. The content of the table and detail depend on the layout of the overall risk management approach and desire to consolidate details in a smaller number of documents.

4.4.1.7 Documentation Summary of the Plan Phase

The plan phase produces documents relevant to the ISMS implementation. First and foremost is the need for a plan phase guideline document to ensure the organization is capturing and executing all the relevant steps for the plan phase. Appendix C, "PDCA Guideline Documents: Outlines," provides a notional outline for an *ISMS—Plan Phase Guidelines* document. The outline, flow, and contents are organizational specific, but this general outline provides a good point in the right direction to begin the ISMS process. Other documents resulting from the plan phase may include:

- Scope document describing the boundary of the ISMS
- ISMS policy
- Organizational security policy
- Information and information technology asset list requiring protection
- Risk assessment:
  - Methodology
  - Results
- Risk treatment plan
- SoA
- SoC
- Standards and procedural guidelines and templates
- Standards and procedures themselves if applicable at the enterprise level
- Measures and metrics to gauge effectiveness of implementation, monitoring, reviewing, and revising the ISMS

All these documents are part of the ISMS and contribute to ISMS implementation. Ensure that all ISMS documentation receives an appropriate classification level that protects what could be proprietary or sensitive information regarding the organization's security posture. With a good set of planning documents to lead the way, it is time to implement—onward to the do phase.

4.5 Do Phase

The plan phase produces documents that guide the implementation of the ISMS, with *implementation* being the focus of the do phase. Figure 4.3 illustrates the do phase process. The core part of the do phase is to implement the risk treatment plan

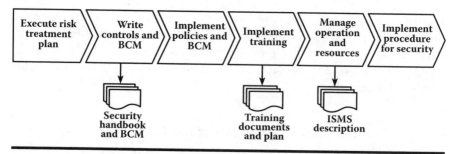

Figure 4.3 Do phase process.

resulting from the risk management process. The ISO 27002 and ISO 27001 standards do not offer guidance on implementation of security controls. The pending security standard ISO 27003 (proposed), *Information Technology—Security Techniques—Information Security Management System Implementation Guidance*, will offer more detail on using the PDCA model to create, plan, implement, operate, and maintain the ISMS.

Implementation of the risk treatment plan begins by writing policies to guide subsequent activities. Procedures provide guidance on *how* to implement and enforce policy. Standards provide guidance on *what* to use to implement and enforce policy. Awareness, training, and education prepare the workforce to take part in the ISMS. Other activities include managing and operating the ISMS, including incident response preparation.

4.5.1 Risk Treatment Plan

The risk treatment plan enumerates risks and identifies organizational responsibilities in addressing risks. The risk treatment plan elaborates governance roles and responsibilities to establish risk management strategy, management actions in turning that strategy into tactics (e.g., operations plans and goals), and operational tasks to administer, monitor, track, and report on risk management activities.

4.5.1.1 Writing Policies and Procedures

The ISMS policy and the organizational security policy support that security (or information assurance) is a necessary part of organizational existence and operations. These policies are high level and do not identify specific security controls. Therefore, the initial step in the do phase is to develop policies for each security control or classification of security controls in the SoC that in turn find justification in the SoA. Policy provides a high-level statement of general objectives for the subject at hand. An organizational security policy may state the need for managing access to information and information technology. The SoA provides a justification for, say, the use of passwords to be applicable to the organization and links that justification to the need for access management. The SoC states that the organization will use passwords as part of an overall access management program. There is now need to write a password policy to provide overall guidance on the use of passwords.

To continue the example, that password policy may state "the use of strong passwords"; remember, a policy statement should be concise. A password standards document may enumerate current industry specifications on what constitutes a strong password, e.g., X number of characters with Y number of special characters and Z number of numeral characters and some number of capital letters mixed with lowercase. A password procedures document explains how to administer a particular system or system type to initially create and enforce the use of strong passwords. Although this may seem cumbersome, decoupling policies, standards, and procedures provides the ability to update one while the others may remain the same. For example, if password-cracking software renders the current standard for strong passwords obsolete, it is relatively straightforward to modify the password standard to reflect a new definition of strong password. The policy for strong password is the same, and the procedures are likely the same; i.e., the administrator will still use the same commands to set up passwords and same configuration screens to set up password enforcement—there is now just a different standard to follow for the construct of the password.

To be ISO 27002 compliant and achieve ISO 27001 certification, use the security controls guidelines to drive the construction of policies, standards, and procedures. An auditor will verify these organizational documents exist and adhere to ISO guidelines. Moreover, the auditor will validate that operational practice adheres to policy, standards, and procedures. A consistent look and feel to all these documents will assist greatly in readability and document maintenance.

Providing explicit traceability from the organizational documents to the specific ISO 27002 controls is preferable both from an audit perspective and to ensure comprehensive creation of all relevant documents. Each ISO control has a section number or control number that the organization can embed in the documents themselves. A better approach is to decouple the ISO control reference from the documents and create a traceability matrix (see tables in the Chapter 6, "Compliance Management," for a framework to create traceability matrices) that links each document or set of documents with a particular ISO security control. The reason for this is, again, maintainability. Better to edit a single document to reflect new security control references than every policy, standard, and procedure.

Each policy begins with a statement of intent that captures the overall objective of the ISO control. This intent guides the specifics of the policy; moreover, standards and procedures are more specific than policy and, as such, may not capture all contingencies for an evolving technical environment. A good heuristic (rule of thumb) is *when in doubt, fall back on the intent*. Although actions may not be in explicit keeping with the letter of the standard or procedure, they may be in keeping with the intent of the policy. The idea is not to open loopholes to circumvent poorly written, vague policies, but to facilitate action and appropriate action when necessary. Yes, there is somewhat of an altruistic expectation here.

The following list provides assistance for writing policy, standard, and procedure for any given control; consider:

- Why was the control selected?
- Who is responsible for the control selection, implementation, enforcement?
- How does one implement the control; enforce the control?
- When does one implement the control; enforce the control?
- What measures and metrics will show the application of the control?
- How do these metrics feed an activity report or other report showing use, effective use, effective security?

Following the writing of policies, standards, and procedures, reflect on the following points:

- Are the policies and procedures clear and realistic? Are they readable?
- Are they too long?
- Do the policies and procedures provide sufficient guidance? Are they actionable?
- Are all parts from the ISO control in the policies, standards, and procedures?
- Is there any means to measure the effectiveness of the policies with help of the procedures?
- What is the performance target? Is it clearly stated?
- What can we measure? How can we measure? Are these adequately presented?
- Is there a publish date in the document?
- Is there a last reviewed date in the document?
- Is it clear who is responsible for the maintenance of the document?

The document objective overall is clear, concise, actionable guidance to adequately protect organizational information and information assets.

4.5.1.2 Metrics and Measurements

> Not everything that can be counted counts, and not everything that counts can be counted.
>
> **—Albert Einstein**

Question is, What can be counted that counts? Metrics and measures discern the existence and quality of policies, standards, procedures, and practice. A metric is an identifiable aspect that an assessor may query. A measure is a determination of some state of the metric (may be intrinsic or artificial value) where that state shows some level of progress, functionality, completeness, level of compliance, etc. The intent of metrics and measures is to capture the state of existence and effectiveness of security preparedness and operations. Some aspects to discern include the following:

- Identify the security control in question.
- Why select this security control?
- What is the goal for this security control?
- Who is responsible for the policy written for that selected control?
- Are they actually performing their responsibilities?
- Is there a policy?
- Is there a standard?
- Is there a procedure?
- Is it a good policy? Capture attributes that define a good policy and compare the attributes of the actual policy.
- Is it a good standard? Is it a good procedure? Perform the same definition and comparison to determine if good standards and good policies exist within the organization.
- Is there organizational practice? Is there good practice? Do organizational practices use the procedures?
- Who is responsible (perhaps a classification of employee) for implementing procedure?
- Who is responsible for tracking the effectiveness of the procedure?
- How does the responsible person measure performance metrics?
- What reports exist to track effectiveness?
- Is there an ability to capture an initial snapshot (baseline) and subsequent snapshots such that a trend analysis is possible?

A metric is an attribute to gauge the quality of performance. For example, the existence of an SWG is one metric. The fact that it exists at all permits definition of metrics to gauge its effectiveness. Metrics to gauge SWG effectiveness may include cross-functional representation, meeting frequency, attendance, committee formations, committee assignments, committee deliverables/deliveries, etc. If all members of the SWG are also members of the IT staff, then the SWG scores low on cross-functional representation.

A measure is the act of comparison. Discerning and recording the types of people who comprise the SWG and comparing against a basis that defines good practice is one measurement regarding the effectiveness of the SWG. The determination of what defines good practice may come from industry standards (e.g., ISO 27001 and ISO 27002), empirical experience within the organization, or vicarious experience from other similar organizations or industry groups (e.g., Computer Emergency Response Team [CERT]).

Table 4.25 provides some initial ideas for developing organizational-specific metrics and measures for the ISMS. The examples are notional and are by no means exhaustive; however, they do provide a good point in the right direction for further development and enhancement. The measures may reflect less than the number of metrics, and likewise for the calculations; the goal is to present enough examples to provide a point in the right direction for the organization to develop its own set of metrics and measures. Some calculations will be a percentage and others may be the simple recording of *yes, no, unknown,* or *not applicable* (NA). It is possible to measure even a subjective compliance assessment in objective terms. Consider a simple scale of nonexistent (no compliance), low compliance, medium compliance, high compliance, and full compliance with stated objectives. No compliance is straightforward. Low compliance may mean there is a piece of paper with the words *Information Security Policy* at the top; that is, the policy exists, but the quality of that policy is low. Medium compliance means a good attempt to achieve a compliant policy, but there are still many missing items. High implies almost there, and a few minor tweaks will achieve full compliance. Translate this subjective judgment into an objective measure of 0, 1, 2, 3, and 4 that represent no compliance, low, medium, high, and full, respectively. Therefore, the calculation column may contain a reference to compliance level that may follow this scale.

The table contents are excerpts from the full metrics and measure development table. Continue to fill in metrics, measures, and calculations for each element in the organization's security management framework. The following material presents useful considerations for completing the table contents.

ISO compliance requires the organization to measure the effectiveness and performance of ISMS implementation; the pending ISO 27004 standard (proposed), *Information Technology—Security Techniques—Information Security Management Measurements*, will provide guidance for metrics and measures. Identifying useful metrics and measures is problematic. Varying levels of the organization are looking for different meanings in the performance results. A firewall administrator wants to know how many blocked packets, how many were potential attacks, and specifics about those potential attacks. The latter requires filtering out expected traffic and isolating exceptions for further analysis to discern attack signatures and patterns. The challenge to the firewall administrator is managing the volume of detail in the logs to identify real threats. A CEO looking for business justification for maintaining a risk management initiative that is costing millions of dollars, Euros, pounds, etc. could care less about the number of blocked packets on a firewall. This difference emphasizes the need for reporting metrics and measures differently throughout the organization.

To solve this problem of relative meaning, consider that metrics at the firewall level gather data points on firewall (FW) operations. The same applies to network intrusion detection systems (NIDSs), antivirus software, antispy, antispam, and all other security mechanisms. These data points roll up to show operational trends over time, which shows the effectiveness of security operations, e.g., FW1 blocked X

Table 4.25   Metrics and Measures Development Guideline: Excerpts

Category/ Subcategory/ Element	Metric	Measure	Calculation (If Applicable)
Security Policy			
Information and Information Technology Security Policy		Measure the existence and quality of the information security policy	
Documentation	Policy exists. Management reviewed. Management approved.	Does the policy exist?	% policies complete = (# existing policies / #target policies)
Dissemination	Policy notifications distributed. Policy accesses and downloads.	Was notification received? Was the policy accessed or downloaded?	% of personnel receiving notification
Policy review	Define review trigger events. Create review board. Assign personnel to review board. Ensure cross-functional representation. Enumerate desired cross-functional representation.	What events trigger the review of the information security policy? Who is responsible for reviewing the information security policy? What business units have representation on the SWG?	% representation = (# business units on SWG / # target business units on SWG)
Security Management Plan		Measure the existence and quality of security controls relevant to the organization of information security.	

(continued)

Table 4.25 Metrics and Measures Development Guideline: Excerpts (Continued)

Category/ Subcategory/ Element	Metric	Measure	Calculation (If Applicable)
Intra-Organization Management			
Executive and management backing	Document management responsibility. Assign management responsibility. Make management actions part of their incentive plan.	Does document exist that expresses management responsibility? Does the document enumerate management responsibilities?	Note: many calculations will be a percentage calculation.
Information security consistency	Awareness program exists. Awareness metrics exist.	Do security awareness, training, and education policy documents exist? Does this document contain the features that comprise a good policy? Including metrics?	Gauge the compliance level according the standards for a good awareness program; e.g. ISO 27002 specifications.
Security roles and responsibilities	Document security personnel within the organization; include credentials that determine their capabilities. Document the positions of these security professionals; ensure they work where most effective.	TBD	TBD

**Table 4.25 Metrics and Measures Development Guideline:
Excerpts (Continued)**

Category/ Subcategory/ Element	Metric	Measure	Calculation (If Applicable)
Authentication and authorization	Configuration management program. Formal identity management program/process. Formal privilege management program/process.	TBD	TBD
Confidentiality agreements	Nondisclosure agreement exists. Legal department review/approve. HR in possession and has policy and procedure when to distribute and how to manage the documents.	TBD	TBD
External authority relationships	Policy exists. Procedures exist on when and how to escalate incidents. Contingency plans exist with default actions given potential for unavailability of key personnel.	TBD	TBD

(continued)

Table 4.25 Metrics and Measures Development Guideline: Excerpts (Continued)

Category/ Subcategory/ Element	Metric	Measure	Calculation (If Applicable)
Professional organizations	List of relevant key groups exists. Memberships exist. Involvement exists where relevant and practical (within budget constraints). Method exists to accept input, discern relevancy to the organization, and disseminate details to appropriate personnel.	How many special interest groups does the organization have an affiliation with? How frequent are the meetings? How many useful inputs are there for organizational security?	TBD
Independent assessments and audits	Policy exists; policy state regular review and provides a specific timeframe (e.g. every 12 months). Retainer or other agreement exists for third-party auditor.	TBD	TBD

Table 4.25 Metrics and Measures Development Guideline: Excerpts (Continued)

Category/ Subcategory/ Element	Metric	Measure	Calculation (If Applicable)
Second Party Management			
Risk management	Establish contractual agreements for contractors, partners, vendors, customers, and other third parties that include the need for security controls. Specify minimum controls for acceptable access. Specify verification and validation methods for compliance.	How many existing standard contracts exist for third parties? How many of these have security clauses that meet minimum standards? How long since the last review of these contracts in context of organizational risk?	TBD
Addressing security when dealing with customers	Ibid	Ibid	TBD
Business agreements	Ibid	Ibid	TBD
Asset Management			
Responsibility and Accountability for Assets			
Inventory	Asset management system exists. Asset prioritization scheme exists.	TBD	TBD
Ownership	Details within asset management system allow for the recording of asset owner.	TBD	TBD

(continued)

Table 4.25 Metrics and Measures Development Guideline: Excerpts (Continued)

Category/ Subcategory/ Element	Metric	Measure	Calculation (If Applicable)
Appropriate use	Policy(ies) exist for acceptable use. The contents of the acceptable use policies adhere to industry standards (e.g. ISO 27002).	TBD	TBD
Information and Information Technology Classification			
Classifications	Establish classification guidelines according to industry standards.	Are there classification guidelines? Do they comply with industry standards?	(# of classifications guidelines / # of target classification guidelines) Compliance level comparing existing against industry standard
Etc.	...	...	...

total packets with Y identified as potential attacks. These operational trends become part of overall security operations reports. Security operations reports in turn roll up to risk management reports that align with motivations behind risk management, e.g., compliance management. At this level, the reports include taking on meaning to track compliance with legislation and regulation driving operational behavior.

The next level of reports is the executive level. Executive interest is in the core reasons for the existence of the organization. This may include justifying investments to a board of directors or reporting to stockholders on performance. An investment of $X millions in security must show a payoff in stakeholder terms. For a public company, the largest group of stakeholders is likely shareholders in varying types of stocks and bonds. Stakeholder terms here include the balance sheet and the income statement. Therefore, measures and metrics reporting at the CxO level are in terms of shareholder value reflected in balance sheet and income statement line items.

From a government perspective, stakeholders include citizens, politicians, soldiers, and government workers, among others. Reporting at the executive level is in terms of these various stakeholders. Money comes into play in any organization; even nonprofits are concerned with revenue and cash flow to support their cause. However, money may not be the only interest and may not be the primary interest. If a politician backs a government initiative, his or her interest may primarily reside in votes for an upcoming election. Therefore, a performance report in stakeholder terms may include the effect the performance is having in the polls. A military commander's primary concern may reside with the safety of his troops; therefore, performance in terms of lives or casualties may be more appropriate. The point is that measures and metrics are becoming more important; however, their application and reporting are not straightforward.

Varying levels of the organization consume operational effectiveness reports in different flavors. The application server administrator and network administrator look for statistics that show uptime or downtime. The security administrator looks for number of viruses blocked by the anti-malware software or number of probes on the firewall. These are data points on individual mechanism performance or individual mechanism uptime. Security management aggregates these mechanistic performance data points into operations reports in terms that reflect overall performance against service level agreements (SLAs). The performance reporting becomes more in business terms of performance at the management level. As the reports reach the executive level, the terms become more of *business value*, not merely performance. The executive invests in operations; one of those operations is security. Executive reports should show the business value of security operations, preferably in terms of ROI with direct correlation to income statement or balance sheet. This is a nontrivial task, but an important one for security to stand and claim business value.

Some thoughts on where to apply metrics to measure the success of the ISMS are the following:

- Quantify the results of risk assessment:
  - Business function value, e.g., e-commerce website in terms of revenue generation and profitability
  - Asset value, e.g., actual value of e-commerce server
  - Vulnerabilities:
    - Known vulnerabilities potentially on server X
    - Actual vulnerabilities on server X discovered via vulnerability assessment
  - Remediation plans:
    - Activities scheduled to fix vulnerabilities

- Vulnerability management:
  - Ongoing activities to raise awareness of new vulnerabilities and patch management to proactively mitigate vulnerabilities
- Threat probabilities, e.g., likelihood of malware
■ Incident handling and reporting:
- Number of incidents
- Time from discovery to notification:
  - Provides insight to security awareness and presence of infrastructure for notification
- Time from notification to triage and escalation:
  - Provides insight to presence of help desk and incident response groups as well as the effectiveness of these groups in responding
- Time from escalation to isolation, fix, and restoration:
  - Provides insight to effectiveness of incident response group in resolving issues
- Time from restoration to complete root cause analysis (RCA) and affect organizational operations:
  - Provides insight to presence of an RCA process and commitment of security to add value to business operations; a lesson learned once is a new defensive mechanism to reduce likelihood of recurrence, or at least reduce the effects of recurrence
■ Management review of ISMS:
- Shows commitment on the part of management to a secure business environment
■ Change management controls
■ Audit log files
■ Findings from internal security audit:
- Baseline for how well the organization knows itself, or at least thinks it knows itself
■ Findings from external security audit:
- Independent collaboration of how well the organization knows itself
■ Testing of business continuity and disaster recovery
■ Tracking of:
- Security awareness, e.g., number of employees who open the e-mail containing awareness material
- Security training, e.g., number of employees attending training webinars
- Security education, e.g., number of certifications obtained or renewed

The list goes on and the nuances become organizational specific. The ideas above provide a good point in the right direction for what can be a most daunting challenge in proving the business value of security.

When writing the policies from selected controls to lower the risk factor, define the goal, the type, and the objective to measure the effectiveness of the policy.

Table 4.26   Definition of Factors

Factor	Description
Goals	Describe the desired result of implementing one or more security controls. Include this detail in the policy.
Type	Type of metric, that is, what type of activity accomplishes the goal. Examples include a result, an output, an implementation, or an activity.
Objective	Describe how to tell when the goal is met.
Purpose	Describe the reason for the metric.
Implementation evidence	Describe the proof that the policy and procedure exist. This is part of internal audit of the ISMS to confirm that the implementation of the metrics is working.
Frequency	Describe how often to collect data, e.g., weekly, monthly, annually, dependent on the business and how often changes are made.
Formula	Describe the calculation and type of expected result, such as a percentage or number.
Data source	List the location of the data.
Indication	Provide information about the meaning of the metrics and measurement and the performance trend.

Table 4.26 shows the definition for these three factors, as well as describes other factors for developing procedures to implement policy. These factors provide guidance for creating consistent procedures that promote clear stating of objectives and measuring the accomplishment of those objectives.

Implementing policy by way of procedure provides guidance for consistency and an audit trail for internal audits to validate the implementation and repeatability of the ISMS operations. This is all part of the PDCA model for continual improvement of a management system.

4.5.2 Selecting and Implementing Controls

Use the ISO 27002 to provide a framework and guidance for selecting and implementing the appropriate controls. Selection of specific controls and implementation is organization specific. In general, consider the section of controls from the abstract perspective of, *Does the organization need this security control at all?* If so, state the reasons. If no, state the reasons. This is essentially the SoA. For all security controls that the organization needs, consider the type of controls and implementation guidance from the perspective of, *What features of this control does the organization need?* Again, ISO 27002 provides guidance with regard to the features of various controls. Using security policy as a guide and balancing security requirements with available resources (budget), the security professional decides what features constitute best practice and what constitute acceptable practice.

At this point, there is a good idea of what security controls are necessary at all and what features of each the organization will implement. Vendor guidance, training, and user groups then provide insight into implementation and deployment of the security controls. **Note:** Protection of the organization is important and the focus of the ISMS. Moreover, the collection of documents that define and make up the ISMS contains sensitive details about organizational operations and security posture. Be sure to protect the distribution and storage of these documents.

4.5.3 Awareness, Training, and Education

There are many philosophies on human learning and many approaches. From academic and professional instruction experience, learning generally progresses through set phases: awareness, understanding, use, and effective use. People start out not knowing what they do not know; awareness overcomes this deficit. In addition, there is a difference between knowing about something and knowing that thing. Security awareness provides knowledge *about* security. As people progress through the understanding phase, they internalize the need for security and start to realize their role. Upon acceptance of that role, they begin to act more securely, that is, they begin to use security measures and apply their awareness. Through using these new skills, they may develop a certain level of competency or even expertise, that is, they begin to use the tools effectively. This is a simplification of a very complex subject, but generally holds true.

Security awareness activities overcome general ignorance of security issues, the need for security, and that there are actions the person may take to contribute to a more secure environment. Security awareness is for all employees, and delivery methods may include new-employee orientation, new-job or new-duties orientation, periodic reminders, posters, and more. Security training is for those directly involved with information and information technology requiring secure use. These people may include system administrators and data capture personnel (e.g., hospital admittance, billing personnel). Security professionals also need training on security mechanisms, e.g., how to operate a firewall, network intrusion detection system, or how to set up a honey pot. Moreover, security professionals need education, which is a broader and deeper perspective on security than just the operation of security mechanisms. Objectives of security education may be a degree specifically in security (e.g., master of science in information assurance) or a certification (e.g., Certified Information System Security Professional [CISSP]).

The presence of security awareness, knowledge, and expertise in the organization is part of the ISO requirements and part of the ISMS audit for ISO 27001 certification. Measures and metrics may track these activities in the following manner:

- Awareness:
  - Number of e-mails sent in awareness campaign
  - Number of return receipts (shows e-mail was opened)
  - Quiz results from awareness activities (shows level of participation as well as understanding)
  - Survey results; may use sampling to extrapolate sample population results to larger employee population
- Training:
  - Number of professional seminars attended
  - Number of product-certified security professionals (e.g., certified firewall administrator or certified firewall engineer)
- Education:
  - Number of degreed professionals in a security-related discipline
  - Number of professionals with security certifications:
    o New certifications
    o Renewed certifications (shows commitment on continuing education to maintain certification)

4.5.4 Managing Operation and Resources

The objective for post-ISMS implementation is effective ongoing operation to manage organizational risk and maintain acceptable levels of confidentiality, integrity, and availability of information and information technology. To accomplish the operational objectives requires allocation of appropriate resources. Resources include knowledgeable security professionals and the appropriate security tools to address risks in the SoA. Operations management includes acquiring personnel, managing personnel, acquiring tools, and managing tools. The first step is documenting procedures for operations activities.

Documentation includes labor category descriptions (expertise needed), skills inventory (existing expertise), change management procedures, personnel assignment procedures (e.g., segregation of duties), tools implementation procedures, and tool operation procedures. The ISMS requires that each activity adhere to ISO standards as well as be repeatable to produce consistent results. Achieving this as well as proving this requires extensive documentation.

4.5.5 Managing Security Incident

Preparing for security incidents requires addressing policy, procedures, infrastructure, and tools to support the following with respect to incidents:

- Monitoring
- Detection
- Notification
- Triage
- Escalation
- Response
- Isolation
- Restoration
- Root cause analysis
- Organizational feedback

4.5.5.1 Monitoring

Security mechanisms, security professionals, and the employee population all provide incident detection. This requires the identification and implementation of appropriate security mechanisms, including firewalls, anti-malware (antivirus, antispam, anti-spyware), intrusion detection systems, and more. The organization invests in knowledgeable security professionals and prepares them with training and education. Awareness programs prepare all employees and primarily assist in helping them avoid dangerous behavior and to be aware of their surroundings and monitor for anomalous activities.

4.5.5.2 Detection

Security mechanisms, security professionals, and the employee population all provide incident detection. A firewall may alert a denial-of-service attack. The antivirus software on the e-mail server may notify of a bombardment of worms. An intrusion detection system may alert of anomalous behavior. An employee may notice that financial information in a database does not match expected values seen the day before. Manual evaluation of an audit log may show clues to insider threat activity. All these and more comprise incident detection.

4.5.5.3 Notification

An infrastructure to support notification of incidents includes a help desk, a security incident response center (SIRC) in the security operation center (SOC), which is typically part of the network operations center (NOC). Depending on the severity of the incident, the organization may have access to subject matter experts (SMEs). SMEs may be in-house expertise available to respond upon need or external resources available on a contractual basis.

The notification infrastructure may include a help desk, e-mail access to the help desk, toll-free access to the help desk, and a ticketing system to track incident notification and response times (metrics and measures).

4.5.5.4 Triage

Prepare the help desk to handle known security issues, e.g., isolating a virus on desktop, deleting infected files, and restoring clean files. Prepare the help desk to triage incidents and to know when to escalate incidents that are beyond its ability to handle effectively. Likewise, prepare the SIRC and SOC teams with triage guidance to involve the SMEs.

4.5.5.5 Escalation

Escalation of incidents requires preparation to engage groups of varying expertise. First, automate mechanistic response, e.g., desktop antivirus system, isolates and treats infected files. The organization should train employees to be aware of their environment and when to escalate detection of anomalous activities to the help desk, as well as provide subsequent escalation guidance from the help desk to SIRC/ SOC and SMEs.

4.5.5.6 Response

The ability to respond presupposes available expertise to respond to security incidents. Ad hoc response is not nearly as effective as a prepared and rehearsed response. Moreover, the response teams need to obtain the appropriate response tools. These tools may include cyber forensics tools, antivirus inoculation software, etc.

4.5.5.7 Isolation

The response teams need to have the authority to isolate the problem. This may mean disconnecting key servers from the network, thus interrupting operations.

4.5.5.8 Restoration

The primary goal is service restoration. Service restoration may mean treating the symptom. The organization should understand the need to identify the problem because without addressing the problem there is high likelihood of recurrence.

4.5.5.9 Root Cause Analysis

The RCA identifies the problem. The root cause may be technical, organizational, personnel, or procedural. The RCA is a methodical process that identifies relevant contributions to incident occurrence. The findings from the RCA provide insight into how to prevent incident recurrence. At the least, an RCA will reduce the effects of recurrence by preparing a more effective response.

4.5.5.10 Organizational Feedback

The RCA results provide details for organizational feedback. Organizational feedback implements activities that address the root cause of the problem. If the root cause is procedural, then modify the procedures and retrain personnel using those procedures. If the root cause is unaware personnel, modify awareness material and delivery (e.g., new-employee orientation).

There are many opportunities to measure incident response effectiveness. These details will contribute to becoming more effective in incident response; more importantly, capturing these details will prove the business value of security. Useful documents for incident reporting include an incident reporting summary and RCA report.

4.5.6 Documentation Summary of the Do Phase

The do phase implements the ISMS and produces documents relevant to ISMS operations, which is the act phase of the PDCA cycle. Similar to the plan phase, the organization may capture details of the do phase to ensure a relevant approach to ISMS implementation. Appendix C provides a notional outline for an *ISMS—Do Phase Guidelines* document. Again, the outline, flow, and contents are organizational specific, but this general outline provides a good start.

The do phase produces at least the following documents:

- Security handbook that includes all the controls that have been written
- Business continuity management plan that includes BCP and DRP
- Awareness, training, and education:
  - Relevant materials
  - Documented awareness, training, and education plan
- ISMS operational description
- Incident management:
  - Incident report
  - RCA report

Policies providing justification for the creation of these documents and procedures on how to use these documents, templates, collection tools, analysis tools, and reporting tools, all contribute to the ISMS audit for certification.

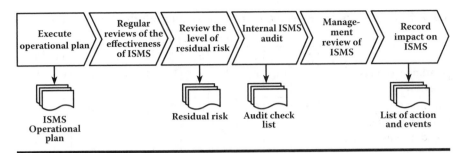

Figure 4.4 Check phase.

4.6 Check Phase

The check phase reviews the policies and procedures to verify they exist, that the organization actually uses them, and that they are effective in supporting organizational objectives in risk management. This process is an internal audit of the ISMS. Figure 4.4 shows the steps of the check phase starting with the last step in the act phase of implementing the ISMS and picking up the regular review of the ISMS for effectiveness in meeting organizational objectives in managing organizational risk.

The next step is to review the residual risk and compare it against acceptable levels of risk, and balance appropriate safeguards with the business value they provide. Management review of internal audit and residual risk validates their understanding and agreement with the ISMS and provides input to potential modifications to the ISMS (the act phase).

4.6.1 Execute Operational Plan

An effective and successful ISMS requires a formal operational plan as well as metrics and measures to ensure the ISMS operates as intended and satisfies organizational objectives in managing business risk. The ISMS can be complex, and various pieces require review at different times. Part of the operational plan is a schedule and checklist for ISMS review. Table 4.27 presents a checklist to track ISMS review, record previous review, and plan subsequent reviews. The table rows list ISMS elements to track, and the columns represent months of the year. The notations within the table are P for a *planned review* and N for *next review* (may not have a formal plan yet).

The following sections present additional details for ISMS operational effectiveness.

4.6.2 Review of the Effectiveness of the ISMS

Metrics to measure the effectiveness of the ISMS may include SLAs in the form of uptime goals (Table 4.28) or downtime tolerance (Table 4.29). The tables provide the

Table 4.27 Security Management Framework and Interpretation Guide

ISMS Element	Months (1 = January, etc.)											
	1	2	3	4	5	6	7	8	9	10	11	12
Finding from last review	P	N	P	P	P	P	P	P	P	P	P	P
Information security policy and operation changes	P	N	P	P	P	P	P	P	P	P	P	P
ISMS policy and operation changes	P	N	P	P	P	P	P	P	P	P	P	P
Internal organization and external parties		N			P			P			P	P
Assets responsible— risk management, residual risk			P									
Employee before, during, and termination or change				P								
Secure area, equipment security						P						
Operational procedures and responsibilities					P							
Access control								P				
Security requirements of information system								P				
Security requirements of information system									P			
Incidents, security events, and weakness management	P	N	P	P	P	P	P	P	P	P	P	P

Table 4.27 Security Management Framework and Interpretation Guide (Continued)

ISMS Element	Months (1 = January, etc.)											
Business continuity management— handbooks, test result					P							
Compliance review		P				P					P	P
Management review			P									

Table 4.28 Annual Uptime Goals Guideline

	Goal	Days	Hours	Minutes
	100.000%	365.00	8,760.00	525,600.00
59 s	99.999%	365.00	8,759.91	525,594.74
49 s	99.990%	364.96	8,759.12	525,547.44
39 s	99.900%	364.64	8,751.24	525,074.40
29 s	99.000%	361.35	8,672.40	520,344.00
	98.000%	357.70	8,584.80	515,088.00
	95.000%	346.75	8,322.00	499,320.00
	90.000%	328.50	7,884.00	473,040.00

Table 4.29 Annual Downtime Tolerance Guideline

	Goal	Days	Hours	Minutes
	100.000%	365.00	8,760.00	525,600.00
59 s	99.999%	0.00	0.09	5.26
49 s	99.990%	0.04	0.88	52.56
39 s	99.900%	0.37	8.76	525.60
29 s	99.000%	3.65	87.60	5,256.00
	98.000%	7.30	175.20	10,512.00
	95.000%	18.25	438.00	26,280.00
	90.000%	36.50	876.00	52,560.00

time implications in days, hours, and minutes for readily understanding the implications of the commitment, meaning 0.04 days of downtime tolerance does not make as much sense to most readers as 52.56 minutes. Likewise, 10,512 minutes does not make as much sense as 7.3 days. Mapping out the implications of committing to 5 to 9 seconds uptime, or providing functionality 99.999 percent of the time, implies no more downtime than 5.26 minutes per year. Be sure to specify if this commitment includes outages due to security issues alone, or if this includes hardware failures, as well as downtime for scheduled maintenance. If indeed 5 to 9 seconds annual operational uptime is a requirement, ensure the design includes the appropriate redundant functionality to support this requirement—bonuses, promotions, and continued employment reside with appropriate management of expectations.

Other metrics may include tracking security events and response to the event. First, the ability to detect security events shows the appropriate tools in place for environmental awareness and the ability to detect anomalies. Second, such tracking shows organizational preparedness to handle the event. Automated tools like anti-virus, anti-spyware, firewall rules, etc. handle most events (hopefully). Tracking performance and reporting results show business value in these preventive tools.

With regard to personnel awareness, training, and education, metrics may include number of prehire investigations and results (e.g., avoided hiring three people with criminal backgrounds). Track the delivery of new-hire orientations with regard to security awareness, including legislative and regulatory awareness and covering material to comply. Another metric may include sending security awareness material via e-mail and tracking how many sent, how many open the e-mail (an awareness metric), and how many acknowledge having viewed the material. If there is value in tracking a level of understanding, present a short quiz and track correct responses. One may also track the progress of security professionals toward obtaining or maintaining professional certifications or degrees related to security.

The above metrics are general and potentially useful to most organizations. Many metrics are organizational specific as well as showing the degree of success. A medium-sized company making floor tile still needs to be security aware to ensure its continued operation; however, focused attacks on such a company are not as likely as on a major international bank or government agency. All organizations can learn from periodic review and may improve operations with implementation of the PDCA process and feedback experiences.

4.6.3 Review the Level of Residual Risk

Residual risk is that risk to the organization after risk sharing, transfer, or mitigation. Periodic review of risk should identify and explain any residual risk, especially that residual risk in excess of *acceptable* risk according to policy. Justifications for residual risk may include acceptably low probability of threat occurrence, mitigation expense greater than asset value, or *additional* mitigation expense generally does not provide business value. Given the pervasive constant in the contemporary business environment is change, and change at an ever-increasing rate, an assumption is the business environment is likely to change quickly. Hence, a periodic review of residual risks in light of new parameters, business direction, threats, safeguards, etc. is advisable.

4.6.4 Conduct an Internal ISMS Audit

An internal ISMS audit determines if policy and procedures exist. Additionally, an audit review policy content and procedure accuracy to implement policy. If policies and procedures exist and are in use, the audit also evaluates the effectiveness of policies and procedures. Generally, relevant questions in the internal audit are: Do policies and procedures exist for a particular security control? Does the organization use them? Does the organization use them effectively?

ISO 27002 provides implementation guidance for policy content (Table 1.2). A series of audit questions modeled after policy content expectations provides support for not only whether the policies and procedures exist, but also the quality of the policies and procedures. During the audit, note which aspects of the security control the organization has implemented and, as importantly, those aspects that are not. The audit gathers justification details for both. Not implementing a particular control or an aspect of a control is fine, providing there is valid rationale behind the decision. Too often, there is omission by oversight; conscious omission due to low threat level, low probability of occurrence, or priorities due to budget constraints is more justifiable to management, stakeholders, or a judge should events come to a litigious end.

As a general guideline for audit questions, consider the following:

- Identify the security control in question.
- Why select this security control?
- Who is responsible for the policy written for that selected control?
- Is there a policy?
- Is there a need for a procedure?
- Is there a procedure?
- Do organizational practices use the procedure?
- Who is responsible (perhaps a classification of employee) for implementing procedure?
- Who is responsible for tracking the effectiveness of the procedure?
- Are there metrics to track the effectiveness of the procedure?
- How does the responsible person measure these metrics?
- What reports exist to track effectiveness?

Table 4.30 presents a notional internal audit form. The details are organizational specific. Generally, the goal is to obtain a snapshot of the organization's

Table 4.30 Notational Internal Audit Form

Auditor name:						Date:
Excellent	Acceptable	Needs Improvement	Unwholesome	Control Change	Enclosures	**Security Control:** <Audit process remarks> **Justification:** <Brief description>
☐	☐	☐	☐	☐	☐	Clear responsibility exists for policy and procedures.
☐	☐	☐	☐	☐	☐	There is a policy and the contents meet or exceed organizational objectives.
☐	☐	☐	☐	☐	☐	There is a procedure and the contents meet or exceed organizational objectives.
☐	☐	☐	☐	☐	☐	Employees use the procedures in their operations.
☐	☐	☐	☐	☐	☐	There are metrics and measures to gauge the effectiveness of this procedure.
☐	☐	☐	☐	☐	☐	There are reports to track effectiveness.
Additional Details:						

security posture at minimum expense. Using an objective third party, using a short, simple form that provides the ability to aggregate the results from many inputs, is an effective process.

Appendix A, "ISMS Assessment Discovery Question Set," contains an extensive discovery question set to discern the organization's security posture. The likelihood of using the entire question set is very low due to its detail and the probable low tolerance an interviewee will have to sit through such questioning. However, the detail is there for the reader to discern what is important and use a subset accordingly.

4.6.5 Regular Management Review of the ISMS

ISO 27001 requires management review of the ISMS on a regular basis. Although management concerns may not extend to the specifics of procedures, standards, and the mechanisms enforcing those standards, their interest should extend to reports on the effectiveness of ISMS in the context of supporting business objectives. Moreover, management's interest in the ISMS should extend beyond the information technology (IT) department's perspective. An effective ISMS requires a cross-function forum consisting of at least IT, business operations (representation of that part of the business for which IT provides support), legal (e.g., legislative compliance), and security professionals.

The cross-function forum manages the generation of the necessary documents for management review. Section 7 of the ISO 27001[1] standard provides an outline of management review input as well as guidelines for management review output. The latter provides feedback to the cross-function forum and generally the organization on the effectiveness of the ISMS and revisions/refinements to organizational policy guiding ISMS activity.

4.6.6 Record Action and Events That Impact the ISMS

The cross-function forum uses the results from the audit and feedback from management review to develop an ISMS revision plan. The intent is to improve the ISMS or otherwise refine the ISMS to reflect changes in business goals or operating environment. The ISMS revision plan provides input to the next phase of the PDCA cycle, the act phase.

4.6.7 Documentation Summary of Check Phase

The check phase monitors ISMS operations and produces documents relevant to potential ISMS revision, or the act phase of the PDCA cycle. The organization may capture details of the check phase to ensure a relevant approach to ISMS monitoring and operational controls. Appendix C provides a notional outline for an *ISMS— Check Phase Guidelines* document. The guideline documents for the PDCA phases are not the ISMS documents themselves, but guidelines for the execution of the PDCA process. Recording details of the process ensures comprehensiveness, consistency, and repeatability—all-important details for achieving ISO 27001 certification.

The check phase of the PDCA cycle reviews the existence and effectiveness of ISMS security policy, procedure, and controls. The documents resulting from the check phase include the following:

- Metrics and measurements for individual selected controls
- Updated list of residual risks
- Audit checklist
- Results from the internal audit
- List of things to do to improve the ISMS operation

As with many documents resulting from ISMS development, review, and management, these documents contain sensitive information with respect to the organization's operations, assets, and security posture. Store and transfer these documents securely to protect organizational interests, e.g., do not send these documents

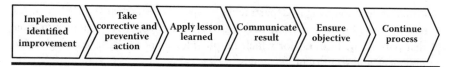

Figure 4.5   Act phase.

over the public network (i.e., Internet) in clear text. If engaging an independent audit firm, establish an industry standard encryption process prior to electronically transferring these or supporting documents.

4.7   Act Phase

The PDCA act phase provides an opportunity to improve the ISMS. This phase acts on the results from the check phase. Figure 4.5 shows the steps of the act phase.

Improvement initiatives come out of the check phase. These initiatives may include modifications, additions, or detractions from preventive measures (defenses, monitoring) and corrective measures (detection, notification, escalation, response). Apply lessons learned to the new initiatives and communicate the results to the appropriate parts of the organization. Repeat our mantra: *Security is a process, not a destination.* The final step prompts continual review and improvement inherent in the PDCA cycle. The following sections elaborate on the act phase steps.

4.7.1   Implement Identified Improvements

The check phase monitors and reviews the effectiveness of the ISMS. Outputs from the check phase include recommendations for ISMS improvements; the act phase implements those improvements. Improvement suggestions may come from monitoring ISMS operations with respect to meeting SLAs, or an internal audit may provide improvement insights. Management input reflecting a changing business environment or evolving compliance requirements provides improvements for ISMS. The least desirable source of improvements is from external auditors verifying and validating ISMS security controls, policies, and procedures. With management approval, the cross-function forum or SWG oversees and performs ISMS improvements.

4.7.2   Apply Lessons Learned: Empirical and Vicarious

4.7.2.1   Empirical

Empirical lessons learned are those that hit and stick home the hardest; after all, once burned, twice cautious. Periodic review of ISMS policy, procedure, and operations results identifies lessons learned across the organization and leverages lessons learned from actual internal experiences.

4.7.2.2 Vicarious

Although the radical empiricist may disagree, a vicarious lesson that gravity does indeed exist and has a deleterious effect with a strong sense of finality on those jumping unaided out of an airplane at 10,000 feet is preferable to firsthand experience. Point is, review of industry experiences from conference proceedings, professional seminars, surveys, or other audit results provides valuable insight to potential ISMS modifications.

Reflect all applications of lessons learned in PDCA guideline documents (i.e., process update) as well as in ISMS policies and procedures. Also, capture modifications to metrics and measures, dissemination of new information throughout the organization, management review, and feedback results, as well as project activity to implement the modifications. All this detail supports the business case for security efforts and provides input to independent audit to achieve or maintain ISO 27001 certification.

4.7.3 Communicate the Results: Organizational Outreach

Like initial implementation, subsequent modification to the ISMS requires outreach to those aspects of the organization affected by the modifications. This outreach may be in variations of awareness, training, and education; awareness for general employees, training for the operations personnel directly affected by the modification, and education for the security professional to address some additional nuance.

4.7.4 Ensure the Objective

Following the implementation of a security control, there is need to verify and validate that control, that is, ensure the control is in place and working as intended. This verification and validation are ensuring that the security controls meet the objectives of the ISMS.

4.7.5 Continue the Process

Security is a process, not a destination. The completion of the act phase leads to a repeat of the plan phase with focus on the effects of new vulnerabilities, changing technical environment, changing business environment, or changing business drivers. A risk assessment should occur not more than 12 months from the previous assessment, and sooner given the aforementioned risk assessment trigger events.

4.7.6 Documentation Summary of the Act Phase

The act phase revises the ISMS according to details from the check phase. The organization may desire to capture details of the act phase to ensure a relevant approach to ISMS revision and dissemination of those revisions throughout the organization from management approval to user awareness, buy-in, and practice. Appendix C provides a notional outline for an *ISMS—Act Phase Guidelines* document.

The documents resulting from the act phase are all revisions of previous documents, including:

- *ISMS—Act Phase Guidelines*
- Metrics and measurements
- Residual risk update
- Audit checklist
- Results from the internal audit
- List of things to do to improve the ISMS

4.8 Summary of Implementing the ISMS

The objectives of this chapter were to apply the PDCA model to the development of an ISMS and overall security program. Each phase covers a different aspect of establishing, implementing, managing, and maintaining the ISMS. The results of these efforts produce the following documents:

- ISMS policy
- ISMS scope:
  - List of important business functions:
    - Distinguish key business functions, that is, those functions critical to organizational mission fulfillment and organizational survival
  - List of important information and information technology assets with classification in context of business function support
- ISMS supporting security policies:
  - Policies that govern the selection and implementation of security controls, e.g., password policy
- ISMS procedures:
  - How to implement policy
- ISMS standards:
  - Specific controls to implement policy
- Risk assessment methodology:
  - Document how the organization performs risk assessment
- Risk assessment findings:
  - Product of the risk assessment methodology when applied to the organization

- Risk treatment plan:
  - Enumerate how the organization will address each risk in terms of accept, ignore, transfer, share, or mitigate
- Procedures:
  - Likely multiple documents to address how the organization will ensure effective planning, operation, and control of information security and related processes and metrics
- Records and logs:
  - Evidence relevant to show conformity to ISO security standards

Though not specifically enumerated in ISO 27001, other useful documents include:

- Security handbook
- BCP, continuity of operations plan (COOP)
- DRP
- Training plan
- Training documents
- Description of the ISMS operation
- Incident response plan
- Metrics and measurements, including alignment with business drivers and business risk management
- Residual risk update
- Audit checklist
- Results from the internal audit
- Process to review and update ISMS, including trigger event to prompt review (e.g., calendar, incident, change of business environment, etc.)
- ISMS improvement list

This long list of documents formally defines the ISMS. These documents support the creation, implementation, and ongoing management of the ISMS and are key in the audit process to obtain ISO 27001 certification. Many additional document templates and actual details will support the ISMS process. These documents include the following common elements in management standards, with all finding foundation in management commitment:

- Roles and responsibility definition
- Document control
- Record management
- Training
- Management review
- Internal audit
- Corrective and preventive actions

- Common model, PDCA
- Audit processes similar
- Accredited assessment schema based on common international standard: ISO 19011:2002, *Guideline on Quality and/or Environmental Management System Audit*[16]
- Requirements based on similar standards
- Certification body responsible for verifying auditor competence

The ISMS is but one of many ISO management systems. The collective of management systems may be called a business management system (BMS), with an overarching goal to implement, maintain, and improve business management. The creation of a single, coordinated BMS provides the ability to leverage experience between many management efforts. Moreover, a single BMS with foundation in ISO standards provides a common look and feel for the organization itself, as well as auditors verifying good practice and granting certification.

Chapter 5

Audit and Certification

Having set up an information security management system (ISMS) using the International Standards Organization (ISO) standards, an organization is able to manage business risk with repeatable processes using many standards-based policies, procedures, tools, and templates. Business benefits from this approach include leveraging initial investments in procedures, tools, and templates across many parts of the organization. Centralized creation and management of these tools support organizational learning where lessons learned by one result in better practices by all. Moreover, the creation of standards-based traceability matrices that align security initiatives with business drivers provides the ability to prove the business value of information security. With this foundation in good security management practices, many organizations desire to pursue the next step of independent audit of their ISMS and obtain certification that their ISMS meets ISO 27001 standards. This chapter presents details of preparing for and obtaining ISO 27001 certification.

5.1 Objectives

The following is a summary of chapter objectives:

- Learning about the audit process:
  - Interweave three perspectives of the audit process:
    - *Preaudit, audit,* and *postaudit*
    - *Four-stage approach* of ISO 27001 certification
    - *Pre-site visit, site visit, post-site visit*
- Facilitating the audit process
- Preparing to achieve ISO 27001 certification

- Definition of an accredited certification body
- Role of an accredited certification body
- Finding and engaging a certifying auditor

5.2 Certification Process Overview

The pending standard ISO/IEC 27006 (proposed), *Information Technology — Security Techniques — International Accreditation Guidelines for the Accreditation of Bodies Operating Certification/Registration of Information Security Management Systems*, provides guidance to accredited certification bodies (third-party auditors) on how to certify and register another organization's ISMS. Because the standard is not yet available, certified accreditation bodies (henceforth called *certifiers* for brevity) perform variations on a very similar process to certify the organization as ISO 27001 compliant. The goal is not 100 percent perfection, given that security is a process and not a goal; the objective is to instill a process to plan, implement, monitor, review, and revise security with changing industry knowledge, business environment, and an evolving threat environment. Therefore, the goal of the certification process is not to prove 100 percent safety, but rather an adequate level of preparedness with appropriate policy, standards, and procedures in keeping with ISO 27001 and ISO 27002.

ISMS certification lasts approximately three years, then requires recertification. A certificate register is available at http://www.iso27001certificates.com/, which shows all organizations that have various ISO certifications and have registered with the site.

The certification process generally consists of the following activities, with slight variations among the certifiers:

- Preaudit
  - Selecting an accredited certification body
  - Audit preparation
- Audit
  - Pre-site visit activity
    - Stage 1
    - Stage 2
  - Site visit activity
    - Stage 3
  - Post-site visit activity
    - Stage 4
- Postaudit

Many certifiers portray their activity in stages and specifically use the term *stages*. Activities in these stages align directly with *pre-site visit, site visit,* and *post-site visit* activities, which in turn align with *preaudit, audit,* and *postaudit* activities.

The reason for introducing the categorization of pre-site visit, site visit, and post-site visit becomes evident in Chapter 6, "Compliance Management," where achieving ISO 27001 certification is one instance of a compliance management process. The intent of these various perspectives is to add clarity that ties together multiple activities to satisfy a larger goal.

Only an accredited certifying body may certify an organization as ISO 27001 compliant, and the organization must choose a certifying body to perform the audit. Audit preparation is the organization compiling all relevant documentation and notifying appropriate personnel regarding pending phone calls and site visits by the certifiers. Pre-site visit consists of documentation review by the certifier. Site visit is the certifier validating that organizational practices are in keeping with documentation. Post-site visit is the certifier analyzing the results and providing a findings report to the organization. At this point, there may be a certification or the need for corrective action prior to receiving certification. The remainder of this chapter expands on each of the phases or stages in the bullet list above.

5.3 Selecting an Accredited Certification Body

Only an accredited certification body may certify the organization as ISO 27001 compliant. The URL http://www.iso27001certificates.com/ contains a list of accredited certification bodies. The applicable National Accreditation Board certifies the certifier to become an accredited certification body. The organization may not certify itself as ISO 27001 compliant; such an audit must be by a third party. Likewise, if a third party plays a role in establishing the ISMS and that third party is also an accredited certification body, that third party may not audit its own work and a different third-party accredited certification body is necessary to perform the certification audit.

The objective of the certification audit is to confirm that the organization has implemented the ISMS, the appropriate procedures exist to operate, monitor, review, and revise the ISMS, the appropriate documentation exists regarding the ISMS, and organizational practices adhere to the ISMS documentation.

5.4 Certification Preparation Checklist

The certification preparation checklist provides a comprehensive list of materials and activities necessary to prepare the organization for an audit; Table 5.1 provides such a checklist. An internal audit verifies the existence of each document as well as the quality of each document compared to the ISO 27001 and ISO 27002 standards. Moreover, it examines organizational practices in light of the documentation. Again, perfection is not necessarily the goal; the goal is a good solid foundation for information security management that includes security policy, standards, procedures, and practice.

Table 5.1 Certification Preparation Checklist

Documentation	Description
Scope	Documentation describing the boundaries of the ISMS.
Information and information assets with classification	Documentation listing important information and information technology assets within scope; include classification of assets specifying importance to the organization.
ISMS policy	Document specifying the organizational policy with respect to the creation and maintenance of an ISMS.
Information security policy	Document that describes the organization's ISMS in layman vocabulary. In some cases, the ISMS policy is part of this document.
Risk assessment	Document describing the risk assessment processes as well as standards, tools, and templates to support the risk assessment activity.
Selection of controls (SoC) from ISO 27001	Document with a list of relevant controls from ISO 27001.
Risk treatment plan	Document with the plan to address organizational risks. The risk treatment plan will evolve from the original document from the plan phase.
Statement of applicability (SoA)	The SoA is a document that includes a list of all ISO 27001 controls and statements for each control on how the organization will address that control in the context of managing business risk.
Information Security Handbook	The Information Security Handbook includes all security controls and procedures for the organization.
Business continuity management	A document to manage the continuity and recovery of the organization in a disaster that includes a business continuity plan (BCP) and disaster recovery plan (DRP).
Training documents and plan	Documents describing the information security awareness, training, and education (SETA) for employees and a plan when each takes place, e.g., new-hire orientation.
Description of ISMS operation	Document that describes the operation and function of the ISMS, including ISMS document locations.
Incident management document	Document describing incident management process.

Table 5.1 Certification Preparation Checklist (Continued)

Documentation	Description
Metrics and measurements	Document describing the creation of metrics and how the organization uses them to measure the effectiveness of the ISMS operations. The metrics and measures show business value as well as provide operational feedback to cross-function forum as well as management.
Residual risk update	Only the rare organization has no residual risk. The organization must review and update knowledge of and treatment of all accepted risk (residual risk). There should be a document that describes this process, a process that works in harmony with the risk treatment plan and the SoA.
Audit checklist	Document describing internal audits. The audit checklist is not mandatory for an external audit; however, the external auditor will look for details on how the organization performs an internal audit.
Results from the internal audit	This document is part of that to operate the ISMS. It is often a basis for input in the risk treatment plan to improve the ISMS operation.
ISMS operation improvement plan	Document describing ISMS improvements as a result of internal audit.

The guidelines, tools, and templates herein use specific versions of the ISO security standards, ISO 27001:2005 and ISO 27002. If the audit is to occur against latter versions, adjust the checklist as well as the preparation activities and materials accordingly. Selecting the certifier and preparing material to support the audit and certification process are part of preaudit activities.

5.5 The Audit Stage Process

Table 5.2 presents the four audit stages and a short description of each. These audit stages vary among the different certifiers; however, they all have the same objective and compare organizational preparedness with the same ISO security standard.

Pre-site visit activity includes stage 1 and stage 2 activities. Site visit activities include stage 3 activities, and stage 4 is in post-site visit activities.

5.5.1 Stage 1: Engaging the Certifier and Audit Kickoff

Upon the organization engaging a certifier, the auditor assigned will request documentation regarding the ISMS. This includes all documentation about the ISMS,

Table 5.2   Audit Process

Audit Stage	Description
1	Engaging the certifier and kicking off the audit process; handing over the documentation for review.
2	Verifying the existence of the appropriate documentation and the quality of the attributes of the documentation. If the auditor finds the documentation sufficient, he or she will agree to conduct an on-site assessment.
3	Performing the on-site visit and validating the claims of the ISMS documentation. After the on-site assessment, the lead auditor will have a meeting to convey the findings.
4	The auditor analyzes results and produces a findings report for delivery to the organization.

Table 5.3   Audit Report after Stage 1

Audit Report	Description
Document review	Report on the review of the documents. Are the documents complete? Is the organization taking the correct measures to document and work with its ISMS? (Are they on the right track?)

risk management, SoA, SoC, implementation plans, management plans, procedures, etc. Remember to convey these documents in a secure manner to the auditor with an appropriate nondisclosure agreement (NDA). (See Table 5.3.) **Note:** A secure manner does not include via plain-text attachments to an e-mail traversing the public network (Internet).

5.5.2   Stage 2: Document Review

The auditor will review the documentation for adherence to ISO 27001 and ISO 27002. The auditor will look for traceable links among ISO 27001, ISO 27002, policy, standards, procedures, and operational practice. He or she is looking for application of the Plan-Do-Check-Act (PDCA) model in the creation and management of the ISMS, and generally a presence of all relevant ISO 27001 features. Because the auditor will map the ISMS to the ISO standards, preparing documents that align with the ISO standards will expedite the process. The security management framework (SMF) and SMF-based templates herein provide such an alignment with the intent to accelerate both the development of the ISMS and the certification process. The auditor will determine if the organization is ready for an on-site audit. If not, the audit process will end with recommendations on improving preparedness.

If the auditor finds the documentation ample, he or she will agree to conduct an on-site assessment. The on-site assessment is looking to validate the existence of the ISMS as described in the documentation. Written policy and procedures are a start; however, the *proof is in the practice,* so to speak. **Caveat:** Practice without supporting policy and procedure is not adequate to achieve certification. Good practices are common; however, capturing those good practices in documentation is not. The good practices are then as good as the people who practice them, and when these people leave the organization, so often does the good practice. Organizational learning and organizational preparedness require adequate documentation to guide all personnel in appropriate action.

Stage 2 is part of the pre-site visit activities. If the audit proceeds to an on-site visit, the auditor should generate a site visit agenda, schedule various interviews and validation activities prior to being on site, and arrange for site contacts that will assist in arranging for the auditor to enter the site and areas relevant to the audit. The on-site contact may also assist in arranging interviews and certifier access to the relevant information and information technology to validate the ISMS security controls. If the auditor is not forthcoming with these materials and this level of planning, suggest that he or she does so to optimize the investment in the audit process.

5.5.3   Stage 3: On-Site Audit

Stage 3 is the on-site visit. The on-site audit occurs after the certifier determines the documentation is in keeping with the ISO security standards. The purpose of the on-site visit is to assess that personnel security awareness and security practices are in keeping with the documentation, that is, to determine the organization actually does what it says it does. This process includes interviews as well as verification and validation of security controls. Verification is ensuring the presence of security services and security mechanisms. Security services may include an incident response center, a help desk, a disaster recovery site, etc. Security mechanisms may include firewalls, intrusion detection systems, anti-malware, etc. However, the presence of these services and mechanisms is one task; determining their quality is another.

Validation determines the quality of the security services and mechanisms, where the quality is gauged against what the organization claims they do. The initial document review determines if policy, standards, and procedures adhere to the ISO standards. Part of the on-site audit determines if practice adheres to these documents. Validation of controls may include the certifier shoulder surfing, or the auditor may perform hands-on validation. For shoulder-surfing validation, the auditor works with the user, administrator, engineer, or other personnel, where those personnel perform activities to show organizational practice is in keeping with policy, standards, and procedures. In other cases, the certifier may request access to perform activities itself. Validation activities will include system log-on (use of unique user IDs and passwords), application log-on, operating system hardening, secure communications (e.g., virtual private network [VPN]), physical security (e.g., cipher locks), and more.

For example, personal experience includes showing up to an interview with the manager, physical security having entered the facility through the loading dock, waving to the security cameras, and entering a backdoor on the other side of the loading dock. Then, walking up several flights of stairs, entering each floor along the way, opening data closet doors, and talking to a few users in offices along the way asking for directions (no one offered an escort or challenged our presence). This is a good example of hands-on validation of physical security. The personnel, including the security manager, were all nice people, professional, security aware, and under the impression their safeguards were adequate. Personnel badges contained pictures and radio frequency identification (RFID) capability to log entry/exit. The assumption was that all personnel would use the official entrance, hardly the preferred path of those with less than virtuous intents.

The breadth and depth of hands-on validation is the critical path in the duration of the on-site visit. Many activities may depend on initial findings. One method is to make a judgment call on personal credibility during the interviews. A high level of awareness, knowledge of security in general, and knowledge of organizational security objectives and practices result in a high level of confidence on the part of the certifier that the organization gets it and is doing the right things. Some on-site activity is standard and will take place as a matter of course, e.g., checking for password and cipher lock (or equivalent) safeguards on the data center. Other activities will be organization specific; e.g., an organization processing credit card information should take steps to protect customer privacy and identity. The audit will still be ISO 27001 focused; however, the ISO security standards support the need to bolster up security in areas of particular concern to that organization. The validation activities will also vary depending on the initial findings; that is, exploring weaknesses to find the break point and maybe pushing a bit further to determine the implications of the break point.

Audits may be intrusive or nonintrusive. Typically, they are the latter, but verify to ensure everyone involved has the same expectations and understanding. An intrusive audit or assessment may include an intent to break into systems by compromising user IDs and passwords. A passive audit or assessment may just discover the user IDs and passwords, but not attempt to use them in a subversive manner. Likewise, an intrusive audit or assessment may attempt denial of service. Although it is good to know where the break points are, this is not good if such activities actually interrupt production operations.

Table 5.4 shows a list of potential reports resulting from stage 3. The reports include the audit findings in a format that states the compliance requirement, the current state of the organization, a gap analysis, a remediation analysis (options for fixing weaknesses), and recommendations for gap closure. The certifier may use the term *nonconformity*. A nonconformity is a condition contrary to the requirements of the ISO 27001[1] standard. The auditor may further categorize findings in three nonconformity classifications: *major*, *minor*, and *observation*. A major nonconformity

Table 5.4 Audit Reports after Stage 3

Audit Reports	Description
Document review	Report enumerating documents that are part of the audit and the status of each document
Summary report	Report of the inspection carried out by the auditor
Audit findings	Report on what the auditor found that is not compliant with the standard and has to be fixed and in place for the next inspection in six months
Recommendation	Report whether the auditor will recommend that the organization should apply for the certification

may be a total breakdown of a system, control, or objective. This may be the complete absence of a particular requirement or the absence of formal documentation or an existing practice. Clauses 4 to 8 are mandatory sections of ISO 27001 to achieve certification; an absence of any of these requirements will likely be a major nonconformity. A major nonconformity will likely result in noncertification against the ISO 27001 standard, and the organization will have to wait for six months to request another audit.

A minor nonconformity results if part of a policy is missing or is sufficiently vague to cause confusion. In this case, the policy (or other document) exists, but the quality of the policy does not meet with the intent of the ISO standards. A minor nonconformity may result as well if the documentation is complete but the practice is incomplete. Similarly, personnel do perform the activities related to the safeguard; however, they do not perform all the activities that constitute conformity with the ISO standards. There may be a grace period shorter than six months to fix minor nonconformities.

The observation nonconformity results if the certifier finds appropriate documentation and practice but sees an opportunity for improvement that will increase the effectiveness of the control or otherwise benefit the organization's security posture. The organization provides a written response to addressing all observations. Similar to the SoA, *addressing* the risk means the organization may rationalize the observed nonconformity through a statement of risk acceptance, or it may state a plan to modify documentation or practice to remediate the risk.

5.5.4 Stage 4: Delivery of Findings

Stage 4 is the formal delivery of the results from the certifier to the organization. Stage 4 is the presentation of findings, gaps (nonconformities), options, and recommendations by the certifier for organization actions. The report(s) will align with specific elements within ISO 27001 and ISO 27002. The certifier provides a classification for each gap (major, minor, observation). The organization provides a written response to each gap, addressing the nonconformities according to its position of accepting the risk or plans to mitigate the risk. The results of stage 4 are either pass (receive certification) or fail. The organization must wait six months to reattempt certification and perform corrective action during that time according to recommendations by the certifier.

If the organization receives ISO 27001 certification, it is valid for three years, after which there is a renewal process. To prepare for and ease the renewal process, the organization and the certifier may agree upon a three-year surveillance plan for the ISMS. The plan will include a series of reviews and visits by the certifier and which sections or clauses of the ISO standards to focus on for each review and visit. The specific plans may vary slightly according to new details in ISO standard updates or a changing business environment (new legislation, regulation, market demands for increase in or otherwise modified security posture). Each visit is a mini-certification audit resulting in a findings report that includes requirements, gaps, options, and recommendations. This ongoing monitoring of the ISMS is good practice and eases the certification renewal process.

Chapter 6

Compliance Management

The purpose of this book is to assist the reader in establishing an effective information security management system (ISMS) and achieving ISO 27001 certification. The process to establish an ISMS is one instance of an overall *compliance management process*, where the compliance requirements in context of achieving ISO 27001 certification are ISO 27001 and ISO 27002. It is possible to abstract the ISO 27001 certification process described thus far into a general compliance management process accommodating many compliance requirements. Other compliance requirements may be Sarbanes–Oxley, Health Insurance Portability and Accountability Act (HIPAA), or legislation applicable to civilian government (e.g., Federal Information Security Management Act [FISMA]). This chapter presents material regarding an abstract approach to compliance management applicable to all these and more.

Additionally, there is the potential to cross-index compliance requirement elements such that showing compliance for a requirement in one standard implies compliance with another or many others. Therefore, achieving ISO 27001 certification implies at least partial compliance with other security-related legislation, regulation, and standards. Building a security management framework (SMF) with foundation in all organizationally relevant security compliance requirements provides the ability to develop a single methodology and single tool set for discovery, analysis, and reporting that establishes, tracks, and proves compliance with all applicable security requirements.

6.1 Objectives

The following list summarizes the objectives for this chapter:

- Distinguish the difference between a comprehensive compliance management program (CMP) and an information assurance (IA) CMP.
- Present details of an IA CMP.
- Present an IA CMP methodology.
- Enumerate a set of processes, tools, and templates to support an IA CMP.
- Discuss the application of the processes, tools, and templates to plan, establish, implement, maintain, review, and revise (sound familiar?) the IA CMP.

6.2 Introduction to Compliance Management

Compliance management is both very broad and specific to the nature of the organization. For example, a healthcare organization may need to comply with legislation governing hazardous waste disposal. Such compliance is absolutely critical to employee and public safety. Such compliance activity is part of a comprehensive CMP. Compliance management with respect to information and information technology is but one part of this comprehensive CMP. The focus herein is on compliance management with respect to information security; that is, the security of information technology, business functions, personnel, infrastructure, and physical aspects that contributes to information security— also known as *information assurance*. That is, the focus is on an *information assurance compliance management program*. With respect to creating an IA CMP, the following are necessary:

- IA CMP framework
- Process to identify all relevant compliance requirements
- Template(s) to enumerate all relevant compliance requirements
- Creation of requirement traceability matrices
- Cross-index to leverage compliance activities across all applicable requirements, and to avoid redundancy, thus minimizing costs

6.3 IA CMP

As previously mentioned, the map of the territory is not the territory. This text is a map of the ISO standards, a map of how to use them in practical application. This text is not a replacement for the ISO standards. To acquire the ISO standards, go to www.iso.org or use an Internet search engine to find an alternative source. The authors intend the material herein as a supplement to the actual standards applicable to the organization, not a substitute. An IA CMP consists of the following useful tools, some of which use ISO 27002 as a foundation:

- Compliance management framework
- Security management framework
- Compliance management requirements engineering
- Compliance assessment methodology
- Compliance management tools
- Compliance metrics

6.3.1 Compliance Management Framework

A CMP enumerates all organizational compliance requirements. An effective CMP starts with a compliance management framework. A compliance management framework provides guidance on how to define all organizational-specific compliance requirements; an IA compliance management framework provides focus on security-related compliance requirements. A compliance management *framework* assists to identify and enumerate all relevant compliance requirements.

Note: There is a hesitation to say *all* compliance requirements or *comprehensive list*, as there is a question of necessity to identify, enumerate, and act upon literally all compliance requirements within the formality of the compliance framework. Under the principle of *best–good–good enough*, there is a practical limit to this exercise. To this end, consider that the framework provides the ability to provide adequate identification, enumeration, and planning for compliance requirements that have a direct effect on operations and organizational viability. Point is, the same framework provides the ability to record requirement details to any breadth or depth necessary. Figure 6.1 provides an overview of the compliance management requirements framework.

External compliance requirements reside outside the organization and are most often legislative or regulatory restrictions or guidance imposed on organizational practices. Internal compliance requirements include mission statement, organizational goals, corporate policy, contractual obligations, and enumeration of stakeholder interests.

Explicit compliance requirements are enumerated in a Request for Proposal (RFP) or in a contract. Implicit compliance requirements are derived from explicit requirements or implied by compliance with explicit requirements. For example, a U.S. federal civilian RFP may require compliance with the Federal Information Security Management Act of 2002. The implied requirements in FISMA include the National Institute of Technology (NIST) standards and guidelines, as well as the Office of Management and Budget (OMB) audit standards, as OMB audits gauge the compliance levels of federal organizations against FISMA. A low FISMA compliance level may jeopardize funding; therefore, enumerating the OMB audit

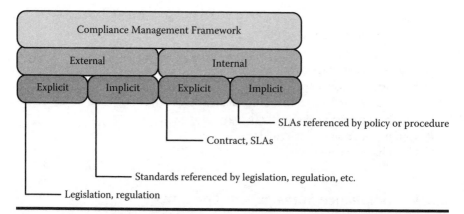

Figure 6.1 Compliance management requirements framework.

guides as an external-implicit compliance requirement is appropriate to mitigate risk of reduced funding.

External-explicit requirements include self-imposed standards of compliance, e.g., ISO 9000, ISO 27001, ISO 27002. The difference is, no legislation compels an organization to become ISO 27001 certified. The organization chooses ISO 27001 as a self-imposed standard for establishing an ISMS. Internal-explicit requirements include organizational mission statement or internal service level agreements (SLAs) between, say, network operations and various business groups. Internal-implicit requirements include adherence to security practices of another organization via business associate agreement. Implicit requirements may also include documents not explicitly enumerated, but part of the project, e.g., principles, constraints, and assumptions (PCAs) or concept of operations (CONOPS). Although not typically thought of as compliance requirements, PCAs, CONOPS, and similar documents provide direction for organization activity, including security; thus, they may fall under at least consideration for the IA compliance management framework.

The intent behind the framework is to provoke thought in various directions and to decompose a larger problem into manageable chunks with a guideline that assists the organization to consider all relevant compliance requirements. The following provides an expansion of the compliance management framework:

■ External compliance requirements:
  ● Explicit:
    ○ Legislation
    ○ Regulation
    ○ Guidelines
    ○ Directives
    ○ Instructions

- Implicit:
  - ○ Any qualification of a necessary supporting activity to adhere to an explicit requirement
  - ○ Any qualification of a supporting activity to minimize organizational risk:
    - For example, litigation management: for example, *Federal Sentencing Guidelines*, Chapter 8, "Sentencing of Organizations"

- Internal compliance requirements:
  - Explicit:
    - ○ Mission statement
    - ○ Policies:
      - For example, ethics policy
    - ○ Procedures
    - ○ Standards
    - ○ Contracts:
      - Partners, vendors, customers
  - Implicit:
    - ○ Any qualification of a necessary supporting activity to adhere to an explicit requirement

6.3.2 Security Management Framework

Traditionally, security is an afterthought. In the past, most executives and managers yielded to the need for door locks, perhaps a security guard, and the need for fire control systems, at least after they saw a drop in insurance premiums to provide a payback for the investment. Adding appropriate controls to protect cyber assets or the facilities housing cyber assets is traditionally a *"nice to have" if there's enough budget left over*. Due to the exploding popularity of computers and the Internet, the business environment is vastly different from just 10 years ago; *security is no longer a nice to have, but a legislative mandate*. In the United States, the Sarbanes–Oxley Act of 2002 (SOX), Section 404 prescribes security controls for financial systems, and the Health Insurance Portability and Accessibility Act of 1996 Final Security Rule (HIPAA FSR) requires the protection of electronic protected health information (ePHI). Other legislation imposes restrictions on data ownership and data custodianship, including the European Directive on Data Protection or the Safe Harbor framework that permits non-European organizations access to data by certifying adequate privacy protection. Moreover, organizations require proof of return on investment (ROI) on all major budget allocations; providing details for return on security investment (ROSI) is difficult to say the least — difficult, but not impossible. The ability to capture details of security planning that align with the business drivers behind them facilitates the ability to show a ROSI, plus more.

An SMF provides the foundation for defining a security program (policies, standards, and procedures), defining the scope of security assessments, performing security assessments, defining common security terms and concepts for organizational reference, aligning security initiatives with business risk management, and much more. Indeed, a well-thought-out SMF is the foundation for considering, discussing, presenting, planning, executing, and tracking security initiatives at every level of the enterprise. The primary goal of the SMF is to provide consistency across the enterprise and completeness on any particular security initiative by using the framework as a checklist of items to address. *Addressing* may mean actual work to comply with the security requirements. Adequate addressing of the requirement may also mean to acknowledge the existence of such a requirement and provide an explanation as to why the organization feels the requirement does not apply to it or that it is willing to accept the risks. A summary of benefits for an SMF includes the following:

- Definition of a framework that provides a list of terms and definitions to promote common understanding
- Enables consistent results
- Tool for business planning, security planning, and preparation
- Tool for effective discovery:
  - Target questions, surveys, automated discovery tools to the right place
  - Focused discovery that does not present questions to people who do not know the answers
- Basis for analysis tools; assessing a level of compliance requires a basis of comparison — a target of acceptable performance, preparedness — using an industry standard to define that the target removes the notion of arbitrariness from the process
  - Also enables comparison of your organizational results with others using the same standards
- Basis for reporting tools
- Completeness
- Consistency
- Understanding — in context of an interpretation guide
- Conveying feedback to operations
- Tracking mitigation and remediation progress
- Basis of comparison for future assessments to gauge progress (or regress) as well as current standing

In the context of compliance management, an SMF provides a foundation within which to define all security requirements. Chapter 3, "Foundational Concepts and Tools for an Information Security Management System," provides an example of an SMF with foundation in ISO 27002. Security professionals within the organization may expand this framework to accommodate all internal, external, explicit, and implicit security requirements. The organization ends up with a security framework specific to its compliance needs. Using Table 3.1 in Chapter 3 as a basis for an ISMS, create a traceability matrix that links all relevant security elements to their compliance requirements. This table then becomes the traceability matrix linking business drivers (compliance requirements) with security initiatives to satisfy those requirements.

Given a framework within which to consider compliance requirements overall and security requirements specifically, there remains the need for a discipline to determine, record, and track requirements through the solution life cycle phases of development, implementation, operation, and dissolution — in short, a *requirements engineering process*.

6.3.3 Compliance Management Requirements Engineering

Systems engineering* (SE) is a disciplined approach to establishing and deploying systems. A system may be a business system, computer hardware system, software system, or functional system (e.g., lunar rocket). Requirements engineering is a subtopic within the discipline of systems engineering. The description of requirements engineering herein is but an introduction to a much more complex process; however, creating security requirements that are comprehensive in meeting compliance requirements and effectively managing organizational risk requires such a disciplined approach. The first step in requirements engineering is to identify and enumerate the compliance requirements; the aforementioned compliance management framework (Figure 6.1) assists with this. The second step is to identify the requirements in context of the challenge at hand — in this case, security compliance requirements. The SMF is a good starting point for this. The security professional aligns each security element in the SMF with compliance requirement documents, as well as articulates the associated risk and method to address that risk (this is very similar to the statement of applicability [SoA] in the ISMS). Articulating the risk requires a systematic approach to addressing each business driver, each business risk (in terms of threat space, asset space, and business functionality), as well as each security element in terms of confidentiality, integrity, and availability (CIA triad).

Security requirements engineering establishes a set of compliance requirements that identify and integrate business drivers, business operations (business functions), risk management, security compliance requirements, and security initiatives. Security initiatives (i.e., projects, operations, services, and tools) align with the security compliance requirements they satisfy. The security compliance requirements align with the risks they address (e.g., risk mitigation). The risk management requirements align with business operations they provide value to, and ultimately to business

---

* See www.incose.org for more information on systems engineering.

drivers of the organization. Business drivers are in direct support of or directly define the reasons the organization exists at all; e.g., a common business driver in the commercial marketplace is to provide investor or shareholder value.

The security requirements engineering process requires identifying and enumerating the security compliance requirement documents; Table 6.1 presents a template for a compliance requirement matrix; this is a high-level view of compliance requirements. Security professionals with requirements engineering skills or a systems engineer must decompose each compliance requirement document into a set of compliance categories and elements. Table 6.2 through Table 6.4 present a series of requirements traceability matrices and provide a template for these categories and elements, one per row. These high-level compliance requirements may come and go (e.g., new legislation and legislative repeal). Therefore, separating these high-level security requirements from security initiatives will assist to maintain the compliance requirement documentation over time. This separation is possible via the traceability matrices based on the organization-specific SMF.

With respect to requirements engineering, define an organizational-specific SMF with foundation in high-level compliance requirements (e.g., SOX, FISMA, HIPAA, ISO 27002, etc.). Use the SMF to create a traceability matrix that links each SMF element to its corresponding high-level requirement document. Use the SMF to record policies that address each element; by default those policies link to the high-level security requirement. Moreover, use the SMF to capture standards and procedures for passwords; by default, these standards and procedures align with the high-level requirement documents. For example, the use of passwords as an element in the SMF will link to SOX, HIPAA, and ISO 27002. Use the SMF to capture the fact that there is a password policy and its location (www.xxx. intranet/security/policies); likewise, capture the fact there is a password standard and password procedures and their locations. Assume there is a legislative reform that includes new password guidelines (e.g., HIPAA FSR now states the need for 22-character passwords that include at least 2 capital letters, 4 numbers, and 3 special characters). The SMF provides traceability from HIPAA FSR to all associated policies, standards, and procedures. A quick review shows the location of the password standards. The traceability tables also show other legislation supported by the password standard, and, upon review, there are no conflicts; so, modify the standard accordingly with surety the modifications satisfy all relevant requirements.

To continue with the example, consider that new vulnerabilities require a modification to a procedure. A reasonable question is, What legislation is this procedure associated with to ensure no modifications to the procedure conflict with legislative directives? The traceability tables provide upward traceability from procedure to legislation supported by the procedure. The SMF may also support the documenting of security services and to which compliance requirements they align, e.g., the security working group as a security service traces to ISO 27002 and HIPAA FSR. The same for security mechanisms; e.g., the antivirus system traces to the need for secure communications, which in turn finds basis in ISO 27002, SOX, and HIPAA.

Table 6.1 Compliance Requirement Matrix

Requirement Reference[a]	Requirement Title	Source	Reference	Comments
EE.1	HIPAA privacy rule	Legislation	http://www.cms.hhs.gov/HIPAAGenInfo/Downloads/HIPAALaw.pdf	Applicable only to those sections of the organization doing business in the United States and subject to this legislation
EE.2	HIPAA Final Security Rule	Legislation	Http://www.cms.hhs.gov/Hipaageninfo/downloads/Hipaalaw.pdf	Applicable only to those sections of the organization doing business in the United States and subject to this legislation
EE.3	European Directive on Data Protection	Legislation	http://europa.eu.int/eur-lex/pri/en/oj/dat/2002/l_201/l_20120020731en00370047.pdf	Applicable only to those sections of the organization doing business in the European area and subject to this legislation
EI.1	U.S. Federal Sentencing Guidelines (FSG), Chapter 8, "Sentencing of Organizations"	Legislation	http://www.ussc.gov/2006guid/TABCON06.htm	Provides guidelines for determining the culpability of organizations in litigation; culpability directly affects fines and other penalties
IE.1	ISO 27002:2005	International standard	www.iso.org	Provides guidance for security controls
IE.2	ISO 27001:2005	International standard	www.iso.org	Provides guidance to develop an ISMS
IE.3	Policy X	Organization policy	www.intranet.xxx	Organizational policy for TBD
Etc.				

[a] *EE = external-explicit; EI = external-implicit; IE = internal-explicit; II = internal-implicit.*

Table 6.2 Requirements Traceability Matrix — Example 1: *Federal Sentencing Guidelines* **(FSG) Excerpt**

FSG Reference Number	Page	Reference	Guideline Verbiage	Interpretation/ Comments
1	476	§8B2.1	Effective compliance and ethics program.	Define compliance program and ethics program (FSG ref. 7). Articulate what it takes for these programs to be effective. Implement effective compliance and ethics program.
2	476	§8B2.1 (a)(1)	Exercise due diligence to prevent and detect criminal conduct.	Implement a risk management program that includes compliance management.
3	476	§8B2.1 (a)(2)	Otherwise, promote an organizational culture that encourages ethical conduct and a commitment to compliance with the law. Such compliance and ethics program shall be reasonably designed, implemented, and enforced so that the program is generally effective in preventing and detecting criminal conduct. The failure to prevent or detect the instant offense does not necessarily mean that the program is not generally effective in preventing and detecting criminal conduct.	Reflect organizational desire for ethical behavior and commitment to complying with relevant legislation in policy, new-employee orientation, and an ongoing ethical awareness program. Implement metrics to track awareness, understanding, and compliance with ethical guidelines and legal requirements.
Etc.				

Table 6.3   PSP Traceability Matrix — Example: Template Outline

Reference Number	Policy, Standard, Procedure	Requirement Description	Degree	Trace to	V&V
PO.AA.001	Policy	Policy for ethics program	Must	FSG.1	TBD
ST.AA.001	Standard	Standard for ethics program	Must	FSG.2	TBD
PR.AA.001	Procedure	Procedure for ethics program	Must	FSG.3	TBD
Etc.					

Table 6.4   Requirements Traceability Matrix — Example 2: Template Outline

Requirement Source	<Project> Requirement ID	Requirement Description	Degree	Trace to	V&V
XYZ RFP	1		Must	< Requirement ID>	
	2		Shall		
	3		May		
	n				

Figure 6.2 provides an overview of the traceability matrices, starting with business drivers and focusing on security as one business aspect within the organization. A business driver of legislative compliance motivates the selection of security compliance requirement documents. The selection of compliance requirements drives the structure of the SMF. Identification and enumeration of business risks in context of the SMF flow from security compliance requirements. Policies align with the business risks they address. Security services align with the policies that drive their creation. Security mechanisms align with the services they support. The level of detail can be large, and there is a bit of effort to create and maintain the documentation. However, the benefits can be very worthwhile in ability, accuracy, confidence, and speed in making security decisions with foundation in business need and the ability to prove the business value of security. The following material provides an example using actual table templates and entries.

The organization may be subject to a very large array of compliance requirements that include municipal codes, county or city codes, state or regional codes, local legislation, national legislation, and even international law. All relevant compliance requirements should comprise the total compliance management program. The focus herein is on the security aspects of compliance management. The organization must

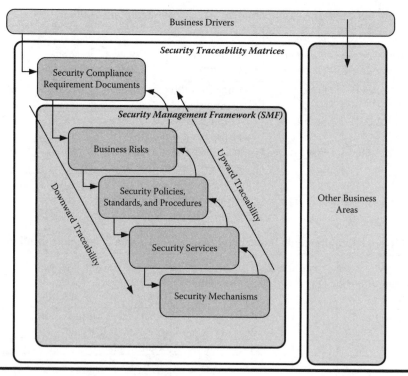

Figure 6.2   Compliance traceability matrices: overview.

decompose each requirement document into a list of requirement elements, align each element with a business driver (upward traceability), and align each requirement with a security initiative (downward traceability). **Caveat**: Select one method of traceability, either downward or upward. Maintaining one direction of traceability usually works fine, especially if using a software package to manage requirements.

Table 6.1 provides a compliance requirement matrix; this is where to record the security compliance requirement document names and details regarding their applicability. This table, like the remainder of the tables showing traceability, is notional and will vary according to the needs of the organization. Table 6.2 selects the FSG as an example of decomposing a compliance requirement into categories and elements. Table 6.3 shows an example of a policy, standard, procedure (PSP) matrix that aligns with the FSG matrix in Table 6.2.

Note: Requirements references do not have to distinguish external-explicit etc. Using a requirements identification that is just a number still provides the ability to trace from one set of requirements to another, which is the point. The examples here provide a variety of nomenclatures to present various options on how to label requirements and create traceability.

Table 6.4 shows a generic example of a traceability table that references an RFP.

Identifying requirement types assists in determining the motivation behind the requirement. Some useful abbreviations to identify requirement types are:

- External-explicit (EE)
- External-implicit (EI)
- Internal-explicit (IE)
- Internal-implicit (II)

There are many kinds of requirement sources. The source may offer insight into how to characterize the degree; i.e., a legislative mandate will likely be a must-do requirement, as are contractual requirements. Some requirement sources are:

- Legislation
- Regulation
- Instruction (e.g., Department of Defense Instruction)
- Directive (e.g., Presidential Directive)
- RFP (Request for Proposal)
- CONOPS (concept of operations)
- Contract
- SOW (statement of work)

The requirement *degree* denotes the degree of flexibility in acting upon that requirement, that is, flexibility in actually implementing the requirement. Some requirements are a must-do; these are nonnegotiable imperatives that find foundation in legislative mandates, contracts, or statements of work. A degree of *shall* denotes a negotiable point. A degree of *may* denotes no obligation, but a good idea if possible within existing budget and schedule constraints. Some requirements with a degree of *may* may actually be accomplished as an inherent part of implementing another requirement. Tracking these enables the security department to show value-add to the initiative officially approved.

The *trace to* column provides a link to the driving requirement. Many instances of requirement tables trace in both directions. This is a very high maintenance and often confusing manner to record requirements traceability. Establishing a principle of *always trace upward* simplifies the process; trace upward is a personal preference. The question may arise as to what security initiative requirements track to legislative X compliance. A trace-down scheme enables the ability to look at legislation X in the requirements tables and follow the links downward. A trace-up scheme enables the ability to look at the various security initiatives and follow the links upward to legislation X. There are benefits to both, and there are arguments to performing traceability either way. If the organization prefers a trace-down scheme, then fine. Choose one over the other; however, do not choose both.

Verification and validation (V&V) describes the manner to test the requirement is met. Verification establishes that the service, mechanism, process, standard, etc.

are actually in place. Validation establishes that the service, mechanism, process, standard, etc. actually work as intended. V&V options include audit, review, inspection, test, simulation, or any number of situational-dependent methods.

6.3.3.1 Requirements Traceability Example

Table 6.5 enumerates various business drivers; for example, a business plan document that specifies a strategic advantage in achieving ISO 27001 certification. Table 6.6 enumerates the compliance requirement documents in support of this strategic initiative. The *trace to* column links these documents to the business driver. One method of linking requirements is to use a table abbreviation as a prefix followed by the number of the requirement in that table. Table 6.7 shows the bare beginning of the SMF as part of a requirements traceability matrix. The SMF defines the organization-specific outline of security; remember the SMF from Chapter 3 and the interpretation guide. The SMF herein finds foundation in ISO 27002; therefore, each category and element are traceable to the IE.2 requirement in Table 6.6. Use of IE.2 is another potential way to assign requirements identifications.

The mix and match of requirement identifications here show that a variety of methods work. Select what works for your organization with the key factor being consistency. Subsequent traceability tables drill down into security initiatives and the specifics of the services and mechanisms. Benefits to following a requirements engineering discipline include consistency, comprehensiveness, ability to justify each security initiative (initial costs) in terms of business drivers, and ability to justify ongoing operations (run and maintain costs) in terms of business drivers. A huge advantage is the ability to review the latest, greatest security wonder-widget and be able to determine if it fits within a strategic initiative. Too many times, organizations implement technology for technology's sake or security for security's sake. Formal alignment and traceability assist to justify security investments in business terms.

6.3.4 Security Compliance Assessment Methodology

Identifying compliance requirements and creating compliance matrices for enumerating requirements and providing for requirements traceability are the first steps in the compliance management methodology. Implementing the security initiatives establishes a baseline for security operations. All these activities contribute to security compliance management. The next step is to ensure ongoing compliance. To accomplish this, the organization needs a *compliance assessment methodology*. A comprehensive compliance assessment methodology consists of:

■ Project management
■ Pre-engagement
■ Engagement

Table 6.5 Requirements Traceability Matrix: Business Drivers (BD)

Requirement Source	*<Project> Requirement ID*	Requirement Description	Degree	Trace to	V&V
Company X business plan	BD1	Achieve ISO 27001 certification to add competitive differentiation to our e-commerce hosting services	Must	<Requirement ID> — perhaps to strategic initiative to gain 5% market share	Receipt of ISO 27001 certification by accredited certifying body
Etc.					

Table 6.6 Compliance Requirement Document Matrix (CRDM)

Requirement Reference[a]	Requirement Title	Source	Reference	Comments	Trace to
IE.1	ISO 27001	Industry standard	www.iso.org	Applicable only to those sections of the organization doing business in the United States and subject to this legislation	BD1
IE.2	ISO 27002	Industry standard	www.iso.org	Applicable only to those sections of the organization doing business in the United States and subject to this legislation	BD1
Etc.					

[a] EE = external-explicit; EI = external-implicit; IE = internal-explicit; II = internal-implicit.

■ Post-engagement
■ Pre-site visit
■ Site visit
■ Post-site visit
■ Delivery and sign-off

This list is from the perspective of an external assessor providing assessment services to an organization. For a self-assessment, the organization can draw upon a subset of the above activities depending on the assessment goal. An internal assessment is good practice prior to engaging an external firm to perform an assessment (more high level) or audit (very granular). An internal assessment provides the ability to identify compliance gaps prior to an external party discovering them. Some legislation requires the assessor or auditor to notify authorities in the event of security violations or upon the finding of inadequate security controls, e.g., SOX. The authors recommend preparing management and executives with a preview of what the external assessors may find; moreover, an internal assessment provides the opportunity to address any particularly egregious violations prior to engaging an external assessor. The following sections expand on compliance assessment.

Table 6.7 Requirements Traceability Matrix Using SMF

Requirement Source	<Project> Requirement ID	Requirement Description	Degree	Trace to	V&V
Internal business driver	1	Establish ISMS	Must	IE.1	ISMS documentation
Etc.					
	2	Information security policy	Must	IE.2	Security policy document
	3	Information security policy document	Must	IE.2	Security policy document
		Review of information security policy	Must	IE.2	Security policy review procedure
Etc.					

6.3.4.1 Project Management

Project management is a metaview of the compliance management process or compliance assessment process. These are the details to plan activity, track progress, and identify deliverables and milestones, as well as earned value. These details include:

- Work breakdown structure (WBS)
- Project plan
- Phase definitions
- Deliverable definitions
- Resource management:
  - Labor
  - Capital
- Earned value

A WBS provides the row entries in a project plan. Table 6.8 presents a notional WBS for development of the ISMS and an ISO 27001 assessment. Most organizations will have very similar work breakdown structures; however,

Table 6.8   ISO 27001 Notional WBS

Task ID	Task	Duration (Days)	Responsibility
	Phase 1: Define ISMS		
	Identify organizational security requirements		
	Define security requirements		
	Define security governance policy		
	Define security policies		
	Security governance policy	0	
	Applicable security policies	0	
	Compliance requirements document	0	
	Define ISMS (to-be) complete	0	
	Phase 2: Risk Assessment		
	Business impact analysis (BIA)		
	ID business functions		
	ID personnel		
	ID supporting infrastructure		
	Vulnerability assessment		
	Threat assessment		
	Risk assessment	0	
	Risk assessment complete	0	
	Phase 3: Develop ISMS		
	Discover current security posture (as-is)		
	Gap analysis (as-is versus to-be)		
	Develop transition plan (as-is (to-be)		
	Develop SoA		
	ISMS development plan document	0	
	Develop ISMS complete	0	
	Phase 4: Deploy ISMS		
	Develop deployment plan		
	Awareness campaign		
	Rollout		
	Track status		
	ISMS deployment plan document	0	
	Deploy ISMS complete		
	Phase 5: Precertification Preparation		
	Internal audit		
	Internal audit findings report	0	
	Analysis		
	Internal audit findings and action report	0	
	Corrective actions		
	Precertification preparation complete	0	

Table 6.8 ISO 27001 Notional WBS

Task ID	Task	Duration (Days)	Responsibility
Phase 6: Audit by Certifying Agency			
	Pre-site visit		
	Stage 1		
	Stage 2		
	Site visit		
	Stage 3		
	Post-site visit		
	Stage 4		
	Audit by certifying agency complete	0	

each organization will vary depending on the complexity of security requirements, internal expertise on information security, current security posture, and available budget to manage business risk. Likewise, the timeline to achieve ISO 27001 certification will vary tremendously according to the size of the organization, scope of applicability, current security posture, in-house expertise, etc.

The WBS provides the rows (tasks) in the overall project plan. Project plan details include much more than shown in Table 6.8, like predecessors, resources per line item, calendar information, and Gantt charts showing dependencies, critical path, and more. The duration times of zero denote milestones or deliverables. Phase definitions are part of the project plan. The six phases in Table 6.8 may vary, but will be close to the actual phases to develop an ISMS and audit it for ISO 27001 certification.

Earned value (EV) is a method to track progress toward completion against budget expenses to date. EV can be very complex and is better for larger, more complex projects. In any respect, the wise project manager projects weekly and monthly burn rates (budget spent) and tracks actual burn rate against projected. Additionally, the project manager tracks completion of deliverables and achievement of milestones. If the burn rate is higher than expected, so should be the completion rate of deliverables and milestones.

6.3.4.2 Pre-Engagement

A compliance management activity, say a *compliance assessment*, requires a meeting of the minds among the activity performer, the assessor, and the activity sponsor. The activity performer may be an accredited certifying body performing an audit for ISO 27001 certification. The performer may also be an internal security professional performing a compliance assessment to discern the organization's compliance posture against that requirement. To achieve this meeting of the minds requires planning, formal documentation, and formal sign-off on scope, tasks, costs, etc. All this activity occurs prior to the sponsor engaging the performer. Pre-engagement activities and documents include the following:

- Proposal material
- Cost models
- Project definition
- Project success criteria

Generating proposal material assumes the presence of a proposal process that discerns the customer (sponsor) objectives and provides a summary of activity to meet those objectives, that is, *a proposal*. The proposal includes activities to perform, the scope of where to perform them, the cost for those activities, and a list of deliverables and milestones. Formal sign-off with regard to scope, deliverables, and cost occurs prior to the engagement. Formalizing all details in documents and requiring sign-off ensure the management of expectations as well as provide a baseline from which to identify scope creep. Activities outside the current scope may be wonderful ideas and even critical to the security of the organization; however, the primary goal is to determine, agree upon, and satisfy success criteria that focus on the current project scope. No one remembers all the good things if the primary goals are not met. Appendix F contains a project definition template that follows an outline of:

- Statement of project intent
- Change history log
- Table of contents
- Objectives
- Scope
- Assumptions
- Project team
- Project plan outline
- Risks
- Project milestones

The intent of the project definition is to capture project objectives; convey the objectives in terms of scope, roles and responsibilities, deliverables, milestones, and overview of a project plan; and define the success factors of the project.

6.3.4.3 Engagement

Following proposal sign-off, essentially a contract, the engagement begins. Engagement activity includes the following; some items should look familiar from Chapter 5, "Audit and Certification":

- Pre-site visit:
  - Participants
  - Agenda

- Schedule
- Site visit
- Post-site visit:
  - Analysis
  - Follow-up
  - Site report generation
- Enterprise:
  - Aggregate site analysis (a.k.a. enterprise analysis)
  - Enterprise reporting
- Delivery:
  - Presentation of initial findings
  - Review and revision
  - Delivery of final findings
  - Sign-off

Pre-site visit prepares for the site visit. Preparation is important to ensure that the site visit is productive given that there is cost involved in travel and labor to perform on-site activities. The pre-site visit activity identifies participants in the compliance assessment and provides an agenda to participants that describes pending activity, as well as a schedule. Pre-site visit activity may also include surveys, questionnaires, phone interviews, and other activity to save time and material costs of an extended site visit. The specifics vary according to the objectives.

The site visit follows the agenda and includes interviews, data collection, document collection, and other tangible evidence supporting the assessment objectives. If verification and validation are necessary, the assessor may shoulder surf on-site personnel, showing the presence and effectiveness of various security measures. The assessor may require hands-on validation, which means direct access to in-scope information technology and physical security.

Post-site visit activities analyze the results of the site visit and may involve follow-up phone calls and e-mails. Ultimately, the assessor generates a report or series of reports reflecting the compliance requirements, the assessment findings, the gaps between the requirements and the findings, options for gap closure, and recommendations for gap closure. These reports are the basis for conclusions (e.g., granting ISO 27001 certification) and activities to maintain an acceptable level of compliance, or activities to attain an acceptable level of compliance.

At times, the assessment process may include multiple sites. Generating individual site reports may be necessary. Generating an enterprise analysis, or an aggregate analysis, is another task. To manage expectations, the project definition or proposal should reflect the reporting levels in the deliverables section. Whether formal reports are necessary at the site level or not, the assessor will benefit from analyzing individual site findings in and of themselves, comparing the site results to each other, and then aggregating the results into an enterprise report. The benefits to this effort are to identify those sites with exemplary practices and those that need assistance in increasing compliance levels. Those with exemplary practices offer the enterprise the opportunity to leverage intraorganizational best practices at other sites; this is a cost savings by not reinventing the wheel. Moreover, the enterprise analysis will likely identify opportunities to leverage central efforts across many, if not all, sites. The principle here is intelligent allocation of resources. If there is a limited security budget, and there always is, spending it wisely with intent and objectives is preferable to individual site efforts. Leveraging central initiatives is more cost effective than redundant efforts across many individual sites.

The actual delivery of the results is an important step. The delivery may be once at the end of the engagement. If the engagement is longer (months versus weeks), and across multiple sites, specify milestones to deliver results consistently along the way. This prepares the customer for the final deliverable as well as presents the opportunity for individual sites to remediate some aspects prior to the final delivery. This latter provision carries many names, like saving face, gaining political capital, or just blatant CYA.* The point is that the site contacts have the opportunity to prepare for their participation in follow-up activities.

6.3.4.4 Post-Engagement

Post-engagement activity includes:

- Capturing lessons learned
- Modifying the process

Every engagement offers lessons learned. These lessons are for project planning and execution, and may be in the compliance assessment process, the process of constructing reports, the material in the reports, customer relations, delivery of results, pricing model adjustments, and other areas. Capturing these lessons learned and modifying the compliance assessment process accordingly ensure continual improvement and competitiveness. Even an internal service competes with an external alternative.

6.3.5 Compliance Management Tools

Compliance management methodology uses a set of tools to facilitate activity. These tools may be organizational specific, but all can find basis in the ISO security standards or other industry security standards. Categories of compliance management tools are:

- Team management
- Project management
- Pre-engagement

---

* Cover your assets.

- Engagement
- Post-engagement
- Pre-site visit
- Site visit
- Post-site visit
- Delivery and sign-off

Capture lessons learned from each engagement, then review and revise the tool set with respect to the lessons learned. Security and every other business process benefit from continual improvement; even if claims of perfection abound, continual verification of that perfection through systematic review is good business practice. For the sake of compliance management and compliance assessment, the term *tools* refers to documents in the form of methodologies, templates, and analysis. The following section elaborates on the list above.

6.3.5.1 Team Management

The *team* is the security team, or specifically the assessment team. Team management tools consist of roles and responsibilities. Leave no doubt of accountability for actions and expectations on the part of the sponsor and team members by clearly enumerating each task and who is responsible for each. Training material to prepare the team at the beginning of the engagement and to train new team members joining mid-engagement includes interpretation guides, templates for all team activities, contact information for each team member, procedures, assumptions, schedule, budget, and scope documents. Communications between the team and customer should be consistent in look and feel as well as content. Provide standard agenda formats, site schedules, e-mail formats, and presentation formats. The assessment should produce consistent results.

6.3.5.2 Project Management

Project management tools include a standard WBS, or at least a standard WBS to start with, and customize according to organization specifics. Other tools include project plan templates, burn rate trackers, budget tracker templates, standard e-mail communication formats, meeting agenda and meeting minutes templates, and status report templates. The burn rate tracker captures labor and material expenses on a weekly basis. Part of the burn rate tracker should be a projection of labor and material expenses and the ability to compare actual and projection. Overages in the current week should cascade out to project end, showing the cumulative effects to overall budget. This is an effective practice to determine problems early and fix them. A budget overage should be no surprise at the end of the project. If there is a budget overage, there should be awareness and expectation management well ahead of project completion.

Project management tools also consist of communication protocol guidance that specifies the official channels of communication. Security is a sensitive issue, and communication to a CIO prior to communication with the CSO may be a breach of protocol; better to know this ahead of time and capture communications protocol in a formal document. The project manager should also gather sample report templates, results analysis guidelines, statistical analysis tools, project plan templates, report/deliverable interpretation guides, site visit schedule/agenda templates, and team communications templates and samples. Managing the planning of the assessment, the execution of the assessment, and the delivery of the assessment results is at least as important as the results themselves.

6.3.5.3 Pre-Engagement

Pre-engagement tools include templates for project definitions, contracts, statement of work, or other documents that express the scope and detail of work to perform. A very important tool is a cost model or pricing model. The cost model captures all project expenses, revenue, and profit. Capturing lessons learned for the cost model provides the ability to perform more accurate pricing for future engagements. If there is downward pressure on costs, having a model that captures all details enables intelligent adjustment of labor and material projections.

6.3.5.4 Engagement

Supporting the engagement are mainly discovery templates, checklists, and methodologies on how to use them effectively. The SMF assists with developing a consistent set of tools to promote completeness, consistency among multiple assessors, and repeatable results for subsequent assessments. An interpretation guide enables all parties to have a list of the security standards and understand the intent of the standards. Discovery includes interviews, hence the need for interview guides. Discovery requires capturing details in findings templates and other report templates. Most assessments are subjective in nature; that is, the assessor compares the findings against the compliance requirements and describes the differences in narrative terms. The recording of these details and the interpretations on the back-end consumption of the reports may vary tremendously among assessors. Providing a tool to quantify the assessment findings or add a quantification of the subjective narrative provides many benefits.

With respect to quantifying compliance assessment results, consider a simple scale of *low*, *medium*, and *high* compliance with corresponding values of 1, 2, and 3. A quantification guideline provides direction on how to determine if compliance is low, medium, or high. This quantification guideline aligns with the SMF and uses the interpretation guide to establish criteria for the compliance levels. Capturing a compliance level of 1, 2, or 3 for each compliance element enables the ability to sum, average, calculate percentages, discover minimum and maximum values, compare one site with another, and aggregate the results from all sites. The initial assessment then provides a quantified baseline compliance level, and subsequent assessments provide quantification that enables trending.

The use of a small scale like low, medium, and high provides more consistent results than a scale of higher granularity of, say, 1 to 20, where 15 to 20 represent degrees of high compliance. Trying to get too specific in the quantification reduces the consistency of interpretation and scoring between assessors. A simple scale increases the likelihood of an apples-to-apples comparison between site results, and aggregating site results at the enterprise level that more accurately reflect the true enterprise posture.

Use the same SMF for the interpretation guide, data collection (recording assessment results), conveying of remediation options and recommendations, and tracking of remediation activity. This framework enables the easy comparison of multiple documents across planning, implementation, monitoring, reviewing, and revising the security program.

6.3.5.6 Post-Engagement

Assuming quantified assessment results, post-engagement tools include the statistical processing of the results both at the site level and at the enterprise level (aggregating site results). Other tools include reporting templates and sample narrative. Reports include findings, gap analysis, remediation analysis, and remediation recommendations. These details may be in separate reports or in a single report, depending on the complexity and volume of the details and the desire of the organization.

6.3.5.7 Delivery and Sign-Off

Delivery tools include standard presentation format (template) and standard sign-off for delivery and project completion.

The intent of these compliance management tools or compliance assessment tools is to produce consistent, comprehensive, repeatable results among sites and over time. There is also the possibility to capture lessons learned in the tools through a process of continual review and improvement, which is the point of ISO 27001 and the creation of an ISMS.

6.3.6 Compliance Metrics

In any practical application of a system, process, methodology, software system, etc., there is the primary goal of getting it to work at all; that is, focus is on getting it into operation, warts and all, so to speak. The next concerns are getting it to work effectively and efficiently; focus here is often on feature management and cost management. The final goal typically is getting it to work securely; focus here is on managing business risk, of which one concern is legislative and regulatory compliance. This simplistic description separates *use, effective use,* and *secure use* into three discrete considerations. The intent is not to portray the thought process as absolute discrete tasks, but rather a predominance of considerations — meaning that security is not entirely absent during planning and development, but is often a thought in development, though more often a minor thought. In addition, the intent is not necessarily to put a feature-poor product in production; however, market demands often result in just that. The widget may enter the marketplace with some security, albeit not the best security in deference to market timing. The principle of best–good–good enough rules; it goes to market if it is good enough to go to market. Is widget X in perfect legislative compliance? No. Is widget X in blatant legislative violation? No. Good — sell it and begin work on the first patch or dot release. Judgments aside, this is the reality that organizations face when acquiring, implementing, and supporting business operations with information technology; perfection rarely rules, nor do best practices despite the nice marketing material behind the phrase — often good enough rules the day. With this premise, there is great need to justify security from project inception so that it is not an afterthought or an annoyance, but an enabler and a marketplace differentiator.

Justification of security efforts overall is moving toward metrics and measures. Legislative mandates require proof of security and secure actions. Even in the most safeguard austere environment, there is still a need for at least minimal security (hopefully a bit more); hence, there is the need to objectively measure the presence and effectiveness of security in business operations — that is, there is need for security metrics. The focus here is on security compliance metrics, a subset of overall security metrics. Compliance metrics include the following:

- Compliance levels:
  - Presence of security measures
  - Quality of security measures
  - Practice of security measures
- Policy, standard, and procedure management:
  - Develop
  - Review
- Dissemination:
  - Awareness
  - Understanding
  - Compliance
- Mitigation/remediation tracking

6.3.6.1 Compliance Levels

The SMF enables a clear articulation of organizational security goals. Security posture includes policies, standards, procedures, security services (e.g., security working group [SWG] or computer security incident response team [CSIRT]), and security mechanisms (e.g., firewall, intrusion detection system [IDS], anti-malware). A compliance assessment determines the current security posture and compares it against the security goals, where security goals incorporate all relevant security compliance requirements. The process of assessing compliance determines *compliance levels*, or the degree of the current situation as compared to the goals. Three categories of compliance-level metrics are *presence*, *quality*, and *practice*.

Presence metrics determine if security measures exist at all: Is there an enterprise security policy? Is there an anti-malware policy? Are there anti-malware mechanisms (i.e., software applications for antivirus, antispam, anti-spyware, etc.)? If the compliance assessment uses ISO 27002 as a foundation, there is the ability to count the number of security measures in ISO 27002 and compare them against the number of elements in ISO 27002. This is an opportunity for a statistical measure: *the organization has X percent of security measures recommended in ISO 27002*. Having the safeguard is the first step. There is still the need to determine if the safeguard is good, and there is the need to determine the quality of the safeguard.

Quality metrics determine if the safeguard contains the features to make it a good safeguard. The standard of *good* is organizational specific and depends greatly on the role of security. A standard of good is available from many industry-accepted security standards. These standards specify features that they consider to make a good safeguard. For example, a good security policy contains the following attributes or qualities:

- A definition of information security to the organization and in terms meaningful to the organization
- The objectives of a security program
- The scope of a security program
- A statement of management intent for security in terms that align with business drivers, such as current strategy, strategic direction, and operational objectives
- The need for a security management program
- A statement of need for security policies, standards, and procedures
- A statement of need for organizational compliance with security policies, i.e., good security practices that apply security standards and procedures
- Risk management requirements of particular importance to the organization, including:
  - Legislative compliance
  - Security awareness, training, and education
  - Business continuity, continuity of operations planning, disaster recovery

For any particular organization, the list may vary. The point is to adopt a standard that defines what comprises a good security policy. Then compare existing policies with that standard to determine the quality of existing policies; moreover, quantify the level of compliance to convey statistical summaries of the current situation and provide an objective baseline from which to measure progress. For example, there are eight high-level bullets in the list above that comprise a good security policy. The simplest method is to count the number of attributes that exist in the policy reviewed. If there are six of eight, then the policy *attribute compliance level* with the standard is 75 percent. Hold this thought as the following paragraph dives a bit deeper into principles of quantification and then applies this 75 percent attribute compliance level in a bigger picture.

Overcomplicating compliance quantification will increase costs, result in inconsistent results, and produce results difficult to understand. An effective but simple method is to use a scale of *nonexistent, low* level of compliance, *medium* level of compliance, *high* level of compliance, and *fully compliant*; then, use a quantification of 0, 1, 2, 3, and 4, respectively, to numerically represent the scale. A determination of nonexistent is straightforward; the safeguard is there, or it is not. Full compliance is when the safeguard contains at least all the attributes in the standard. The organization then determines and publishes an internal guideline on what constitutes low, medium, and high compliance. Some percentage of attributes greater than 0 and less than 50 percent may constitute low compliance, 50 to 84 percent may constitute medium, and 85 to 99 percent may constitute high. Using this guideline, the 75 percent example above is a medium compliance, or a compliance level of 2 using the 0-to-4 scale and a compliance-level percentage of 50 percent ((2/4) * 100 = 50%).

Use the compliance attributes to determine the attribute compliance level and translate the attribute compliance level to a compliance level using the 0-to-4 scale. Then perform a similar calculation on each security element in the security standard. Assessing attribute level compliance on its own also permits the addition of weighting. For example, perhaps the security policy leaves out the objectives of the security program as well as mention of legislative compliance. The organization may decide that stating security program objectives is more important than stating legislative compliance; therefore, the security program objectives attribute is given a weight of 2. Using a weighted scale (Table 6.9) with the two missing elements, 1 being the weighted attribute, yields an attribute compliance level of 66.67 percent. If the weighted attribute is there and two nonweighted attributes are missing, the attribute compliance level is 77.78 percent. Weighting adds a bit of complexity, but yields a more accurate picture by reflecting what is important to the organization. Note that any weighting becomes part of the published guidelines and is not left up to individual assessors. The goal is to produce consistent results among many assessors and from one assessment engagement to the next. This consistency provides for accurate statistics and trending that translate into proof for the business value of security.

There is a difference between the presence of a good procedure document and whether that procedure is actually used in day-to-day operations. Moreover, the organization may not capture many excellent day-to-day operations in a formal procedure document. The presence of a good procedure does not necessarily

Table 6.9 Weighted Scale Example

Attribute	Weight	Present	Score
x	1	1	1
x	2	0	0
x	1	1	1
x	1	0	0
x	1	1	1
x	1	1	1
x	1	1	1
x	1	1	1
	9	6	6
	Compliance level	66.67%	

imply good practice, and good practice does not necessarily imply the presence of a good procedure — hence the need to distinguish the difference in a compliance assessment. Assessing practice is similar to assessing any other safeguard. First, is there a practice at all? Second, what is the quality of that practice? The same attributes that denote a good safeguard denote a good practice. If there are procedures, then level of adherence to the procedures yields a practice level.

Important note: When gauging a compliance level and a percentage, the results are what they are. There is no intent to point fingers, blame, or otherwise make judgment. A compliance level of 50 percent is not failing per se, nor is it passing. A 50 percent compliance level means that the security control contains approximately half the features enumerated in the security compliance requirements — it is that simple. This point of nonjudgment is a hard lesson learned from personal experience. Years ago, a set of compliance assessment reports used the terms *compliance score* and *report card*. The association of report card and score brought forth connotations of school and tests and passing or failing. Any compliance score below 60 percent was perceived as failing when in fact the intent was never to pass or fail, merely to discern and fix. The point of the lesson is that terminology and perception matter a lot. The term *compliance level* carries a more neutral connotation and promotes focus on fixing existing security programs rather than defending them.

6.3.6.2 Policy, Standard, and Procedure Management

In general, policy specifies *why*, standards specify *what*, and procedures specify *how*, *when*, *where*, and *who*. Policy drives organizational behavior by specifying practices and aligning them with strategic business drivers; one generic business driver is *risk management*. One silo of risk management is compliance management. Standards specify the services, tools, and mechanisms to implement policy. Procedures specify how to use the standards to implement policy, when to apply the standards, where to apply them, and roles and responsibilities in applying them. An SMF will assist in identifying policies necessary to state the organization's desired security posture. There will be a finite number of these, and they will be traceable to business drivers such as risk management and legislation X.

A series of metrics and measures emerge by tracking the number of policies necessary and the number of policies written. Ongoing metrics emerge out of tracking periodic reviews against changing business, legislative, and regulatory environments. The same principle applies to standards and procedures. The point of quantifying is to enable summary graphs in executive reports. From personal experience, more than one criticism has been cast on an executive summary of 20 pages or more. In a situation where the report detail is in the 50,000-page range, a 20-page summary is not so bad. However, the same summary with quantified graphs in 10 pages is often more palatable to the time-challenged executive.

6.3.6.3 Dissemination

The quantification aspects attempt to measure awareness, understanding, and compliance. Tracking awareness presumes the presence of a dissemination program that provides access to security awareness. Access may be online, via live sessions, or even through the receipt of a manual or memo. Whatever the dissemination method, there is a need to verify that people have received and read the material. Sending security awareness material via e-mail enables the tracking of how many are sent and the number of return receipts upon opening the e-mail. There is an assumption that if opened, the user actually reads the material.

The next step beyond awareness is the measure of understanding. This may take the form of a quiz or test or survey. The score will represent the level of understanding of the issue, the organizational stance, expectations of employees, and their individual roles and contributions to establish and remain in compliance. A short self-assessment questionnaire often compels more complacent employees to actually read the material and attempt to understand it.

Measuring compliance may include follow-on compliance assessments. Establishing a baseline of quantified compliance levels, disseminating security awareness and training, and then reassessing compliance levels over time using the same quantification techniques enable trend analysis. Upward trends show effectiveness of the awareness and training programs.

6.3.6.4 Mitigation/Remediation Tracking

The SMF enables the ability to develop templates for compliance assessment discovery tools, recording findings, performing a gap analysis, making remediation recommendations, defining remediation projects, and tracking remediation projects. The use of a consistent SMF promotes easy comparison of each of the above efforts between multiple documents. Moreover, creating metrics and measures in context of the framework promotes the use of those metrics in establishing and implementing the security management program, as well as ongoing review and revision.

After the initial compliance assessment, there will be a number of security initiatives for risk mitigation. Tracking the number of initiatives and the accomplishment of them is another measure of progress.

6.3.6.5 Benefits of Metrics and Measures

The key benefit of metrics and measures is an objective reflection of the business value of security to the organization. Business justification for security comes from a return on investment analysis. Business value comes from determining operational effectiveness of security and linking that operational effectiveness to the business functions it supports. *Key business functions* define the very reason for the existence of the organization. For a bank, a key business function is transaction processing, e.g., consumer ATM use or commercial funds transfer. Loss of the transaction processing business function results in great customer dissatisfaction, if not lawsuits, due to deals falling through because the funds transfer did not occur. Security measures that ensure the *availability* of this business function add business value. Security measures that ensure *confidentiality* in transaction processing (privacy of parties involved and transaction details) add business value. Security measures that ensure the *integrity* of the transaction — that the transaction occurs without error — also add business value. Metrics and measures attempt to capture this business value.

Another benefit is the ability to engage in performance-based contracts to ensure high levels of service delivery. A world economy and intense competitive demands are forcing organizations to focus on core competencies, and many organizations are outsourcing noncore operations. One such outsourcing is managed security services (MSS). The business arrangement is not so much to deliver widget X, but to provide ongoing security services. A performance-based contract establishes SLAs, performance metrics that measure the quality of the service. SLAs link payment for services to the quality of those services. Achieving at least minimal levels of performance results in payment; higher levels of performance may result in bonuses; less than minimal performance may result in financial penalties. Creating, understanding, monitoring, and tracking performance metrics is one aspect of security metrics and measures. Another aspect resides with deliverable-based contracts.

6.3.6.5.1 Deliverables-Based Contracts

Security organizations may install enterprisewide firewalls to provide secure Internet connectivity. Upon delivery and successful acceptance testing, money changes hands and the security company is off to the next engagement. In short, it was engaged to deliver a product; it did, and so was paid according to successful and timely delivery. This is an example of a deliverables-based contract. Metrics and measures center around initial delivery and successful testing.

6.3.6.5.2 Performance-Based Contracts

Security organizations may perform an ongoing service, e.g., firewall management. This service may include installing, configuring, and monitoring the firewalls. The contract terms reflect the need for effective performance for delivery, configuration, and monitoring. The contract terms may be in the form of SLAs. SLAs may be X number of firewalls installed by Y date, or the ability to manage all firewalls from a central management location, or penetration testing will result in no more than X percent of policy violations. Such SLAs are the basis for a performance-based contract. The goal is not so much delivery of a firewall solution as it is the effective overall management of the security services provided by the firewall.

One key difference between the two types of contracts is the need for metrics and measures under a performance-based contract. From both a customer perspective and a delivery perspective, determining what to measure, how to measure it, and what constitutes acceptable performance is nontrivial. The customer wants perfect performance, and the provider does not want to commit to SLAs so high that it loses revenue in nonperformance penalties. A disciplined approach, a set of tools based on the SMF, will provide the ability to identify, define, implement, monitor, and track security metrics and measures.

6.3.7 ISO Certification: An Instance of IA CMP

An information assurance compliance management program (IA CMP) is an attempt at a comprehensive framework approach to security management. The SMF is organizational specific and incorporates many compliance requirements that include legislation, regulation, and security standards. No single legislation or security standard represents a comprehensive security solution; organizational security needs change constantly with new business challenges, new risks, new threats, and new vulnerabilities. The best security solution is agile and extensible to meet unforeseen circumstances. The IA CMP provides such an agile and extensible solution. The IA CMP framework herein accommodates the use of ISO 27001 and ISO 27002 security standards. Indeed, achieving ISO 27001 certification is one instance of the IA CMP approach.

This chapter attempts to be neutral in wording and phrasing, that is, non-ISO specific where the details in the other chapters are ISO specific. The point is to use language relevant to the objectives of the security program. If an objective is ISO 27001 certification, tailor the IA CMP to accommodate ISO 27001 and call the security management program an ISMS. The IA CMP should not contend with the auditor expectations; rather, it should help satisfy those expectations with an ISO 27001-compliant ISMS, plus the ability to expand that ISMS to meet many other security goals.

Table 6.10 provides a format in which to define a security program in the context of the SMF. The author's preferences lean toward using an industry standard as a baseline for the SMF, then modifying the framework to fit organizational-specific needs. The foundation framework herein is the ISO 27002 security standard. Alternative or supplemental industry standards include Control Objectives for Information and Related Technology (COBIT), NIST SP 800-53, Department of Defense Directives (8500.x), and others.

6.4 Conclusion and Commentary

Compliance is conformity to a set of requirements. Those requirements may be legislative, regulatory, contractual, operational, or SLAs, and others. *Management* is the coordination of resources and activities to accomplish a goal. *Compliance management* is the coordination of resources and activities to conform to a set of requirements; that set of requirements is collectively called *compliance requirements*. As shown in Figure 6.3, an effective CMP is a continuous cycle of:

■ Plan
■ Do
■ Check
■ Act

These phases interweave organizational structures of *governance, management,* and *operations* to identify business drivers, articulate business risks, identify

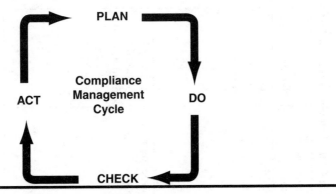

Figure 6.3   Compliance management cycle.

Table 6.10 Sample Format for Defining a Security Management Program

Requirement Number	Security Element	Security Standard Description	Security Plan Details	Responsibility	Trace to
Requirement ID	Security element description	Summary of security plan standard	Define the security plan specifics to satisfy the security plan element.	Define the security plan implementation and maintenance responsibilities.	Cross-reference to unique requirements identifier.
Unique identifier for security plan element	<Standard reference from outline>	<Brief description of the requirement>	Specify a security plan for the particular security element.	The security plan provides actionable items and specifically denotes responsibility for implementation and operations and maintenance.	Provide cross-reference to other requirements or initiatives; e.g., HIPAA remediation efforts will also satisfy security program requirements; likewise, security program efforts may satisfy HIPAA requirements. Cross-referencing will minimize duplicate efforts.
Etc.					

compliance requirements, implement compliance management, and perform ongoing compliance assessments in a continual cycle of awareness and preparedness.

6.4.1 PDCA Overview

The Plan-Do-Check-Act (PDCA) cycle is an industry standard to manage continuous improvement of a business function. The PDCA model applies to compliance management to identify initial compliance requirements, align those requirements with business drivers in terms of risk management, and define a CMP. PDCA continues with support to implement and operate the compliance management process, as well as implement measures to monitor and track the effectiveness of compliance management. And PDCA supports review and revisions to the compliance management process to initiate a cycle of continuous improvement.

6.4.1.1 Plan

Planning consists of determining compliance management challenges in terms of business risk, identifying security compliance requirements, and using security compliance requirements to develop a security management program that includes policy, standards, procedures, and practices to define, plan, implement, enforce, monitor, and track security compliance. Planning activity produces an implementation plan to enforce security compliance requirements. Strategic direction for compliance management comes from risk governance. Risk management converts the strategic direction into actionable tasks.

6.4.1.2 Do

Doing entails implementing the plan to enforce security compliance requirements. Risk management facilitates this implementation and works with developers to establish security operations. Security operations administer, monitor, and track security products that enforce compliance policy.

6.4.1.3 Check

After the initial development of security operations, there is need to review the effectiveness of operations. One measure of effectiveness comes from a compliance assessment. The results of the check phase include review of the compliance requirements to ensure they accurately represent the current compliance environment (e.g., new legislation governing security or risk management). Moreover, a compliance assessment determines current compliance levels with existing compliance requirements. The process identifies gaps and addresses each gap in terms of an appropriate risk management strategy: ignore, accept, transfer, share, or mitigate.

6.4.1.4   Act

Actions following the check phase include providing and implementing organizational feedback of the findings.

6.4.2 Melding Compliance Management with PDCA

The organization provides strategic direction by way of a *governance* process that identifies business drivers, articulates strategic direction, and produces policy governing organizational behavior. The executive-level and senior management provide the governance function. *Management* produces tactical guidance to implement the strategic direction. This tactical guidance takes the form of performance objectives and operational plans, among others. *Operations* implements the management plans and performs the tasks of administration, monitoring, tracking, and reporting on operational effectiveness.

Table 6.11 presents key imperatives of a compliance management program in context of PDCA and with cross-references to the organizational functions of governance, management, and operations. The following sections expand on each task and describe compliance management in terms of inputs to that task, actions under that task (a process), and outputs from that task. Compliance management should be a pragmatic sequence of events with well-defined deliverables and milestones to contribute to the identification and management of business risk.

6.4.2.1   Identify

The imperative is to identify relevant compliance requirements. The business environment and type of business drive compliance requirements. A U.S. public company has different compliance requirements than a U.S. federal agency. This requires input of business background material that provides assistance to identify applicable legislation, regulation, standards, contractual obligations, and other compliance requirements that influence organizational behavior. Learning the business background and environment leads to a list of applicable compliance requirements. The results are a list of relevant compliance requirements to the organization.

6.4.2.2   Establish

Define a compliance management program using the security compliance requirements as guidance. Decompose the requirements into categories and elements that support the creation of a traceability matrix and requirements definition matrix. Outputs from activities to define a compliance management program include:

- Strategic goals for compliance management program
- Compliance management scope

Table 6.11 Compliance Management PDCA Breakdown

Imperative	PDCA	GRO	Comments
Identify	Plan	Governance, management	Identify compliance requirements.
Establish	Plan	Governance, management	Define a compliance management framework and compliance management initiatives.
Plan	Plan	Management	Develop plans to implement compliance management initiatives.
Implement	Do	Management, operations	Implement compliance management initiatives.
Monitor	Check	Operations	Monitor effectiveness of compliance management operations, e.g., compliance assessment.
Maintain	Check	Governance, management, operations	Report and review the results of monitoring. As the reports flow up the chain from operations to management to governance, each level provides maintenance for its respective scope of responsibility. The reports contain compliance gap details. Review of the reports produces options and recommendations for gap closure in terms of managing business risk.
Improve	Act	Governance, management, operations	Provide organizational feedback with respect to revising the compliance management program; essentially, implement initiatives to close compliance gaps or otherwise address the risks inherent in the gaps.

- ■ Templates to support compliance management:
  - • Base templates on compliance requirement categories and elements that result from the decomposition process
- ■ Compliance objectives

The governance process establishes business strategic goals and objectives that drive compliance management.

6.4.2.3 Plan

To satisfy the strategic objectives, use the framework/templates resulting from the decomposition of the compliance requirements to develop project plans that implement the compliance management initiatives. Planning develops an action plan to implement security initiatives; security initiatives affect the security posture of the organization with the intent to align that security posture with compliance requirements and to be able to prove compliance. In terms of managing business risk, many of these initiatives will be security controls found in ISO 27002. The results of planning include project definitions and plans.

While the tasks and roles below expand beyond just the planning phase, consider the following insights for the planning effort:

- Governance:
  - Establish strategy.
  - Approve policy.
- Management:
  - Interpret strategy into actionable tactics.
  - Provide input to the development of strategy.
  - Develop the standards that define what to use to enforce policy.
  - Develop the procedures that define how to enforce policy.
  - Plan for the development of operations.
  - Establish operations.
- Operations:
  - Implement the services and mechanisms to enforce policy using standards and procedures.
  - Provide input to the development of standards and procedures.

Governance occurs at the executive and senior management levels with a variety of inputs that span strategic business drivers and tactical constraints. Governance produces strategic plans. Management occurs at the senior and mid-management levels and acts according to strategic directives. Management produces tactical plans to implement strategy. Operations, under management directives, implement the tactical plans in the form of operational constructs, security services, and security mechanisms.

6.4.2.4 Implement

Implementation takes the plans for compliance management and produces the operations that meet initial compliance objectives as well as provide the ability to review and maintain compliance objectives. The implementation process establishes the security posture of the organization to mitigate risk, risk that aligns with compliance objectives. Note, given budget and resource constraints, and there are always budget and resource constraints, a 100 percent compliance level may not be an objective, let alone attainable. The objective is to establish an ongoing process of continual review and improvement with the goals to maintain acceptable levels of compliance. Implementation results in security operations. Operations personnel administer, monitor, track, and maintain the security services and mechanisms, and report on their effectiveness.

6.4.2.5 Monitor

To maintain an effective security posture that keeps risks at an acceptable level and satisfies compliance requirements requires monitoring. Monitoring assesses the compliance levels of existing security practices against security compliance requirements; this requires the development of an assessment methodology, tools, and templates to support the compliance assessment process. The results of monitoring activity include compliance assessment methodology, tools, and templates, and the results of using these, i.e., compliance assessment findings.

The act of monitoring compliance levels results in a collection of discovery data. Subsequent activity (see next step) compiles the discovery data into a series of reports.

6.4.2.5.1 Compliance Assessment Process

The compliance assessment process includes a methodology to guide discovery, analysis, and reporting:

- Discovery — compliance sources, requirement titles
- Analysis — determine requirement driver, requirement type
- Reporting — recording details

Additionally, the compliance assessment process uses tools and templates that find basis in the SMF. Using the same framework to assess compliance as to define the requirements on which to base the assessment promotes consistency and comprehensiveness in the assessment task itself and in reporting the results. The compliance assessment process is an ongoing endeavor that compares the current security posture against security objectives, as well as the current compliance assessment results against previous results. The ability to provide consistent results to produce these valid comparisons (current compliance level and compliance-level trends) requires tools and templates that normalize the process from assessment to assessment, as well as from assessor to assessor.

6.4.2.6 Maintain

Monitoring tasks overlap with maintenance tasks where both, together, perform discovery, analysis, and reporting of compliance assessments. The formal process and output from maintenance are the gap analysis reports and gap closure reports. The gaps highlight compliance deficiencies; the analysis provides insight on how to address those deficiencies in terms of business risk: ignore, accept, share, transfer, or mitigate. Again, the reports use the same SMF to promote consistency and comprehensiveness.

There may be many levels of reports as a result of compliance maintenance. The language and tone of the report take on different characteristics depending on organizational level of the report consumer. An auditor gauging the effectiveness of security controls wants technical details in terms of the compliance requirements he or she is auditing against, e.g., SOX. A security operations manager wants a report in terms of meeting contractual SLAs or other tactical objectives. A CEO wants a report in terms of meeting strategic objectives, business value, stakeholder value, and shareholder value, and preferably aligned with the income statement and balance sheet.

6.4.2.7 Improve

The compliance assessment process results in recommendations for improvement. Review and acceptance of the recommendations result in modifications to any aspect of the security environment:

- Policy, standards, procedure, and practice
- Modifying existing security services; adding new services; eliminating security services that no longer provide justifiable business value
- Modifying, adding, or removing existing security mechanisms; e.g., adding additional virtual private networks (VPNs) to ensure secure communications with business partners or eliminating in-house security operations center due to new outsourcing arrangement
- Modifying compliance requirements due to discovery of new risk management requirements

Outputs from improvement are proposals and project plans to implement the improvements.

6.4.3 ISO 27001 Certification: An Instance of Compliance Management

The compliance management program provides the ability to insert any compliance requirement, including ISO 27001. The governance process identifies ISO 27001 certification as a strategic goal. Therefore, ISO 27001 is one external-explicit requirements document, and ISO 27002 is an external-implied requirements document. Decomposing these documents into categories and elements yields the SMF in Chapter 3. The SMF then becomes the foundation for defining an interpretation guide; defining the ISMS; creating tools and templates in support of ISMS development, implementation, operation, monitoring, maintaining, and improving — and we come full circle in accomplishing an effective, extensible compliance management program that supports the attainment of ISO 27001 certification.

Appendix A: ISMS Assessment Discovery Question Set

The question set follows a distinct pattern throughout. The shaded question is of the format *does your organization have X?* Valid responses may include *yes, no, unknown,* or *not applicable.* All answers provide insight to the current compliance level as well as levels of awareness or understanding of the organization's security position. If the answer is yes, the subsequent set of questions discerns the quality of X; that is, does it possess attributes that constitute a good X? The values of X in this question set are *policy, procedure,* and *practice.* Does your organization have a policy for Y? Does your organization have a procedure for Y? Does your organization actually practice Y?

For example, assume the initial question is *does your organization have a password policy?* If so, the next set of questions discovers if it is a good password policy relative to the compliance requirements. If not, this detail enters as a *gap* in the gap analysis report. The remediation report then proposes the development or the enhancement of a password policy. To this end, the remediation report suggests attributes of a password policy that make it a good policy for this particular organization. What makes for a good password policy for this organization? Attributes of a good password policy come from industry standards (e.g., International Standards Organization [ISO] or National Institute of Standards and Technology [NIST]), industry best practices, recommendations from consultants, security professionals employed by the organization (you, perhaps!), or legislative or regulatory requirements.

Following policy questions are questions regarding organizational procedure and organizational practice. Questions regarding organizational procedure address

213

the existence and attributes of how policy is implemented and enforced. Even with the existence of policy and procedure, there is still the question of the organization practice; that is, does the organization actually perform what is in policy and procedure? Many organizations have fine policy; however, no one knows about it or there are no implementation and enforcement of policy. The distinction between policy and practice is an important one to make during a compliance assessment.

The question set in Table A.1 is organized by various categories; add/modify/delete categories to fit organizational need. The question set herein is a sampling of what will be a much larger, more detailed question set that will accommodate all relevant legislation, regulation, and security standards applicable to the organization. No static question set can be exhaustive and 100% applicable to all organizations; therefore, consider the enclosed question set as a starting point. As a security professional, supplement this question set with specifics relevant to your industry, organization, situation, and experience. The specifics will change with time, among industries, and among organizations, with introduction of new threats, new technologies, and new business drivers.

Applicable questions to all sections in Table A.1 include whether the [policy, standard, procedure, practice] requires, specifies, or otherwise addresses:

Assigning responsibility for policy, standard, procedure, practice
    Creation, dissemination, tracking awareness, understanding, and use
    Implementation and enforcement
Inclusion of policy, standard, procedure, practice in awareness, training, and
    education programs
Referencing an appropriate sanction policy for non-compliance
Using metrics to objectively capture organizational preparedness (policy, standard, procedure) and practice
Tracking awareness, understanding, and practice
Reporting to management and executives on effectiveness

The role of information assurance (security) is to effectively address and manage business risk. Business risk management is the primary business driver behind information assurance. One business risk is compliance management, e.g., to remain in compliance with applicable legislation. A compliance management program is part of effective business risk management. Compliance management and risk management lead to the need for formal security management that aligns security initiatives with compliance requirements and with the business benefit of addressing and mitigating business risk. The question set categories of Table A.1 are as follows. These categories are generic and flexible to align with many security standards including ISO 27002.

Risk Management
Risk Assessment

Compliance Management
External Compliance Requirements
Legislation, Regulation
Internal Compliance Requirements
Security Policy (in alignment with external compliance requirements)
Self-Imposed Security Standards
Security Management
Security Policy
Security Management
Security Principles
Confidentiality
Cryptography
Integrity
Availability
Prevention
Defense Management
Monitoring
Access Management
People Management
Privacy Management
Asset Management
BC/DR
Operations Management
ELCM
Media Management
Mobile Code
Mobile Computing
Communications Management
Appropriate Use
Audit Management
Data Management
Incident Management
Configuration Management
Vulnerability Management
Work Area Management
Workstation Management
Solution Quality Assurance (SQA) Management
Physical Security

Table A.1 provides a list of sample questions to discern the current organizational security posture. The *Categories* are those in the list above. The *Ref #* is a Table A.1 internal reference for ease of question identification and reference. The cross-reference (*X-Ref*) is an empty column to accommodate the insertion of an appropriate security standard, legislative, or other reference number. For example, if ISO 27002 is the baseline standard, ISO 27002 section 4 discusses risk management; therefore, insert 4, 4.1, and so on as appropriate in the *X-Ref* column to denote the cross-reference between the question set and the ISO standard.

Table A.1   ISMS As-Is Discovery Question Set

Category	Ref #	X-Ref	Question
Risk Management	1		
Risk Mgmt	1.1		Does your organization have a policy that addresses the need for risk management?
Risk Mgmt	1.2		Does this policy require, specify, or otherwise address the following:
Risk Mgmt	1.2.1		Identification of an acceptable risk posture for the organization?
Risk Mgmt	1.2.2		Risk assessment?
Risk Mgmt	1.2.3		Multi-perspective on risk, including: Threat space? Asset space? Vulnerability space? Business impact assessment?
Risk Mgmt	1.2.4		Reporting results of risk assessment, e.g., gap analysis between acceptable risk posture and current risk posture?
Risk Mgmt	1.2.5		Remediation analysis report, i.e., specify how to increase security posture or reduce risk to a more acceptable level?
Risk Mgmt	1.2.x		*Note:* Add questions that determine the quality of this security control specifically for the organization. Consider risks in this area, threats, vulnerabilities, dependent business functions, organization-specific operational demands, special situations, etc.
Risk Mgmt	1.3		Does your organization have a procedure describing how to implement and enforce risk management policy?
Risk Mgmt	1.4		Does this procedure require, specify, or otherwise address the following:

Table A.1 ISMS As-Is Discovery Question Set (Continued)

Category	Ref #	X-Ref	Question
Risk Mgmt	1.4.1		Scope breadth: threat space, asset space, vulnerability space, business impact assessment?
Risk Mgmt	1.4.2		Scope depth: Interviews—asking? Verification—seeing? Validation—hands on?
Risk Mgmt	1.4.x		*Note:* Provide questions that discern organizational procedure that implements policy. All procedure questions are variations of the policy questions. "Do you have a policy that prescribes X?" turns into a question of "do you have a procedure that describes how to X?" All policy questions below may have the procedure and practice questions added as described above. In the interest of space, these practice questions are not included.
Risk Mgmt	1.5		Does your organization *practice* the procedures as described above?
Risk Mgmt	1.6		Does this practice include or otherwise address the following:
Risk Mgmt	1.6.x		*Note:* Provide questions that discern organizational practice. All practice questions are variations of the policy and procedure questions. "Do you have a policy that prescribes X?" turns into a question of "do you actually perform X?" All policy questions below may have the procedure and practice questions added as described above. In the interest of space, these practice questions are not included.
Compliance Management	2		
Compliance Mgmt	2.1		Does your organization have a policy for compliance management?

(continued)

Table A.1   ISMS As-Is Discovery Question Set (Continued)

Category	Ref #	X-Ref	Question
Compliance Mgmt	2.2		Does this policy require, specify, or otherwise address the following:
Compliance Mgmt	2.2.1		The scope of compliance management: explicit business requirements, implicit risk management (therefore, security) requirements, and explicit security requirements?
Compliance Mgmt	2.2.2		The need to identify and enumerate relevant legislative, regulatory, and other requirements with which the organization must comply?
Compliance Mgmt	2.2.3		Specify an industry security standard that specifies a baseline for an organizational security program, e.g., ISO 27002, NIST, or COBIT?
Compliance Mgmt	2.2.4		A formal compliance management program (CMP) to define, document, and maintain the organizational approach to comply with relevant legislative and regulatory requirements?
Compliance Mgmt	2.2.5		Scope: explicitly articulate a broad intent to adhere to legislative compliances as well as provide a list of examples of contemporary issues, including digital rights, copyright, music sharing, software sharing, videos, e-books, etc.?
Compliance Mgmt	2.2.6		Legal use of information (organizational, partners, vendors, customers, contractors, and other second parties)?
Compliance Mgmt	2.2.7		Legal use of information technology (including software) (organizational, partners, vendors, customers, contractors, and other second parties): Right to use (RTU)? Licensing? Purchased, freeware, shareware, open source, etc.?
Compliance Mgmt	2.2.8		Inclusion of compliance management in awareness, training, and education programs?

Table A.1   ISMS As-Is Discovery Question Set (Continued)

Category	Ref #	X-Ref	Question
Compliance Mgmt	2.2.9		The rights of duties of the organization in monitoring for compliance?
Compliance Mgmt	2.2.x		*Note:* Add questions that determine the quality of this security control specifically for the organization. Consider risks in this area, threats, vulnerabilities, dependent business functions, organization-specific operational demands, special situations, etc.
Compliance Mgmt	2.3		Does your organization have a procedure describing how to implement and enforce compliance management policy?
Compliance Mgmt	2.4		Does this procedure require, specify, or otherwise address the following:
Compliance Mgmt	2.4.1		Creation of an effective compliance management program?
Compliance Mgmt	2.4.x		*Note:* Provide questions that discern organizational procedure that implements policy. All procedure questions are variations of the policy questions. "Do you have a policy that prescribes X?" turns into a question of "do you have a procedure that describes how to X?" All policy questions below may have the procedure and practice questions added as described above. In the interest of space, these practice questions are not included.
Compliance Mgmt	2.5		Does your organization have a policy for compliance assessment?
Compliance Mgmt	2.6		Does this policy require, specify, or otherwise address the following:
Compliance Mgmt	2.6.1		Compliance assessment aligns with compliance requirements?
Compliance Mgmt	2.6.2		Specifically articulates the need to assess compliance with security management program?

(continued)

Table A.1   ISMS As-Is Discovery Question Set (Continued)

Category	Ref #	X-Ref	Question
Compliance Mgmt	2.6.3		The level of assessment: Interview—ask and believe the response? Verification—document review; existence and quality? Validation—shoulder surfing or hands-on proof of existence and quality of function?
Compliance Mgmt	2.6.4		The strength of assessment (intended for automated scans): Discover and map—systems, Oss, patch levels, software installations, etc.? Low intrusive—low intensity intrusion? High intrusive—more accurate assessment of vulnerabilities, but danger of denial of service?
Compliance Mgmt	2.6.5		The use of formally documented testing, including test criteria and procedures?
Compliance Mgmt	2.6.6		That all assessments be performed by trained and competent security professionals?
Compliance Mgmt	2.6.7		The schedule for assessments: Non-busy times for the organization? Non-critical times to the organization? No/low business disruption? Annually, quarterly, monthly, as befits the expense of assessment and evolving threat space?
Compliance Mgmt	2.6.8		The need to track, trend, and report gaps, risk evaluations, and remediation activities?
Compliance Mgmt	2.6.9		Differentiate between internal compliance assessments (performed by organization personnel) and external compliance requirements (independent)?
Compliance Mgmt	2.7		Does your organization *practice* the procedures as described above?
Compliance Mgmt	2.8		Does this practice include or otherwise address the following:
Compliance Mgmt	2.8.1		Existence of a compliance management program?

Table A.1   ISMS As-Is Discovery Question Set (Continued)

Category	Ref #	X-Ref	Question
Compliance Mgmt	2.8.2		Compliance management governance and adjudication working group, with cross-representation from business management, business operations, technical management, and legal?
Compliance Mgmt	2.8.x		*Note:* Provide questions that discern organizational practice. All practice questions are variations of the policy and procedure questions. "Do you have a policy that prescribes X?" turns into a question of "do you actually perform X?" All policy questions below may have the procedure and practice questions added as described above. In the interest of space, these practice questions are not included.
Security Management	3		
Security Policy	3.1		Does your organization have a policy that addresses the need for executive backing and management support of security?
Security Policy	3.2		Does this policy require, specify, or otherwise address the following:
Security Policy	3.2.1		The articulation of security objectives and aligning these objectives with business risk?
Security Policy	3.2.2		Formal processes to define, write, review, and approve information security policy?
Security Policy	3.2.3		Management support of security through actions and clear delineation of responsibilities?
Security Policy	3.2.4		Review of the security policy awareness, understanding, and effectiveness?
Security Policy	3.2.5		Appropriate resources allocation?
Security Policy	3.2.6		Assignment of security roles and responsibilities?
Security Policy	3.2.7		Ensure enterprisewide application of security controls?

(continued)

Table A.1   ISMS As-Is Discovery Question Set (Continued)

Category	Ref #	X-Ref	Question
Security Mgmt	3.3		Does your organization have a procedure describing how to implement and enforce security policy? Policy for a security management program?
Security Mgmt	3.4		Does this procedure require, specify, or otherwise address the following:
Security Mgmt	3.4.1		Risk assessments?
Security Mgmt	3.4.2		Articulation and assessment of the threat-space; implications to operations, people, infrastructure, and information?
Security Mgmt	3.4.3		Security control evaluations in light of risk and threat assessments?
Security Mgmt	3.5		Does your organization have a policy for outsourced, in-house, or other variation of managed security service (MSS)?
Security Mgmt	3.6		Does this policy require, specify, or otherwise address the following:
Security Mgmt	3.6.1		All applicable security controls to effectively manage business risk?
Security Principles	4		
Security Principles	4.1		Does your organization have a policy that specifies or otherwise addresses security principles?
Security Principles	4.2		Does this policy require, specify, or otherwise address the following:
Security Principles	4.2.1		That which is not explicitly permitted is denied?
Security Principles	4.2.2		Adherence to the principles of confidentiality, integrity, and availability: Safeguard the integrity of business operations, information, and information technology? Safeguard the confidentiality of information as an information owner and an information custodian? Safeguard the availability of business operations, information, and information technology?

Table A.1   ISMS As-Is Discovery Question Set (Continued)

Category	Ref #	X-Ref	Question
Security Principles	4.2.3		Security management program with foundation in industry standards (e.g., ISO 27001)?
Security Principles	4.2.4		Safety of people first?
Security Principles	4.2.5		Promotion of personal and professional ethics?
Security Principles	4.2.6		Business need drives security?
Security Principles	4.2.7		Security initiatives align with and address business risks?
Security Principles	4.2.x		*Note:* As a security professional, consider the philosophy of security and driving principles behind security as a value-added business function. Moreover, consider this from the perspective of ensuring the continued viability of the organization you represent, and add to these principles accordingly.
Confidentiality	5		
Confidentiality	5.1		Does your organization have a policy for information confidentiality? *Note:* Use of the term *information* implies documents, data, databases, etc. in any format, including paper, electronic media, bits on a wire, and bits in the air. Bits on a wire may include data network or telephone network transmitting voice, fax, etc.
Confidentiality	5.2		Does this policy require, specify, or otherwise address the following:
Confidentiality	5.2.1		Employee responsibilities?
Confidentiality	5.2.2		Information classification levels: that they exist, that they are displayed prominently?
Confidentiality	5.2.3		Employee access capabilities?
Confidentiality	5.2.4		Existence of a governance and adjudication process to grant/revoke access privileges?

(continued)

Table A.1   ISMS As-Is Discovery Question Set (Continued)

Category	Ref #	X-Ref	Question
Confidentiality	5.2.5		Tracking privileges: who, what, when, where, how, explicit and default privilege termination?
Confidentiality	5.2.6		Contracts with partners, vendors, contractors, and others who may access organizational information?
Confidentiality	5.2.7		Trust levels?
Confidentiality	5.2.8		Risk management requirements: Security controls? Insurance?
Confidentiality	5.2.9		Mutual access to respective records to validate compliance?
Confidentiality	5.2.10		Responsibilities of the organization when in possession of second-party information?
Confidentiality	5.2.11		Of data in-transit, including: Inside organization network (intra-network)? Outside organization network (inter-network)? Private use (e.g., partners, vendors, customers)? Public use (e.g., the Internet)?
Confidentiality	5.2.12		Of data at-rest, including: PC, workstation? Server? Backups? Archives?
Confidentiality	5.3		Does your organization have a policy for cryptography?
Confidentiality	5.4		Does this policy require, specify, or otherwise address the following:
Confidentiality	5.4.1		Application of cryptology on information of specified classification levels?
Confidentiality	5.4.2		Application of cryptology on information in specified states: in-transit, at-rest, mobile information on removable media?
Confidentiality	5.4.3		Use of open-source cryptography (contrary to proprietary)?

Table A.1   ISMS As-Is Discovery Question Set (Continued)

Category	Ref #	X-Ref	Question
Confidentiality	5.4.4		Cryptography of a specified strength and quality?
Confidentiality	5.4.5		Use of approved products? Including the specification to publish cryptographic standards in support of the cryptographic policy?
Confidentiality	5.4.6		Cryptographic key management? Requesting? Generation? Issuance? Distribution? Use? Revocation? Destruction? Escrowing?
Confidentiality	5.4.7		Dealing with compromised keys?
Confidentiality	5.4.8		Consideration of key management within Business Continuity (BC) and Disaster Recovery (DR) planning?
Confidentiality	5.4.9		Use of keys as unique identifiers (e.g., digital signatures)?
Confidentiality	5.4.10		Use of keys as part of log management?
Cryptography	5.5		Does your organization have a policy for the use of cryptography?
Cryptography	5.6		Does this policy require, specify, or otherwise address the following:
Cryptography	5.6.1		Appropriate use of encryption: who, when, where?
Cryptography	5.6.2		The use of appropriate encryption: what, how?
Cryptography	5.6.3		The scope (breadth and depth) for the use of cryptography: Breadth: system types, desktops, servers, backups? Depth: information in-transit, at-rest?
Cryptography	5.6.4		Transport of information technology with cryptographic capability, e.g., among countries with varying laws governing the use of encryption?
Integrity	6		

(continued)

Table A.1   ISMS As-Is Discovery Question Set (Continued)

Category	Ref #	X-Ref	Question
Integrity	6.1		Does your organization have a policy for information integrity? *Note:* Use of the term *information* implies documents, data, databases, etc. in any format, including paper, electronic media, bits on a wire, and bits in the air. Bits on a wire may include data network or telephone network transmitting voice, fax, etc.
Integrity	6.2		Does this policy require, specify, or otherwise address the following:
Integrity	6.2.1		Employee responsibilities with respect to information integrity?
Integrity	6.2.2		Data in transit (i.e., intra-network, inter-network, Internet, other transport [e.g., courier of tapes, CDs])?
Integrity	6.2.3		Transaction integrity (e.g., e-commerce transaction)?
Integrity	6.2.4		Use of encryption to ensure integrity of transmission?
Integrity	6.2.5		Data at rest?
Integrity	6.2.6		Encryption to ensure integrity of data at rest?
Integrity	6.2.7		Physical placement of information or information technology for protected access by authorized persons or entities?
Integrity	6.2.8		Data integrity on publicly accessible systems, initial storage, periodic review (e.g., checking the integrity of information on organization Web site)?
Integrity	6.2.9		Validation of information received from second-party sources?
Availability	7		
Availability	7.1		Does your organization have a policy to ensure the availability of information and information technology? If not an explicit policy for prevention, is the intent of the features below captured in another policy?

Table A.1   ISMS As-Is Discovery Question Set (Continued)

Category	Ref #	X-Ref	Question
Availability	7.2		Does this policy require, specify, or otherwise address the following:
Availability	7.2.1		Equipment maintenance?
Availability	7.2.2		Use of defense in depth to ensure continued operation of business functions?
Availability	7.2.3		Monitoring for degraded service?
Availability	7.2.4		Monitoring for continued service?
Availability	7.2.5		Awareness training for users to detect and notify of unavailable services?
Availability	7.2.6		Distinguish tiers of availability: Loss of access to asset: building is inaccessible, but equipment may continue to operate? Loss of asset: business function continues under degraded performance? Loss of business function asset supports?
Prevent	8		
Prevent	8.1		Does your organization have a policy to prevent compromise of information and information technology? If not an explicit policy for prevention, is the intent of the features below captured in another policy?
Prevent	8.2		Does this policy require, specify, or otherwise address the following:
Prevent	8.2.1		Consideration of information technology mean time between failures (MTBF) prior to purchase?
Prevent	8.2.2		Consideration of and verification of manufacturer's claim of up-time (95, 99, 99.999 percent, etc.)?
Prevent	8.2.3		Servicing of information technology by qualified personnel? *Note:* Qualifications include trained (authorized) and trustworthy (cleared).
Prevent	8.2.4		Use of automated calendaring (reminders) of maintenance tasks?

(continued)

Table A.1   ISMS As-Is Discovery Question Set (Continued)

Category	Ref #	X-Ref	Question
Prevent	8.2.5		Tracking, trending, and reporting on actual performance?
Defense Management	9		
Defend	9.1		Does your organization have a policy to defend information and information technology? If not an explicit policy for defense, is the intent of the features below captured in another policy?
Defend	9.2		Does this policy require, specify, or otherwise address the following:
Defend	9.2.1		Network defense in depth that includes at least: Perimeter defenses (e.g., firewalls)? Demilitarized zones (i.e., buffers between internal organizational network and external networks)? Anti-malware (i.e., anti-virus, anti-spam, anti-spyware)? Content filters? Intrusion detection systems (IDS)?
Defend	9.2.2		Separation of defense responsibilities: Networks? Servers & desktops?
Defend	9.2.3		Wired and wireless networks?
Defend	9.2.4		Specific articulation of security controls for organizational network zones (perimeter, internal, core)?
Defend	9.2.5		Associate defense mechanisms with BC/DR goals (e.g., down-time tolerance, up-time goals, other performance service level agreements [SLAs])?
Defend	9.3		Does your organization have a policy for wireless networks?
Defend	9.4		Does this policy require, specify, or otherwise address the following:
Defend	9.4.1		Controlled connectivity to wired network?
Defend	9.4.2		Use of encryption?

Table A.1 ISMS As-Is Discovery Question Set (Continued)

Category	Ref #	X-Ref	Question
Defend	9.4.3		Restricted data and functions on wireless networks?
Defend	9.4.4		Authorized wireless access points, no rogue access devices?
Monitoring	10		
Monitor	10.1		Does your organization have a policy to monitor information and information technology?
Monitor	10.2		Does this policy require, specify, or otherwise address the following:
Monitor	10.2.1		Intrusion detection?
Monitor	10.2.2		Content scanning outbound information in any format for restricted or hidden data?
Monitor	10.2.3		Personnel activities on organizational assets (i.e., appropriate use or misuse of organizational assets)?
Monitor	10.2.4		Appropriate notifications of personnel monitoring, including employees, contractors, visitors, etc.?
Monitor	10.2.5		Monitoring activity reporting, and use of information to manage employee behavior?
Monitor	10.2.6		Highlight the need to monitor privileged activities: Log-on (entry), e.g., admin, super user, or similar accounts? Transactions? Start/stop applications? Start/stop network services?
Monitor	10.2.7		Highlight the need to monitor anomalous activities: Unscheduled reboots? Connection of unauthorized devices (e.g., USB drives)? User log-on failures (above an expected threshold)? Policy violations?

(continued)

Table A.1   ISMS As-Is Discovery Question Set (Continued)

Category	Ref #	X-Ref	Question
Monitor	10.2.8		Highlight the need to monitor for alerts from security controls: IDS? Anti-malware? Firewall policy violation? External attack signatures? Insider threat signatures? Audit log mining? Physical entry failures (e.g., false PIN, false card swipe, false RFID)?
Monitor	10.2.9		Alert aggregation analysis, e.g., what may appear as minor anomalies in four different areas may together be a serious issue?
Monitor	10.2.10		Link monitoring activity to key: Personnel? Business functions? Systems? Applications? Infrastructure?
Access Management	11		
Access Mgmt	11.1		Does your organization have a policy for access management?
Access Mgmt	11.2		Does this policy require, specify, or otherwise address the following:
Confidentiality	11.2.1		Assign access authorization responsibility (e.g., application owner)?
Access Mgmt	11.2.2		Enumerate assets and associated security controls?
Access Mgmt	11.2.3		Asset tags or other unique identification?
Access Mgmt	11.3		Does your organization have a policy for identity management?
Access Mgmt	11.4		Does this policy require, specify, or otherwise address the following:
Access Mgmt	11.4.1		Unique identities for users?
Access Mgmt	11.4.2		The need for standards and procedures for identity request, adjudication, grant, revoke?

Table A.1   ISMS As-Is Discovery Question Set (Continued)

Category	Ref #	X-Ref	Question
Access Mgmt	11.4.3		Prohibition against sharing identity with another person such that he or she uses the identity for access?
Access Mgmt	11.5		Does your organization have a policy for privilege management?
Access Mgmt	11.6		Does this policy require, specify, or otherwise address the following:
Access Mgmt	11.6.1		The need for standards and procedures for privilege request, adjudication, grant, revoke?
Access Mgmt	11.6.2		Separation of identity (identification) and privilege (authorization)?
Access Mgmt	11.6.3		Application of privilege assessment for system access?
Access Mgmt	11.6.4		Application of privilege assessment for information access?
Access Mgmt	11.6.5		Who may grant privileges?
Access Mgmt	11.6.6		Formal application for privileges?
Access Mgmt	11.6.7		Formal registration?
Access Mgmt	11.6.8		Formal notification of privilege revocation?
Access Mgmt	11.6.9		Logging, tracking, and reporting privilege assignments and revocation?
Access Mgmt	11.6.10		Define trigger events for privilege review: New hire? Leave a position? Start a new position or take on new responsibilities? Separation from the organization? No activity (no exercise of privilege)?
Access Mgmt	11.7		Does your organization have a policy for external access to organizational assets?
Access Mgmt	11.8		Does this policy require, specify, or otherwise address the following:
Access Mgmt	11.8.1		Discovery, evaluation, and approval of what organizational assets will be accessed and consumed by the second party?

(continued)

Table A.1   ISMS As-Is Discovery Question Set (Continued)

Category	Ref #	X-Ref	Question
Access Mgmt	11.8.2		Access method?
Access Mgmt	11.8.3		Scope of access: Physical? Cyber? Entry points? Systems? Information?
Access Mgmt	11.8.4		Network connectivity?
Access Mgmt	11.8.5		Required security controls?
Access Mgmt	11.8.6		Non-disclosure agreements?
Access Mgmt	11.8.7		Information custodian responsibilities (e.g., protection from third-party access)?
Access Mgmt	11.8.8		How to identify and authenticate an entity (e.g., service, system, application) or person?
Access Mgmt	11.8.9		How to present claim of privilege and authorize an entity (e.g., service, system, application) or person?
Access Mgmt	11.9		Does your organization have a policy for digital signatures?
Access Mgmt	11.10		Does this policy require, specify, or otherwise address the following:
Access Mgmt	11.10.1		Use of digital signatures for activity requiring non-repudiation, e.g., transaction logs in support of audits and digital forensics?
Access Mgmt	11.11		Does your organization have a policy for logging accesses?
Access Mgmt	11.12		Does this policy require, specify, or otherwise address the following:
Access Mgmt	11.12.1		Physical and cyber use or attempted use of identity and privilege credentials?
Access Mgmt	11.12.2		Review of logs for anomalous activity?
Access Mgmt	11.12.3		Reporting and investigation of anomalies?
Access Mgmt	11.13		Does your organization have a policy for access management of automated services (e.g., service-oriented architecture [SOA])?

Table A.1   ISMS As-Is Discovery Question Set (Continued)

Category	Ref #	X-Ref	Question
Access Mgmt	11.14		Does this policy require, specify, or otherwise address the following:
Access Mgmt	11.14.1		Definition of a service, service environment/infrastructure?
Access Mgmt	11.14.2		Security of service environment and infrastructure?
Access Mgmt	11.14.3		Service security guidelines: Service development? Introduction of service to organizational environment? Access privileges of service? Trust inheritances from service-to-service invocations?
People Management	12		
People Mgmt	12.1		Does your organization have a policy that distinguishes the need for security professionals?
People Mgmt	12.2		Does this policy require, specify, or otherwise address the following:
People Mgmt	12.2.1		Security roles and responsibilities of all personnel, especially security professionals?
People Mgmt	12.2.2		Distinguish security professional roles and responsibilities from those of other employees?
People Mgmt	12.2.3		For positions involving the planning, development, or execution of safeguarding organizational assets and operational viability: Recruit and hire qualified personnel? Preference to degreed and certified security professionals? Orientation program that includes details of the organizational security posture (policy, standards, procedures, practices)? Ongoing training and education in relevant areas? Encourage or sponsor memberships in professional security societies?

(continued)

Table A.1   ISMS As-Is Discovery Question Set (Continued)

Category	Ref #	X-Ref	Question
People Mgmt	12.3		Does your organization have a policy that addresses employee management with respect to security of information and information technology?
People Mgmt	12.4		Does this policy require or specify the following:
People Mgmt	12.4.1		Pre-hire activities: Background checks (criminal, financial, references)? Credential validation (degrees, certifications, training, experience)?
People Mgmt	12.4.2		Orientation activities: New hires or new to position? Roles and responsibilities?
People Mgmt	12.4.3		Refresher activities: Annual reminders? Ongoing awareness programs?
People Mgmt	12.4.4		Separation activities: Voluntary separation versus involuntary separation? Identity and privilege credential revocation and reclamation? Account revocation? Backup of data on personally managed information technology (e.g., laptops, PCs, USBs)? Contingency plans for unfriendly separations, i.e., expedited identity revocation and physical removal?
People Mgmt	12.4.5		Security responsibilities as part of employment agreement: Confidentiality? Non-disclosure? Non-solicitation?
People Mgmt	12.4.6		Standards, procedures, and checklists in support of all the above?
People Mgmt	12.5		Does your organization have a policy for management responsibilities with regard to security awareness, implementation, and enforcement?

Table A.1 ISMS As-Is Discovery Question Set (Continued)

Category	Ref #	X-Ref	Question
People Mgmt	12.6		Does this policy require or specify the following:
People Mgmt	12.6.1		Management role and responsibility in achieving and maintaining a secure work environment to safeguard the well-being of employees and to protect organizational interests?
People Mgmt	12.6.2		Duty to attain and maintain a high level of awareness of organizational security policy?
People Mgmt	12.6.3		Provide incentives for management's active involvement?
People Mgmt	12.7		Does your organization have a security information dissemination policy?
People Mgmt	12.8		Does this policy require or specify the following:
People Mgmt	12.8.1		Distinction among awareness, training, and education?
People Mgmt	12.8.2		Awareness program for new hires? New promotions?
People Mgmt	12.8.3		Training program for user (e.g., user procedures)?
People Mgmt	12.8.4		Professional memberships and participation in professional activities for general awareness and vicarious learning from events and incidents outside the organization?
People Mgmt	12.9		Does your organization have a sanction policy for non-compliance with organizational policies?
People Mgmt	12.10		Does this policy require, specify, or otherwise address the following:
People Mgmt	12.10.1		Disciplinary actions for first-time offense, repeat offenses?
People Mgmt	12.10.2		Clearly enumerate management responsibilities?
People Mgmt	12.10.3		Investigatory procedures?
People Mgmt	12.10.4		Consideration of circumstances and level of intent?

(continued)

Table A.1   ISMS As-Is Discovery Question Set (Continued)

Category	Ref #	X-Ref	Question
People Mgmt	12.10.5		Consideration of organizational impact?
Privacy Management	13		
Privacy Mgmt	13.1		Does your organization have a privacy management policy?
Privacy Mgmt	13.2		Does this policy require, specify, or otherwise address the following:
Privacy Mgmt	13.2.1		Inclusion of privacy requirements in the compliance management program?
Privacy Mgmt	13.2.2		Protection of information and information technology in keeping with privacy requirements?
Privacy Mgmt	13.2.3		Inclusion of privacy provisions in partner, vendor, customer, contractor, and other second-party dealings?
Privacy Mgmt	13.2.4		Identify a single point (or office) of responsibility for privacy issues, including: Identification of compliance requirements? Representation of these requirements in organizational policy, standards, and procedures? Dissemination of privacy guidance? Monitoring and responding to privacy-related issues?
Asset Management	14		
Asset Mgmt	14.1		Does your organization have a policy for asset management?
Asset Mgmt	14.2		Does this policy require, specify, or otherwise address the following:
Asset Mgmt	14.2.1		Identification and enumeration of all organizational assets?
Asset Mgmt	14.2.2		Asset tracking?
Asset Mgmt	14.2.3		Assigning of unique identifier for each asset (e.g., asset tag)?

Table A.1 ISMS As-Is Discovery Question Set (Continued)

Category	Ref #	X-Ref	Question
Asset Mgmt	14.2.4		Relative asset importance in context of: Key—critical to core function of the organization? Support—supports non-critical functions (overhead)?
Asset Mgmt	14.2.5		Asset classification guidance?
Asset Mgmt	14.2.6		Asset ownership (responsibility for establishing asset classification and protection)?
Asset Mgmt	14.2.7		Custodianship (responsibility for care)?
Asset Mgmt	14.2.8		Recording of each unique identifier and associating asset attributes in a database? *Note:* Asset attributes may include type (e.g., PC, router), operating system (OS), version, standard configuration, current configuration, patch levels, etc.
Asset Mgmt	14.3		Does your organization have a policy for the processing of organizational information on personally owned devices?
Asset Mgmt	14.4		Does this policy require, specify, or otherwise address the following:
Asset Mgmt	14.4.1		Permissible information to transfer to personally owned devices?
Asset Mgmt	14.4.2		Security controls for use of information?
Asset Mgmt	14.4.3		Security controls for transfer of information back to the organization (e.g., virus scan)?
Asset Mgmt	14.4.4		Destruction of information?
Asset Mgmt	14.5		Does your organization have a policy for the removal of information and information technology from organizational premises?
Asset Mgmt	14.6		Does this policy require, specify, or otherwise address the following:
Asset Mgmt	14.6.1		What may be removed?

(continued)

Table A.1   ISMS As-Is Discovery Question Set (Continued)

Category	Ref #	X-Ref	Question
Asset Mgmt	14.6.2		Explicit statement to obtain authorization prior to removing information or information technology?
Asset Mgmt	14.6.3		How to remove: Obtain authorization? Fill out appropriate paperwork? Attend security training for managing assets off site? Log-out/log-in process?
Asset Mgmt	14.6.4		Storage of assets off site: traveling, at home, second-party business site?
BC/DR	15		
BC/DR	15.1		Does your organization have a policy for business continuity (BC) and disaster recovery (DR)?
BC/DR	15.2		Does this policy require, specify, or otherwise address the following:
BC/DR	15.2.1		Threat assessment to identify potential threats and likely threats?
BC/DR	15.2.2		Business impact assessment (BIA) to evaluate organizational impact of threat realization?
BC/DR	15.2.3		Vulnerability assessment to evaluate organizational asset vulnerabilities?
BC/DR	15.2.4		Risk assessment to evaluate organizational posture with respect to being aware of, understanding, and addressing risks to the organization in light of the threat assessment, vulnerability assessment, and BIA?
BC/DR	15.2.5		Clear articulation of how to address the risk in terms of: Risk acceptance? Risk transfer/share (e.g., outsource, insurance)? Risk mitigation (i.e., security controls)?

Table A.1   ISMS As-Is Discovery Question Set (Continued)

Category	Ref #	X-Ref	Question
BC/DR	15.2.6		Identification of: Key business functions? Key personnel fulfilling key business functions? Key technology used by key personnel in fulfilling key business functions? Distinguishing the above from support or overhead functions, personnel, and technology? Giving priority in BC/DR to key areas?
BC/DR	15.2.7		Express the need for BC/DR metrics, including at least: Downtime tolerance? Uptime objective? Identification of problem (time from event occurrence to event awareness)? Notification (time from awareness to escalating problem to appropriate personnel)? Restoration (time from event awareness to restoration of service)? Problem identification (time from event awareness to identifying root problem)? Problem resolution (time from identifying root problem to implementing solution to minimizing or eliminating recurrence)?
BC/DR	15.2.8		Use the above findings as drivers behind the specifics for BC/DR?
BC/DR	15.2.9		Incorporate the principle of people safety first?
BC/DR	15.2.10		Physical architecture to accommodate threat space (e.g., data center on higher floor in flood plain areas)?
BC/DR	15.2.11		Backup and recovery: Formal plan? Standards: media, frequency? Procedures: full backup, incremental backup, transaction backup? Backup validation? Storage: on site, off site?

(continued)

Table A.1   ISMS As-Is Discovery Question Set (Continued)

Category	Ref #	X-Ref	Question
BC/DR	15.2.12		Testing of backups?
BC/DR	15.2.13		Testing of restoration, including: Building of restoration systems? Installing necessary software, applications, and data? Establishing appropriate voice and data communications?
BC/DR	15.2.14		Backup site plans: Hot site? Warm site? Cold site?
BC/DR	15.2.15		Table top exercises to increase awareness of personnel roles and responsibilities in BC/DR scenarios?
BC/DR	15.2.16		Vendor agreements to expedite replacement of key technology?
BC/DR	15.2.17		Communication plan: Intra-organization notification of disaster? Backup communications for key personnel? Account for all personnel on site or in vicinity of disater?
BC/DR	15.2.18		Clear description of security expectations during a BC/DR situation; i.e., security principles, policies, and practices are still in effect during BC/DR?
Operations Management	16		
Operations Mgmt	16.1		Does your organization have a policy for *secure operations management* and *security operations management*?
Operations Mgmt	16.2		Does this policy require, specify, or otherwise address the following:
Operations Mgmt	16.2.1		Operations management services that include: Network operations? Security operations? System operations?

Table A.1   ISMS As-Is Discovery Question Set (Continued)

Category	Ref #	X-Ref	Question
Operations Mgmt	16.2.2		Centralized operations or centralized reporting of operations for an aggregate view of operational activity and effectiveness?
Operations Mgmt	16.2.3		Aggregate collection and review of audit log data?
Operations Mgmt	16.2.4		Standardizing [security] operational features to ensure consistent enterprise operations: Policy? Standards? Procedure? Clock times (for audit log review and valid chronologies for digital forensics)?
ELCM	17		Enterprise Lifecycle Management (ELCM)
ELCM	17.1		Does your organization have a policy for consideration of security in ELCM?
ELCM	17.2		Does this policy require, specify, or otherwise address the following:
ELCM	17.2.1		Definition of solution to ensure understanding of scope; e.g., *solution* includes software, system, technology, or service?
ELCM	17.2.2		A standard for security expectations, e.g., ISO 27001?
ELCM	17.2.3		Security controls as part of the solution selection criteria?
ELCM	17.2.4		Security aspects of: Solution acquisition? Solution integration? Check lists for expected characteristics (security, performance, monitoring, recovery), test procedures, sign-off, accountability?
ELCM	17.2.5		Obtaining solutions from authorized sources?

(continued)

Table A.1   ISMS As-Is Discovery Question Set (Continued)

Category	Ref #	X-Ref	Question
ELCM	17.2.6		Prohibiting the installation of solutions from unauthorized sources, with specific prohibitions against: Downloading and installing unauthorized software, files, documents, etc.?
ELCM	17.2.7		Contracts with vendors, service providers, outsourcers, or other solution providers include: Security features? Security metrics? Security SLAs?
Media Management	18		
Media Mgmt	18.1		Does your organization have a policy for secure media management?
Media Mgmt	18.2		Does this policy require, specify, or otherwise address the following:
Media Mgmt	18.2.1		Reusable media (secure removal of data), including at least: Hard drives? Rewritable CDs?
Media Mgmt	18.2.2		Removable media, including at least: USBs, CDs, DVDs, tapes, external hard drives, cell phones, cameras, audio recording devices, etc.? Laptops—organizationally owned? Laptops—personally owned? Clear specification of whether use of these devices is permissible and when, where, how, and by whom; e.g., organizational employees may be OK, but not contractors?
Media Mgmt	18.2.3		Appropriate destruction of data for: Media reuse within the organization? Media reuse outside the organization, e.g., selling of old equipment?
Media Mgmt	18.2.4		Appropriate destruction of media prior to discarding media, including: Electronic storage (hard drives, CDs, DVDs, digital cameras, etc.)? Paper documents?

Table A.1 ISMS As-Is Discovery Question Set (Continued)

Category	Ref #	X-Ref	Question
Media Mgmt	18.2.5		Secure disposal of media?
Media Mgmt	18.2.6		Media handling, storage, and refresh (to avoid loss of data due to media deterioration) according to manufacturers' guidance?
Media Mgmt	18.2.7		Media labeling: Contents? Classification? Creation date? Expiration date?
Media Mgmt	18.2.8		Creating and maintaining logs of media treatments according to policy?
Mobile Code	19		
Mobile Code	19.1		Does your organization have a policy for the use of mobile code (transfer of code to local machine for execution, e.g., executable scripts during Web browsing)?
Mobile Code	19.2		Does this policy require, specify, or otherwise address the following:
Mobile Code	19.2.1		Permissibility of allowing mobile code use on organizational assets?
Mobile Code	19.2.2		The need for standards and procedures to configure devices to handle mobile code according to policy?
Mobile Code	19.2.3		Providing a list of explicitly permissible mobile code?
Mobile Code	19.2.4		Providing a list of non-permissible mobile code?
Mobile Computing	20		
Mobile Computing	20.1		Does your organization have a policy for mobile computing (use of information technology not physically connected to the organization to access organizational information)?
Mobile Computing	20.2		Does this policy require, specify, or otherwise address the following:

(continued)

Table A.1 ISMS As-Is Discovery Question Set (Continued)

Category	Ref #	X-Ref	Question
Mobile Computing	20.2.1		Enumeration of risks associated with mobile computing?
Mobile Computing	20.2.2		Security measures to mitigate the risks, including: Appropriate use? System configuration? Application configuration? Security controls? Guidance on use of security controls?
Mobile Computing	20.2.3		Security controls that include at least: Encryption, e.g., for hard drives, for network communications, for file transmissions, e-mail? Backups? Anti-malware (virus, spam, spyware, etc.)? Physical security of mobile devices?
Mobile Computing	20.2.4		Secure use of mobile computing technology: Physical proximity to potential observance, surveillance, eavesdropping?
Mobile Computing	20.2.5		Secure connectivity of mobile computing technology to organizational networks and information assets?
Mobile Computing	20.2.6		Guidance for the transport of mobile devices: Site to site? Site to home? Domestic travel? International travel?
Communications Management	21		Secure communication with vendors, partners, contractors, customers, and other second parties
Comms Mgmt	21.1		Does your organization have a policy for communications management?
Comms Mgmt	21.2		Does this policy require, specify, or otherwise address the following:

Table A.1 ISMS As-Is Discovery Question Set (Continued)

Category	Ref #	X-Ref	Question
Comms Mgmt	21.2.1		Information exchange policy, standards, and procedures: Network exchange? Other cyber-based exchange (e.g., USB, CD, DVD)? Paper exchange? Use of voice equipment (speaker phones, mobile phones, voice mail, answering machines)? Faxes? Allowable transmissions, procedures for monitored receipt of sensitive data, clearing memory or cache?
Comms Mgmt	21.2.2		Information ownership: Owner identification? Owner responsibilities (e.g., establishing information classification and access)?
Comms Mgmt	21.2.3		Information custodian responsibilities: Appropriate use? Security responsibilities? Handling and storage?
Comms Mgmt	21.2.4		Labeling standards, including form, content, and display?
Comms Mgmt	21.2.5		Avoiding the dissemination of malware, i.e., malware scanning prior to transmission?
Comms Mgmt	21.2.6		Avoiding the dissemination of unauthorized material, i.e., content filtering prior to transmission?
Comms Mgmt	21.2.7		Use of cryptography in communications: Secure transmission? Digital signatures? Traceability? Non-repudiation?
Comms Mgmt	21.2.8		Incorporate communications management in awareness, education, and training: New employee/new promotion orientation? Annual refresher? Periodic reminders?

(continued)

Table A.1 ISMS As-Is Discovery Question Set (Continued)

Category	Ref #	X-Ref	Question
Comms Mgmt	21.2.9		When to request automated receipts or manually verify receipt of communication transmission?
Comms Mgmt	21.2.10		Packaging requirements for physical communications to ensure privacy and protection, including: Envelopes? Boxes? Pouches? CD/DVD holders?
Comms Mgmt	21.2.11		Policy to use and an enumeration of reliable couriers?
Appropriate Use	22		
Appropriate Use	22.1		Does your organization have a policy for appropriate use of information and information technology?
Appropriate Use	22.2		Does this policy require, specify, or otherwise address the following:
Appropriate Use	22.2.1		Description of authorized use and appropriate use?
Appropriate Use	22.2.2		Examples of inappropriate use: Productivity reduction, time wasters (e.g., Internet sports sites)? Potential legal liability (e.g., Internet porn sites)?
Appropriate Use	22.2.3		Articulate organizational rights and duties of the organization to monitor for inappropriate use: Executive responsibilities to stakeholders and legislative mandates? Management guidance for consistent application of monitoring? Employee guidance for reporting inappropriate use?
Appropriate Use	22.2.4		Reference an appropriate sanction policy of inappropriate use?
Appropriate Use	22.2.5		Addition of appropriate use guidance to awareness, training, and education program?
Appropriate Use	22.2.6		Implementation of warnings during log-on or use of information technology?

Table A.1   ISMS As-Is Discovery Question Set (Continued)

Category	Ref #	X-Ref	Question
Audit Management	23		
Audit Log Mgmt	23.1		Does your organization have a policy for audit log management?
Audit Log Mgmt	23.2		Does this policy require, specify, or otherwise address the following:
Audit Log Mgmt	23.2.1		Activities to log?
Audit Log Mgmt	23.2.2		Details to include in log: Identification of activity initiator (person, service, device)? Identification of activity performer (person, service, device)? Date/time? Event (e.g., log-on, shutdown, start-up)? Activity summary (e.g., activity code)? Failures (e.g., wrong user ID/password)? Error code (if applicable)?
Audit Log Mgmt	23.2.3		Log review?
Audit Log Mgmt	23.2.4		Reporting?
Audit Log Mgmt	23.2.5		Archiving, including how, where, and duration?
External Audit	23.3		Does your organization have a policy for external audits?
External Audit	23.4		Does this policy require, specify, or otherwise address the following:
External Audit	23.4.1		Independent review of: Compliance levels with applicable legislation, regulation, and standards regarding security controls and other risk management perspectives? Policy? Standards? Procedures? Practice?
External Audit	23.4.2		Method to capture an objective measurement of organizational security posture, e.g., security metrics?
External Audit	23.4.3		When to engage independent audits, e.g., semi-annually, annually?

(continued)

Table A.1   ISMS As-Is Discovery Question Set (Continued)

Category	Ref #	X-Ref	Question
External Audit	23.4.4		Reporting of findings to appropriate organizational levels?
External Audit	23.4.5		Method to address these findings, i.e., addressing organizational risk in an appropriate manner, including risk acceptance, transfer, sharing, and remediation?
Data Management	24		
Data Mgmt	24.1		Does your organization have a policy for data management?
Data Mgmt	24.2		Does this policy require, specify, or otherwise address the following:
Data Mgmt	24.2.1		Validation of data input into organizational databases and applications?
Data Mgmt	24.2.2		Data access management?
Data Mgmt	24.2.3		Data distribution guidelines?
Data Mgmt	24.2.4		Data distribution methods (data in transit)?
Data Mgmt	24.2.5		Data distribution restrictions: Intra-organization (among departments, personnel)? Inter-organization (among partners, vendors, customers, etc.)?
Data Mgmt	24.2.6		Data storage methods and guidelines (data at rest): PCs and workstations? Servers? Backup media? Archive media?
Data Mgmt	24.2.7		Data in use, including: Storage in RAM for use by applications or inter-process communications? Caching?
Data Mgmt	24.2.8		Appropriate encryption methods?
Data Mgmt	24.2.9		Data management in compliance with relevant legislation and regulation: Storage methods? Privacy protection? Archive duration?

Table A.1   ISMS As-Is Discovery Question Set (Continued)

Category	Ref #	X-Ref	Question
Data Mgmt	24.2.10		Data removal from the organization; use off-site?
Data Mgmt	24.2.11		Organizational data on personally owned information technology, including, but not limited to, PCs, cell phones, PDAs, USB storage devices, etc.?
Incident Management	25		
Incident Mgmt	25.1		Does your organization have a policy for incident management?
Incident Mgmt	25.2		Does this policy require, specify, or otherwise address the following:
Incident Mgmt	25.2.1		Establishment of a computer security incident response team (CSIRT) or similar function?
Incident Mgmt	25.2.2		The need for CSIRT procedures to accommodate appropriate actions upon notification of an incident?
Incident Mgmt	25.2.3		A formal incident monitoring, detection, and notification capability consisting of: Monitoring—automated and personnel? Notification—help desk or other formal group? Prioritization—guidelines to prioritize routine and exceptional events? Escalation—subject matter experts (SMEs) to process exceptions? Identification—finding the problem? Isolation—isolating the problem? Treatment—treating the problem? Restoration—restoring normal operations? Organizational feedback—providing feedback to minimize likelihood and effects of recurrence?
Incident Mgmt	25.2.4		Periodic and ad hoc reporting of incidents to management?

(continued)

Table A.1   ISMS As-Is Discovery Question Set (Continued)

Category	Ref #	X-Ref	Question
Incident Mgmt	25.3		Does your organization have a policy for employee and second-party responsibilities with regard to security incidents?
Incident Mgmt	25.4		Does this policy require, specify, or otherwise address the following:
Incident Mgmt	25.4.1		Inclusion of incident management in awareness and training programs?
Incident Mgmt	25.4.2		Responsibilities of employees and other second parties working in organization facilities, on organizational information technology, or in use of or observing organizational information?
Incident Mgmt	25.4.3		Duty for employees or second parties (relevant personnel) to report suspect events, anomalies, and vulnerabilities?
Incident Mgmt	25.4.4		Restrict relevant personnel from taking matters into their own hands but to notify appropriate authorities within the organization?
Configuration Management	26		
Config Mgmt	26.1		Does your organization have a policy for configuration management?
Config Mgmt	26.2		Does this policy require, specify, or otherwise address the following:
Config Mgmt	26.2.1		Standard system images, including OS installation, application installation, patch levels, including: PCs, laptops? Servers? Infrastructure (e.g., routers)? Security mechanisms (e.g., firewalls)?
Config Mgmt	26.2.2		Changes made to standard images, including: Hardware? Software? Firmware?
Config Mgmt	26.2.3		Standard configurations: Parameters governing operations, especially those governing secure operations?

Table A.1   ISMS As-Is Discovery Question Set (Continued)

Category	Ref #	X-Ref	Question
Config Mgmt	26.2.4		User ability to modify standard image and configuration parameters?
Config Mgmt	26.2.5		Procedures for authorized system administrators to perform updates; formal change control procedures?
Config Mgmt	26.2.6		Testing procedures for new configurations?
Config Mgmt	26.2.7		Test data for new configuration, new software applications?
Config Mgmt	26.2.8		Security controls and procedures to ensure the proper handling of test data: Dissemination? Use? Storage? Discarding?
Config Mgmt	26.2.9		Distinguish among development, test, and production environments?
Config Mgmt	26.2.10		Need to maintain controls in moving data and software among these environments?
Config Mgmt	26.2.11		Rollback or recovery procedures if problems are encountered as a result of movement among environments (especially any modifications to the production environment)?
Config Mgmt	26.2.12		Project and monitor capacity requirements for: Network traffic (bandwidth) Server capacity (e.g., data storage, log storage) Backup capacity Electric Heating and air conditioning (HVAC) Voice lines to avoid denial of service due to exceeding existing capacity?
Config Mgmt	26.2.13		Monitor for usage trends from a capacity perspective, e.g., organization adopting video streaming as a business tool?

(continued)

Table A.1 ISMS As-Is Discovery Question Set (Continued)

Category	Ref #	X-Ref	Question
Config Mgmt	26.2.14		Enumerate performance parameters and monitor them for effective performance?
Config Mgmt	26.2.15		Monitor for degraded performance as warnings of anomalous activity or early warnings of imminent failure?
Vulnerability Management	27		Vulnerability Management includes Patch Management
Vuln Mgmt	27.1		Does your organization have a policy for vulnerability management?
Vuln Mgmt	27.2		Does this policy require, specify, or otherwise address the following:
Vuln Mgmt	27.2.1		Roles and responsibilities for vulnerability management?
Vuln Mgmt	27.2.2		Vulnerability assessment to identify potential vulnerability points: Physical? Hardware? Software OS? Applications? Etc.?
Vuln Mgmt	27.2.3		Monitoring of vulnerabilities?
Vuln Mgmt	27.3		Does your organization have a policy for patch management?
Vuln Mgmt	27.4		Does this policy require, specify, or otherwise address the following:
Vuln Mgmt	27.4.1		Enumerate all relevant devices and aspects of those devices: PCs, laptops, servers, technical infrastructure (e.g., routers), security infrastructure (e.g., firewalls)? OS patches, application patches?
Vuln Mgmt	27.4.2		Monitor for industry news of new vulnerabilities?
Vuln Mgmt	27.4.3		Monitor for vendor patch releases?
Vuln Mgmt	27.4.4		Contingency planning for unavailable patches, e.g., modifications to turn off vulnerable feature?

Table A.1   ISMS As-Is Discovery Question Set (Continued)

Category	Ref #	X-Ref	Question
Vuln Mgmt	27.4.5		Automated notification of available patches?
Vuln Mgmt	27.4.6		Automated service to push or prompt for user updates?
Work Area Management	28		
Work Area Mgmt	28.1		Does your organization have a policy for work area management?
Work Area Mgmt	28.2		Does this policy require, specify, or otherwise address security control with regard to the following:
Work Area Mgmt	28.2.1		Clear desk policy?
Work Area Mgmt	28.2.2		Use of screen savers?
Work Area Mgmt	28.2.3		Secure storage (lock and key) for sensitive information?
Work Area Mgmt	28.2.4		Correspondence points: Mail room? Fax machines?
Work Area Mgmt	28.2.5		Printing: Sensitive documents? Attended versus unattended?
Work Area Mgmt	28.2.6		Copying: Sensitive documents? Attended versus unattended?
Workstation Management	29		
Workstation Mgmt	29.1		Does your organization have a policy for workstation management?
Workstation Mgmt	29.2		Does this policy require, specify, or otherwise address the following:
Workstation Mgmt	29.2.1		Workstation classifications?
Workstation Mgmt	29.2.2		Physical access to workstations: Restrict to authorized personnel only?
Workstation Mgmt	29.2.3		Physical access to workstation attributes, e.g., on/off button, USB and other ports, CD drive?

(continued)

Table A.1   ISMS As-Is Discovery Question Set (Continued)

Category	Ref #	X-Ref	Question
Workstation Mgmt	29.2.4		Non-installation or removal of attributes not necessary to operation, e.g., floppy disk drive?
Workstation Mgmt	29.2.5		Grouping of workstations for: Common physical protection? Placement on a separate network segment with security controls between that segment and remainder of the enterprise network?
Workstation Mgmt	29.2.6		Security controls between workstations and remainder of enterprise network: Firewalls? IDS with focus on group of critical workstations or servers? Content filtering on inbound/outbound traffic? Etc.?
Workstation Mgmt	29.2.7		Distinguish workstation with wireless network access?
Workstation Mgmt	29.2.8		Enumerate specific safeguards with respect to wireless workstations?
SQA Management	30		Solution Quality Assurance (SQA) Management
SQA Mgmt	30.1		Does your organization have a policy for SQA management or a policy of similar intent?
SQA Mgmt	30.2		Does this policy require, specify, or otherwise address the following:
SQA Mgmt	30.2.1		Security as part of a solution (software, service, other technology): Development process? Testing prior to implementation? Implementation? Integration into existing environment? Including formal check lists for security control expectations, test procedures, acceptance sign-off, and accountability?
SQA Mgmt	30.2.2		Specifically requires integration testing to ensure no adverse effects on existing environment (operating system, other applications, services, business functions)?

Table A.1 ISMS As-Is Discovery Question Set (Continued)

Category	Ref #	X-Ref	Question
SQA Mgmt	30.2.3		Existence and testing for features contributing to BC/DR: Backup? Shutdown? Restart? Monitoring for performance degradation or anomalous behavior?
SQA Mgmt	30.2.4		Training and documentation for: Administrators? Network operations? Security operations? Users?

SQA Mgmt	30.2.5		Restrict access to:
			Development environment
			  Source code?
			Testing environment
			  Test data?
			Production environment
			  Servers, applications, and data?

SQA Mgmt	30.2.6		Source code reviews that include: Treatment of security flaws as software bugs? Introduction of backdoors? Introduction of malicious code?
Physical Security	31		
Physical Security	31.1		Does your organization have a physical security policy?
Physical Security	31.2		Does this policy require, specify, or otherwise address the following:
Physical Security	31.2.1		Draw distinctions (as appropriate) among: Campus security? Building security? Floor security? Room security (including wiring or data closets)? Asset security?
Physical Security	31.2.2		Specify levels of physical security appropriate to protect the classification of information and information technology?

(continued)

Table A.1   ISMS As-Is Discovery Question Set (Continued)

Category	Ref #	X-Ref	Question
Physical Security	31.2.3		Specify use-appropriate identity and privilege credentials?
Physical Security	31.2.4		Entry requests; request adjudication; decision notification; privilege review; privilege revocation?
Physical Security	31.2.5		Physical barriers: fences, gates, walls, exterior doors, windows, interior doors?
Physical Security	31.2.6		Physical environment monitors for: Intruders? Fire? Flood? Temperature (i.e., loss of HVAC)?
Physical Security	31.2.7		Architecture and construction specifications for physical barriers and related safeguards: Placement Vehicle barriers (BFRs), pedestrian management? Strength? Type: bars, locks, biometric, card reader, pin entry, combination lock?
Physical Security	31.2.8		Guards, lighting, video monitoring, motion sensors (or other presence sensors)?
Physical Security	31.2.9		Log entry and exit?
Physical Security	31.2.10		Label interior doors so as to not draw attention to sensitive areas (e.g., Room 3A032 versus Data Center)?

Appendix B: Sample Statement of Applicability

Table B.1 provides an outline for the statement of applicability (SoA) as well as some sample entries for an organization called ABC Inc. Note that some entries are intentionally left blank.

Table B.1 Statement of Applicability Template

SoA Ref	Category/Sub-Category/Element	Statement of Applicability	Control Summary
	Security Policy		
	Information and Information Technology Security Policy		
	Documentation	Applicable to ABC Inc.	The organization will provide a general security policy, an ISMS policy, and policies that address each applicable security control in this framework.
	Dissemination	Applicable to ABC Inc.	The organization recognizes the need to provide periodic review of security policies and will do so on a periodic basis not more than 12 months from the previous review.

(continued)

Table B.1 Statement of Applicability Template (continued)

SoA Ref	Category/Sub-Category/Element	Statement of Applicability	Control Summary
	Policy review	Applicable to ABC Inc.	
Security Management Plan			
	Intra-Organization Management		
	Executive and management backing	Applicable to ABC Inc.	ABC Inc. will create a security governance board consisting of cross-functional representation from the various business units. The governance board will consist of senior-level management and executives. Additionally, there will a security working group (SWG) at the security management level also consisting of cross-functional representation... etc.
	Information security consistency	Applicable to ABC Inc.	Etc.
	Security roles and responsibilities	Applicable to ABC Inc.	
	Authentication and authorization	Applicable to ABC Inc.	
	Confidentiality agreements	Applicable to ABC Inc.	
	External authority relationships	Applicable to ABC Inc.	
	Professional organizations	Applicable to ABC Inc.	
	Independent assessments and audits	Applicable to ABC Inc.	
Second-Party Management			
	Risk management	Applicable to ABC Inc.	

Table B.1 Statement of Applicability Template (continued)

SoA Ref	Category/Sub-Category/Element	Statement of Applicability	Control Summary
	Addressing security when dealing with customers	Applicable to ABC Inc.	
	Business agreements	Applicable to ABC Inc.	
Asset Management			
	Responsibility and Accountability for Assets		
	Inventory	Applicable to ABC Inc.	ABC Inc. will create and maintain an inventory of assets, especially those assets that house or process information… etc.
	Ownership	Applicable to ABC Inc.	
	Appropriate use	Applicable to ABC Inc.	
	Information and information technology classification		
	Classifications	Applicable to ABC Inc.	
	Labeling and handling	Applicable to ABC Inc.	
Personnel Security			
	Pre-Hire		
	Security-related roles and responsibilities	Applicable to ABC Inc.	The SWG will provide policy and guidelines to HR.
	Background checks	Applicable to ABC Inc.	The SWG will provide policy and guidelines to HR.
	Agreements	Applicable to ABC Inc.	The SWG will provide policy and guidelines to HR.
	Tenure		

(continued)

Table B.1 Statement of Applicability Template (continued)

SoA Ref	Category/Sub-Category/Element	Statement of Applicability	Control Summary
	Awareness	Applicable to ABC Inc.	The SWG will provide security policy and guidelines to HR; HR will issue an official HR policy and procedures for management.
	Security education, training, and awareness (SETA)	Applicable to ABC Inc.	Ibid.
	Sanctions	Applicable to ABC Inc.	Ibid.
	*Change of Employment Status*		
	Termination	Applicable to ABC Inc.	The SWG will provide security policy and guidelines to HR; HR will issue an official HR policy and procedures for management.
	New position	Applicable to ABC Inc.	Ibid.
	Asset accountability	Applicable to ABC Inc.	Ibid.
	Access management	Applicable to ABC Inc.	Ibid.
	**Physical Security**		
	Physical Proximity		
	Perimeter	Applicable to ABC Inc.	Perimeter controls include to be determined (TBD).
	Entry/exit	Applicable to ABC Inc.	Physical entry controls include TBD. Hallways are monitored via electronic surveillance at each floor entry/exit point.
	Rooms	Applicable to ABC Inc.	Office security includes nondescript room numbering, cipher locks, and key locks as befits the situation.

Table B.1 Statement of Applicability Template (continued)

SoA Ref	Category/Sub-Category/Element	Statement of Applicability	Control Summary
	External threats	Applicable to ABC Inc.	Data center facilities for Site A must be higher than the second story due to its position in a flood plain.
	Sensitive areas	Applicable to ABC Inc.	Access to secure work areas is via cipher lock. All secure work areas require individual alarm systems with log capabilities for activation and deactivation.
	Public areas	Applicable to ABC Inc.	All loading door entrances to the main building are via cipher lock and must be shut at all times. All doors left open for X minutes send notification to the security and require an in-person visit to validate the security status.
Asset Security			
	Asset safeguards	Applicable to ABC Inc.	
	Wiring	Applicable to ABC Inc.	
	Maintenance	Applicable to ABC Inc.	
	Asset reuse	Applicable to ABC Inc.	
	Asset disposal	Applicable to ABC Inc.	
	Off-site use of assets	Applicable to ABC Inc.	
Operations Management			
	Operational Procedures and Responsibilities		
	Operations	Applicable to ABC Inc.	

(continued)

Table B.1 Statement of Applicability Template (continued)

SoA Ref	Category/Sub-Category/Element	Statement of Applicability	Control Summary
	Configuration management	Applicable to ABC Inc.	
	Log management	Applicable to ABC Inc.	
Outsourcing and Managed Services			
	Service delivery	Applicable to ABC Inc.	
	Monitor and audit	Applicable to ABC Inc.	
	Change management	Applicable to ABC Inc.	
Capacity Planning			
	Capacity management	Applicable to ABC Inc.	All system acceptance criteria include a capacity management section that, at the least, addresses the effects on the LAN, WAN, server room physical space, server resource usage in terms of hard drive, RAM, and processor.
Acceptance Management			
	System acceptance	Applicable to ABC Inc.	
Malware and Malware Carriers			
	Malware	Applicable to ABC Inc.	
	Malware carriers	Applicable to ABC Inc.	
Backup Management			
	Backup	Applicable to ABC Inc.	
Network Security Management			
	Data in transit	Applicable to ABC Inc.	
	Network infrastructure	Applicable to ABC Inc.	

Table B.1 Statement of Applicability Template (continued)

SoA Ref	Category/Sub-Category/Element	Statement of Applicability	Control Summary
	Media Management		
	Removable media	Applicable to ABC Inc.	
	Media disposal	Applicable to ABC Inc.	
	Media storage and transport	Applicable to ABC Inc.	
	Communications Management		
	Information transfer	Applicable to ABC Inc.	
	External connectivity	Applicable to ABC Inc.	
	E-Commerce Management		
	Electronic commerce	Applicable to ABC Inc.	
	Transactions	Applicable to ABC Inc.	
	Organizational information and image	Applicable to ABC Inc.	
	Monitoring		
	Audit logs	Applicable to ABC Inc.	
	Information technology activity	Applicable to ABC Inc.	
	Administrator and power user logs	Applicable to ABC Inc.	
	Error logging	Applicable to ABC Inc.	
	Clock synchronization	Applicable to ABC Inc.	
	Access Management		
	Access Control Policy		
	Access Control Policy	Applicable to ABC Inc.	

(continued)

Table B.1 Statement of Applicability Template (continued)

SoA Ref	Category/Sub-Category/Element	Statement of Applicability	Control Summary
		User Access	
	Identity management	Applicable to ABC Inc.	
	Privilege management	Applicable to ABC Inc.	
	Review of privileges	Applicable to ABC Inc.	
	Information access	Applicable to ABC Inc.	
	Segregation	Applicable to ABC Inc.	
	User Responsibilities	Applicable to ABC Inc.	
	Password configuration	Applicable to ABC Inc.	
	Unattended information technology	Applicable to ABC Inc.	
	Work area management	Applicable to ABC Inc.	
		Network Services	
	Entity identification	Applicable to ABC Inc.	
	Network communities	Applicable to ABC Inc.	
	Traffic management	Applicable to ABC Inc.	
		Operating Systems	
	User identification	Applicable to ABC Inc.	
	Identity authentication	Applicable to ABC Inc.	
	User privileges	Applicable to ABC Inc.	
	Privilege authorization	Applicable to ABC Inc.	

Table B.1 Statement of Applicability Template (continued)

SoA Ref	Category/Sub-Category/Element	Statement of Applicability	Control Summary
	Identity validation management	Applicable to ABC Inc.	
	System utilities	Applicable to ABC Inc.	
	Inactive sessions	Applicable to ABC Inc.	
	Connection time restrictions	Applicable to ABC Inc.	
	**Remote Workers**		
	Mobile workers	Applicable to ABC Inc.	
	Teleworkers	Applicable to ABC Inc.	
	**Solution Quality Assurance (SQA)**		
	Information Technology Security		
	Compliance requirements	Applicable to ABC Inc.	
	**Information Accuracy**		
	Input integrity	Applicable to ABC Inc.	
	Internal integrity	Applicable to ABC Inc.	
	Output integrity	Applicable to ABC Inc.	
	**Cryptography**		
	Cryptography policy	Not applicable to ABC Inc.	ABC Inc. chooses not to implement cryptographic controls at this time due to the prohibitive costs of the infrastructure.
	Key management	Not applicable to ABC Inc.	NA
	**File Security**		
	Production applications	Applicable to ABC Inc.	

(continued)

Table B.1 Statement of Applicability Template (continued)

SoA Ref	Category/Sub-Category/Element	Statement of Applicability	Control Summary
	Test data	Applicable to ABC Inc.	
	Source code protection	Applicable to ABC Inc.	
	Development Environment		
	Change control	Applicable to ABC Inc.	
	Operating system (OS) upgrades	Applicable to ABC Inc.	
	Application upgrades	Applicable to ABC Inc.	
	Memory and other leaks	Applicable to ABC Inc.	
	Acquisition	Applicable to ABC Inc.	
	Vulnerability Management		
	Patch management	Applicable to ABC Inc.	
	Incident Management		
	Computer Security Incident Response Teams (CSIRT)		
	CSIRT operations	Applicable to ABC Inc.	
	Detection	Applicable to ABC Inc.	
	Notification	Applicable to ABC Inc.	
	Preemptive	Applicable to ABC Inc.	
	CSIRT Management		
	Roles and responsibilities	Applicable to ABC Inc.	
	Lessons learned	Applicable to ABC Inc.	

Table B.1 Statement of Applicability Template (continued)

SoA Ref	Category/Sub-Category/Element	Statement of Applicability	Control Summary
	Submissibility	Applicable to ABC Inc.	
Business Continuity (BC) and Disaster Recovery (DR) Management			
	Information Security Aspects of Business Continuity Management		
	BC/DR management process	Applicable to ABC Inc.	
	Threat assessment	Applicable to ABC Inc.	
	Risk assessment	Applicable to ABC Inc.	
	BC/DR plan	Applicable to ABC Inc.	
	BC/DR maintenance	Applicable to ABC Inc.	
Compliance Management			
	External Compliance Requirements		
	Legislation, regulation, codes, and standards	Applicable to ABC Inc.	
	Record retention	Applicable to ABC Inc.	
	Privacy management	Applicable to ABC Inc.	
	Data protection	Applicable to ABC Inc.	
Internal Compliance Requirements			
	Security policies, standards, and procedures	Applicable to ABC Inc.	
	Security controls	Applicable to ABC Inc.	

(continued)

Table B.1 Statement of Applicability Template (continued)

SoA Ref	Category/Sub-Category/Element	Statement of Applicability	Control Summary
	Audit Management		
	Security control audits	Applicable to ABC Inc.	All security devices are to create log entries that provide the ability to audit usage.
	Security audit tools	Applicable to ABC Inc.	Ibid.

Appendix C: PDCA Guideline Documents—Outlines

The documents *ISMS — [Plan, Do, Check, and Act] Phase Guidelines* have generally the same outline and flow from one organization to another. However, the contents are specifically relevant to the organization, the scope of the ISMS, and organizational objectives for the ISMS overall, whether organization interest is in just good security practices (still laudable) or in ISO 27001 certification. To assist with capturing organizational intent for ISMS and execution of ISMS planning, implementation, review, maintenance, and continual improvement, the following sections provide notional outlines for guideline documents in support of the PDCA process.

C.1 ISMS—Plan Phase Guidelines: Document Outline

The document *ISMS — Plan Phase Guidelines* is organization specific and provides direction for the organization to plan the plan phase. This document captures the details of what the organization perceives to be relevant to the plan phase, what the objectives are for the plan phase, and how to accomplish those objectives. The outline below provides a notional table of contents for the plan phase guidelines.

> **CONTENTS**
> **Introduction**
> > Establishing the ISMS

Scope and Boundaries
Organization
    Background
    Location(s)
Information and Information Technology
    Information
    Information Technology
ISMS Policy Statement
    Objectives
    Principles, Constraints, and Assumptions
Compliance Requirements
    Legislative
    Regulatory
    Other
Risk Management Overview
    Risk Management Objectives
    Risk Management Guidelines
        Ignoring Risk
        Risk Acceptance
        Risk Sharing
        Risk Transfer
        Risk Mitigation
    Risk Assessment Guidelines
        Business Function Space
        Asset Space
        Threat Space
        Vulnerability Management
Security Controls
    Security Control Objectives
    Security Management Framework
Management Approval Guidelines
Statement of Applicability Guidelines

C.2 ISMS—Do Phase Guidelines: Document Outline

The document *ISMS — Do Phase Guidelines* is organization specific and provides direction for the organization to plan the do phase. This document captures the details of what the organization perceives to be relevant to the do phase, what the objectives are for the do phase, and how to accomplish those objectives. The outline below provides a notional table of contents for the do phase guidelines.

    CONTENTS
    Introduction
        Implement and Operate the ISMS

Risk Treatment Plan Guidelines
    Management Action Guidelines
    Risk Management Responsibilities
    Risk Management Priorities
    Risk Management Budget
    Security Controls Implementation Guidelines
    Security Controls Metrics and Measures
Awareness, Training, and Education
    Awareness
    Training
    Education
ISMS Management Plan
    ISMS Operations Plan
Defensive Safeguards
    Monitoring
    Detection Safeguards
    Response Safeguards
    Business Continuity
    Disaster Recovery

C.3 ISMS—Check Phase Guidelines: Document Outline

The document *ISMS — Check Phase Guidelines* is organization specific and provides direction for the organization to plan the check phase. This document captures the details of what the organization perceives to be relevant to the check phase, what the objectives are for the check phase, and how to accomplish those objectives. The outline below provides a notional table of contents for the check phase guidelines.

CONTENTS
Introduction
    Monitor and Review ISMS
Monitor and Review Procedures
    Monitor
    Review
ISMS Effectiveness Assessment
    Metrics
    Measures
    ISMS Assessment Process
        Discovery
        Analysis
        Reporting
        Tracking
        Organizational Feedback

ISMS Internal Audit Process
Discovery
Analysis
Reporting
Tracking
Organizational Feedback

C.4 ISMS—Act Phase Guidelines: Document Outline

The document *ISMS — Act Phase Guidelines* is organization specific and provides direction for the organization to plan the act phase. This document captures the details of what the organization perceives to be relevant to the act phase, what the objectives are for the act phase, and how to accomplish those objectives. The outline below provides a notional table of contents for the act phase guidelines.

CONTENTS

Introduction

Maintain and Improve the ISMS

Management Assessment

Cross-Function Assessment

Prioritization Guidelines

ISMS Improvement Implementation Guidelines

Standard WBS

Budget

Earned Value Tracking

Deliverables and Milestones

Deliverables

Milestones

Verification and Validation Plan

Organizational Outreach Program

Expectation Management

Objectives

Agenda

Schedule

Risk

Mitigation Plan

Appendix D: Policy, Standard, and Procedure Sample Templates

Each of the templates contains instances of *zzz* or text between the symbols < >. These denote areas to fill in details specific to the organization.

D.1 Sample Policy Template

Policy   <Name>

Policy Header

	Details
Submitted by	Company X Department Y [group, member] zzz
Approved by	Security working group
Regions	*Note:* Use if there is the likelihood of policy applying to a subset of regions versus a single region or the entire enterprise.
Policy scope	[Enterprise, region, division, site]
Policy number	Zzz-ENT-SEC-AA001. *Note:* The AA provides for a security policy categorization and the ### a number within that categorization; security policy categorization may be physical, personnel, information, information technology, organizational, etc.
Policy type	*Note:* Use if Company X desires to define a series of policy types.
Effective date	DD-Month-CCYY	**Version**	1.0

Policy Statement

Zzz insert policy statement.

Purpose

This policy addresses zzz for all Company X personnel [who zzz].

Scope/Applicability

This policy addresses the Company X [enterprise, region, division, site] level and applies to all [employees, contractors, visitors, etc.].

Level of Compliance

All persons covered by the scope and applicability are expected to [adhere as closely as possible, 100%, maintain the spirit, etc.] of this policy.

Special Circumstances and Exceptions

Where it is impractical to zzz, Company X personnel must zzz and use common sense to prevent zzz.

Definitions, Key Terms, and Acronyms

Term	Definition

Roles and Responsibilities

Roles and responsibilities in security policy development include the details in the following table:

Role	Description	Details
Sponsors	Those providing the financial backing and corporate clout	
Initiators	The point of accountability who starts the process	
Developers	The researchers and writers	
Submitters	The formal provider to reviewers; may be the same as initiator	
Reviewers	Peer or management team to validate content	
Approvers	Formal set of approvers; often take recommendation of reviewers	
Implementers	Apply policy to business operations, technical infrastructure, and solutions	

Roles and responsibilities in policy implementation, monitoring, and enforcement include the details in the following table:

Role	Description	Details
Business management		
Technical management		
Data security		
Risk management		
Systems operations		
Application development		
Network engineering		
Systems administration		
Internal audit		
Legal		
Human resources		

Supporting Documentation

Document	Source	Applicability

Precedence

Zzz insert any precedence for this policy. Precedence may include organization experience either direct or vicarious that supports the development, implementation, monitoring, and enforcement of the policy.

Sanction Guidelines

See zzz sanction policy for guidelines for reporting and escalation of policy violations.

Review Record

		Reviewed by	
Ver	*Date*	*Name*	*Title*

Approval Record

		Approved by	
Ver	Date	Name	Title

Revision Record

Ver	Name	Date	Revision Description

References

ISO 27002
ISO 27001

Resources

<List support resources if applicable.>

Supporting Procedures, Guidelines, and Standards

Type[1]	Description	Hotlink

[1]*P = procedure; G = guideline; S = standard.*

D.2 Sample Standard Template

Security Standard   <Name>

Standard Header

	Details
Submitted by	Company X Department Y [group, member] zzz
Approved by	Security working group

	Details		
Standard scope	[Enterprise, region, division, site]		
Effective date	DD-Month-CCYY	**Version**	1.0
Comments	TBD		

Purpose

This standard addresses zzz for all Company X [personnel, division, sites] [who, that] zzz.

Standard

The following standard(s) apply in context of supporting Company X Security Policy ZZZ:

■ TBD

Special Circumstances and Exceptions

Where it is impractical to zzz, Company X personnel must zzz and use common sense to prevent zzz. Exceptions to this standard are truly exceptions and must be in the interest of:

■ Company X mission statement
■ Company X financial viability
■ Personnel and public safety
■ Operational continuity
■ Public perception

Regions, divisions, and sites are expected to adhere to the enterprise standard where possible and migrate toward the enterprise standard during technology refreshing when possible. Adhering to these standards promotes centralized support capability (i.e., help desk), leveraging of enterprise purchasing agreements, and other economies of scale that promote optimal operations.

Supporting Documentation

Document	Source	Applicability

Review Record

		Reviewed by	
Ver	Date	Name	Title

Approval Record

		Approved by	
Ver	Date	Name	Title

Revision Record

Ver	Name	Date	Revision Description

References

ISO 27002
ISO 27001

Resources

<List vendor/product website or other support resources.>

D.3 Sample Procedure Template

Security Procedure <Name>
Procedure Header

	Details	
Submitted by	Company X Department Y [group, member] zzz	
Approved by	Security working group	
Standard scope	[Enterprise, region, division, site]	
Effective date	DD-Month-CCYY	**Version**	1.0
Comments	TBD	

Purpose

This procedure addresses zzz for all Company X personnel who perform the following business functions or tasks:

■ zzz

Procedure

The <role> is accountable for zzz using the following procedure:

1. Step 1
2. Step 2

Special Circumstances and Exceptions

Where it is impractical to zzz, Company X personnel must zzz and use common sense to prevent zzz. Exceptions to procedure are truly exceptions and must be in the interest of:

■ Company X mission statement
■ Company X financial viability
■ Personnel and public safety
■ Operational continuity
■ Public perception

Supporting Documentation

Document	Source	Applicability

Review Record

Ver	Date	Reviewed by	
		Name	Title

Approval Record

Ver	Date	Approved by	
		Name	Title

Revision Record

Ver	Name	Date	Revision Description

References

ISO 27002
ISO 27001

Resources

<List vendor/product website or other support resources.>

Appendix E: ISMS Policy and Risk Treatment Templates

The templates herein are notional and will vary according to the needs of the organization. The website references are fictitious and represent a useful construct to establish the organization's intranet site. Each of the templates contains instances of *zzz* or text between the symbols < >. These denote areas to fill in details specific to the organization.

E.1 ISMS Policy Template

ISMS Policy for Widgets, Inc.

Policy Header		
	Details	
Submitted by	Widgets, Inc. security working group (SWG)	
Approved by	Widgets, Inc. management review board	
Regions	This policy is applicable at the enterprise level and is relevant to all regional practices within Widgets, Inc.	
Policy scope	Enterprise	
Policy number	ENT-SEC-A001	
Effective date	01-January-2007	**Version**	1.0

Policy Statement

The business objective of this policy is to minimize risks to Widgets, Inc. key business functions. Key business functions define the purpose of Widget, Inc. and carry out those activities that fulfill stakeholder interests in Widgets, Inc. This security policy addresses personnel, information, information technology, and infrastructure that support the successful execution of these key business functions. The Management Review Board (www.widgetsincintranet.com/isms/documents/mrb.doc) approves this policy.

ISMS policy requires the creation of the following in support of the purpose and objectives of this policy:

■ Security management framework (SMF)
■ Definition of business drivers behind security initiatives
■ Use of the SMF to establish planning, implementation, maintenance, review, and revision objectives to minimize organizational risk in terms of confidentiality, integrity, and availability
■ Establishment of criteria with which to measure risk
■ Institution of a comprehensive compliance management program that, at the least:
  • Enumerates all applicable compliance requirements, including but not limited to:
    ○ Legislation
    ○ Regulation
    ○ Contractual obligations
■ Establishment of criteria with which to measure compliance levels
■ Provision of a formal procedure to obtain management review and approval of all information security initiatives

Note: These high-level statements describe the ISMS policy, which advocates the formal management of information security. There are many supporting policies that break down the details of the information security management program. These supporting policies will include but are not limited to:

■ Business continuity
■ Security awareness, training, and education
■ Incident reporting and response
■ Information security control effectiveness metrics and measures

Purpose

This policy addresses the need for all Widgets, Inc. personnel to ensure the confidentiality, integrity, and availability of key business functions that support the very reason Widgets, Inc. exists. Moreover, it minimizes risks to key personnel, information, information technology, and infrastructure that support these key business functions. To this effect, this policy addresses the need for both information security and a management system for information security. The former covers the business drivers behind the need for information security and establishes the framework to develop additional security policies, standards, procedures, and practices. The latter addresses how to formally manage information security within Widgets, Inc.

Scope/Applicability

This policy addresses the Widgets, Inc. enterprise level and applies to all employees.

Level of Compliance

All persons covered by the scope and applicability are expected to adhere to 100% of this policy.

Special Circumstances and Exceptions

Where it is impractical to adhere to this policy, Widgets, Inc. personnel must submit written descriptions of circumstances needing exception. Management review will determine the appropriateness of exception. Management does not anticipate exceptions to this policy.

Definitions, Key Terms, and Acronyms	
Term	*Definition*
SMF	A security management framework provides an outline that covers all security needs of Widgets, Inc. The basis for this outline is in ISO 27001 and ISO 27002, with supplements from National Institute of Standards and Technology (NIST) and Control Objectives for Information and Related Technology (COBIT) as necessary.
Etc.	

Roles and Responsibilities

Roles and responsibilities in security policy development include:

Role	Description	Details
Sponsors	Those providing the financial backing and corporate clout	TBD
Initiators	The point of accountability who starts the process	
Developers	The researchers and writers	
Submitters	The formal provider to reviewers; may be the same as initiator	
Reviewers	Peer or management team to validate content	
Approvers	Formal set of approvers; often take recommendation of reviewers	
Implementers	Apply policy to business operations, technical infrastructure, and solutions	

Roles and responsibilities in policy implementation, monitoring, and enforcement include:

Role	Description	
Business management	TBD	TBD
Technical management		
Data security		
Risk management		
Systems operations		
Application development		
Network engineering		
Systems administration		
Internal audit		
Legal		
Human resources		

Supporting Documentation

The table below provides supporting documents for the development of the ISMS policy.

Document	Source	Applicability
ISO 27001	ISO	Provides the ISMS framework
ISO 27002	ISO	Provides the security controls framework
Xyz legislation	TBD	<Provide description>
Etc.		

Sanction Guidelines

See sanction policy (www.widgetsincintranet.com/isms/documents/ SanctionPolicy.doc) and sanction guidance (www.widgetsincintranet. com/isms/documents/SanctionGuide.doc) for guidelines for reporting and escalation of policy violations.

Review Record			
		Reviewed by	
Ver	Date	Name	Title
1.0	28-Dec-2006	TBD	Chief information officer (CIO)
		Etc.	

Approval Record			
		Approved by	
Ver	Date	Name	Title
1.0	28-Dec-2006	Management review board	

Revision Record			
Ver	Name	Date	Revision Description
1.0	TBD	27-Dec-2006	Initial policy

References

ISO 27002
ISO 27001

Resources

N/A

Supporting Procedures, Guidelines, and Standards		
Type[1]	*Description*	*Hotlink*
TBD		

[1]*P = procedure; G = guideline; S = standard.*

E.2 Risk Treatment Template

Risk Treatment Plan for Company X

Statement of Applicability

Note: May be a separate document; if so, reference the document rather than copy it. A single occurrence is difficult enough to maintain; multiple occurrences are manually intensive and confusing.

Note that some of the table entries are intentionally left blank as part of the template.

Table zzz Statement of Applicability (Excerpt Only)

Category/Subcategory/ Element	Requirement	Statement of Applicability
Security Policy		
Information and Information Technology Security Policy		Fill in details explaining how the organization will address this control. The answer may be to accept the risk with an explanation/rationale as to why.

Table zzz Statement of Applicability (Excerpt Only) *(Continued)*		
Category/Subcategory/ Element	*Requirement*	*Statement of Applicability*
Documentation	Management produces an overarching security policy that includes control of information security and clear implementation guidance.	
Dissemination	Disseminate policy into enterprise initiatives for security awareness.	
Security Management Plan		
Intra-Organization Management		
Executive and management backing	Executives are accountable to stakeholders; fiduciary duties, and should be involved in risk management. Management identifies business risk drivers behind security, then implements and provides oversight to information security functions within the organization.	
Etc.		

Appendix F: Project Definition Template

The project definition template provides the ability to capture and present details surrounding the planning, execution, and delivery of the project. Explicitly defining the objectives, scope, assumptions, deliverables, roles and responsibilities, and success criteria promotes the managing of expectations and scope creep. Every project encounters the opportunity to perform more than officially defined within the contract. Adding value with additional services is not bad and is actually good business practice. However, performing additional services such that core deliverables and milestones are not met is not good. The clear articulation of expectations within a formal project definition document ensures everyone is on the same page with regard to what is going to be done and what constitutes completion and successful delivery.

The project definition is not necessarily a replacement for a contract, statement of work, or request for proposal (RFP) response. The project definition is more often supplemental to these documents. Even in the presence of an overriding document like an official contract, the project definition adds clarity to the task at hand and often refines vague contractual terms into actionable items. The template below is notional and the specifics will vary according to organizational need and project details.

\<Project Name\>   **\<Date\>**

Project Definition [Template] for \<Project Name\>

Statement of Project Intent

This document summarizes the tasks, scope, roles, responsibilities, deliverables, and milestones for \<project name\>.

Table F.1   Project Definition Acceptance

Document Acceptance
Approver: <Name>
Title: <Title>
Date: <DD-Month-CCYY>
Signature: <Signature>

Change History Log

Table F.2   Change History

Project Definition Version No.	Release Date	Description
1	DD-Month-CCYY	
.		

Table of Contents

<TOC>

Objectives

State objectives in concise language that conveys deliverables, services, or other results that this project will produce; may be in narrative format or bullet points.

Scope

State the scope in terms of:

■ Deliverable, service, or other result
■ A description of each
■ Who is responsible
■ Criteria on which to judge the successful completion

Assumptions

Clearly state the assumptions with regard to the objectives and scope. This language clarifies the intent of the activity provider to the activity sponsor. Use the following categories to specify assumptions:

■ Business functions
■ Business lines

- Information
- Information technology
- Infrastructure
- Performance
- General
- Accommodations

Business functions defines the functions or functional areas that are in scope. Elaborate on details of the assumptions with regard to these functional areas.

Business lines defines the groups within the organization that are in scope and any assumptions surrounding these groups.

Information provides assumptions around the scope of data, information, knowledge, intellectual property, etc., relevant to the project at hand. There may be a need to clarify who owns the results of the activity.

Information technology provides assumptions around the information technology that is in scope. This includes PCs, servers, mainframes, mobile devices, phone system, etc.

Infrastructure covers anything not covered under information technology with regard to network infrastructure, buildings, and other physical attributes that enable the presence and operation of information technology or business functions. *Note:* An appendix of in-scope locations may be appropriate to ensure all understand the basis of travel requirements and costs.

Performance defines metrics and measures that define successful completion. At the least, this section should specify deliverables and assumptions with regard to producing and conveying those deliverables to the sponsor. This may include report types, formats, and who should receive copies of materials (e.g., CDs, paper copies, etc.).

General assumptions capture anything not captured in other topic areas.

Accommodations includes any on-site equipment necessary for the successful completion of the activities or any facilities necessary. The assessor may assume access to the Internet while on-site; this requires a network drop and access to the public network. The assessor may need office space, cube space, or no space.

The format of the assumption statements follows this outline:

- In scope:
  - <Bullets defining in-scope assumptions>
- Out of scope:
  - <Bullets defining out-of-scope assumptions>

For example:

Business Functions

- In scope:
  - Security operations center located at <address>
- Out of scope:
  - This does not include the network operations center at the same location.
  - Any business function not explicitly listed as in scope is out of scope.

Note the general out-of-scope statement that captures all remaining business functions. This is similar to the standard firewall rule of "anything not explicitly permitted is denied." Such should be the final out-of-scope statement for each category.

General Assumptions

- ABC, Inc. will provide access to in-scope sites, information technology, and other areas in the previous in-scope statements.
- ABC, Inc. personnel will cooperate and provide the discovery data in a timely manner.
  - Enumerate parameters in a timely manner (e.g., within X work days of initial request).

Project Team

Table F.3 Project Team

Organization	Role	Team Member	Contact Information	Comments
	Project manager	<Name>	<E-mail/phone #>	
	Security engineer			
	Compliance management officer			
	Etc.			

Project Plan Outline

Provide a bullet list of project plan phases and action items. This is not the project plan, but rather a description of the project plan, so the detail can be high level. However, this document defines the project and requires formal sign-off; therefore, be accurate, as any variations may require a formal project change, which adds to schedule and cost. A generic project outline includes the following:

- Project initiation:
  - Select project manager
  - Identify roles and responsibilities
  - Select team players
- Discovery:
  - Pre-site visit
  - Site visit
  - Post-site visit
- Analysis:
  - <List activities and milestones>
- Report generation:
  - <List reports>; these will be deliverables
- Report dissemination:
  - Define communications protocol
  - Deliver
- Project wrap-up:
  - Obtain sign-off

Each of the above project plan details may be converted to a tabular format in terms of an action item list:

Table F.4   Action Items

Who	Deliverable/Milestone	Action	Description

Risks

The table below presents potential risks to the project and solution deliverable; probable impacts are in terms of low, medium, and high.

Table F.5   Risks and Mitigation

Risk	Effects	Impact	Mitigation

Project Milestones

Provide a description of project milestones that may include:

- Project definition delivery
- Project definition sign-off
- Project plan review
- Project plan baseline

Useful Bits of Knowledge*

Useful bits of knowledge (UBOKs) convey pithy details regarding the subject at hand. Some are in the form of questions and answers, and others just provide an insight that the reader may find useful. The following are some information security management and management system (ISMS) UBOKs to help understand information security, information security management, and the ISMS.

1. Can all types of organizations benefit from implement in an ISMS?

   No, insofar as all organizations are compelled to do so by some external authority. Yes, from the perspective of ISMS being an effect tool for managing business risk. Legislative and regulatory compliance requirements increasingly address the need for effective security programs to protect customer interests (e.g., privacy) and stakeholder interests (e.g., investors). Moreover, there is a fiduciary responsibility (due diligence) on the part of the corporate officers to maintain a level of performance that requires a sound business risk management program, part of which is an ISMS. Traditionally, organizational value was in hard assets (e.g., land, buildings, equipment), and transactions required transfer of currency or another tangible payment medium (e.g., gold). Security focus on these tangible assets was more on physical security in the form of guards, vaults, window bars, and alarm systems. Today, corporate assets include information in the form of intellectual property (e.g., strategic plans, financial details, engineering plans, etc.), and transaction payments are reducing numbers on a page here and increasing numbers on a page there, often via transfer

---

* Frequently asked questions (FAQs) imply some effort toward actually capturing questions from users or customers; these facts are not FAQs, but rather UBOKs, which are answers to anticipated questions.

of bits on a wire. Asset protection and financial protection requirements are well beyond the mere physical focus and require increased awareness on the part of all personnel, and protection of the technical infrastructure as well as the technical systems housing assets and facilitating transactions.

2. Are the organizations required to implement the ISMS in its entirety (refer to ISO 27001, clauses 4 to 8) prior to the stage 1 audit (desktop review)?

No. However, the use of ISO security standards provides a solid foundation for building an organizational security program that promotes comprehensiveness and consistency as well as removes the arbitrariness from a purely homegrown framework. Moreover, use of these standards provides the ability to apply for and achieve certification. Such a distinction may be competitive (i.e., we protect customer interests better than our competition) and useful in the event of litigation. The goal of a good security program is to avoid litigation in the first place; however, in the event an incident ends before a judge, documentation with regard to ISO security standard compliance will assist in reducing organizational culpability.

3. Should a stage 1 audit be on site given the large number of documents to review?

No. At least not necessarily. The auditor will request access to the documentation, which the organization can post securely or provide a hard copy to the auditor. Mark all ISMS documentation as confidential and proprietary according to direction from the organization's legal department.

4. Should the organization provide documentation supporting an audit in electronic format?

Yes. It is easier for the auditor to work with, but remember that these documents are confidential. Consider delivering in a format that may not be copied or altered, but still is searchable for key points to assist in expediting the audit. Such a format may be PDF that includes password protection and copy restrictions.

5. What will the auditors look for in the stage 3 audit?

Audit stage 3 is an on-site audit. The auditor compares written policy, standards, and procedure to actual practice. The auditor will review the appropriate documentation and request to validate the practices either hands-on or via shoulder surfing authorized personnel.

6. Does the auditor need to check whether the controls are configured and implemented correctly?

Yes. This is one of the key elements of the audit, to look for differences between documentation and practice.

7. Will the auditors visit the site together with their technical specialists?

Likely. Validating practice is a detailed and time-consuming process, so usually a team works through the audit under a lead auditor.

8. What is the ISMS going to protect? Should the policies focus on the protection of information or information technology?

The ISMS is in place to protect both information and information technology relevant to the organization. Both information and information technology are assets to the organization. One of the first steps is to categorize the information assets to find out what is important and what is not.

9. What impact can it have on your organization if the information is compromised?

When writing a policy you are protecting assets that can be information (processed data with value), paper documents (contracts, certificates), physical assets (hardware, property, equipment), software (systems, applications), services (electricity, telecoms, water), people (staff, customers), the organization's brand, image, and reputation (information held in the minds of stakeholders), public (potential customers or contractors), and others. The standards will give you information on what should be included in the policies.

10. In an organization with many sites, can I have the scope for one site and get certified?

Yes. It is possible, but not common, and not easy, as you have to describe all the connectivity to the other sites. That can be more work than to include some of the other sites.

11. Can a consultant help with implementation and then do the audit?

No. That is a conflict of interest. If you audit an organization, you may not have been part of implementation or consulting.

12. Can an external auditor give advice on implementation when he or she is auditing an organization?

No. If the external lead auditor advises on an implementation strategy, the external organization has conducted actions that are in conflict with governance guidelines.

13. How easy is it to implement an ISMS?

Depending on the current security posture of the organization, it will take some time to implement an ISMS; however, you only have to implement the controls you need. Implementing an acceptable ISMS to the organization is different than implementing an ISMS with the intent of achieving ISO 27001 certification; the preparation for the latter will take longer.

14. If the organization has already implemented ISO 9001,[19] can ISO 27001[1] and an ISMS be integrated into the existing quality system?

Yes. Both of these standards are management standards and use the same model (PDCA) for implementation. The organization may choose to implement the ISMS independently or to develop an integrated management system.

15. What is a certification body?

    An accredited certification body is a third-party organization that assesses/certifies the ISMS against the standard. That is, the certification body (third-party organization) has the right to audit and recommend certification according to the specific standard.

16. Who are the accredited certification bodies for the standard?

    There are a growing number, as the standard is gaining momentum and acceptance as an ISO standard. However, the following are just a few: BS 7799: BSI, Certification Europe, DNV, JACO IS, KEMA, KPMG, SFS-Sertifiointi Oy, SGS, STQC, SAI Global Limited, UIMCert GmbH.

17. How does this standard fit with the ISO 9001?

    ISO is harmonizing ISO 27001 with other management standards, including ISO 9001 and ISO 14001.

18. Who originally wrote the security standard?

    There is no straightforward answer to this question. The "History of ISO Information Security Standards" in Chapter 1 contains some details.

19. What is ISO/IEC Guide 62?

    This is largely for those bodies operating certification schemes and contains general requirements applicable to them.

20. What is the difference between accreditation and certification?

    Essentially, an accreditation body is an organization (usually national) that grants third parties the authority to issue certificates (the ability to certify). An accredited organization issues certificates (certifies) against standards, etc. The former confers the right to do this on the certification company. Therefore, you would need a firm that has been accredited by an appropriate body to get a certificate.

21. What does ISO 19011:2002, *Guideline on Quality and/or Environmental Management System Audit*,[16] have to do with ISO 27001?[1]

    This is a guideline for an accredited assessment schema based on common international standards for the accreditation of a body operating a certification/registration quality or environmental and information security. It is largely for those bodies operating within a certification schema.

22. Where can I get a copy of the standards?

    You can get them from www.iso.org, other organizations, and most national institutes of standards in individual countries.

23. What is the difference between old and new standards?

    The difference between BS 7799 and ISO 27001 is the changes to the structure of the controls. Some BS 7799 controls have been deleted, some have been moved, and some have been integrated with other controls.

24. What is ISO 27001?

    ISO 27001 is the name of an international standard that was BS 7799 and has the full name ISO/IEC 27001, *Information Technology — Security*

Techniques — Information Security Management System — Requirements.
This standard in short describes the requirements for implementing an
ISMS.

25. What is ISO 27002?

    ISO 27002 is the new name for the ISO 17799^2 standard.

26. What is SC27?

    This is the abbreviation for Subcommittee 27 (SC27), which is part of the
    joint technical committee (JTC1) set up by ISO and IEC. SC27 Working
    Group 1 (WG1) focuses on security management standards, including new
    developments of standards in information security and the development of
    ISMS standards.

27. Can NIST standards be used to implement ISMS?

    Yes. There are many special publications from NIST (www.nist.gov) that cover
    computer security and information security management. No single stan-
    dard covers everything, mainly because organizational needs vary so much.
    Select a single standard as a basis for an ISMS; supplement the details with
    other standards as organizational need governs.

28. How long does it take to implement an ISMS?

    It depends on the size and status of information security in the organization.
    The first challenge is to find a strategy and starting point; this book pro-
    vides that. Implementation can be from as short as a few months up to
    years, depending on the size of the organization and resources available
    (i.e., personnel and budget). An important point, though, is that security
    is a process, not a destination. Therefore, there is the goal of achieving
    an acceptable level of compliance and the ongoing effort to maintain an
    acceptable level of compliance.

29. Is it possible to calculate return on investment (ROI) on an ISMS?

    There is still a shortage of long-term information on operating an ISMS to
    calculate the ROI; however, some information and calculations are avail-
    able. A good source for information is the Computer Security Institute's
    CSI/FBI annual computer and crime survey at www.gocsi.com. An Inter-
    net search on security and ROI or return on security investment (ROSI)
    will yield a wide variety of approaches and methods.

30. How can you see that the ISMS is working?

    By using metrics to measure the effectiveness of the ISMS operation. There
    is the pending standard ISO 27004, *Metric and Measurements*, that will
    provide guidance in tracking performance. Also, this text provides some
    information on how to implement metrics.

31. Is implementing an ISMS too much for smaller organizations?

    The general rule is the cost of protecting an asset should not be greater
    than the value of the asset. A multi-million-dollar security initiative is
    appropriate for a multi-billion-dollar company, but not necessarily for
    the eight-person small business serving the local community. However,

even the small business needs to protect its assets. Therefore, go through the steps of business justification for ISMS certification. If local needs and local budget support less than a comprehensive ISMS according to ISO standards, select what is appropriate and use the ISO standards as guidance.

32. Is it important that an organization obtain certification?

The certification is the assurance that the organization has actually implemented an ISMS. The value of the certification is in the eye of the beholder. The organization may use certification in a marketing strategy, as a competitive advantage, or to create internal compliance requirements in the name of due diligence. A certified ISMS may assist in litigation management to show a judge that indeed the organization takes risk management.

33. Is it a good idea to include security requirements in all contracts?

Yes. Such a provision in a litigious world of fuzzy liabilities is prudent. Include such provisions in new contracts, and consider addendums to existing contracts if necessary. Seek legal advice for appropriate wording and processing.

Glossary

Information security requires a lexicon and phraseology to convey the complexities and nuances of the discipline. Many information security terms are misused due to a lack of understanding or because the meanings of the terms are different in different contexts. This text uses the terms and phrases as defined below.

Term	Definition
Asset	Something that has value to the organization, e.g., information, information technology, facilities, intellectual property, key customers, etc. The organization may own an asset, the obvious perspective of asset. Also, consider providers of significant revenue as external assets and treat them accordingly.
Asset categorization and criticality	The process of assessing the asset space, including enumeration of contents and relative importance to the organization.
Availability	The information or information technology is ready for use upon demand.
Business continuity management (BCM)	A process that provides for ongoing operations in the event of an incident with the potential to interrupt operations.
Business functions	A generic term referring to an activity performed with the aggregation of personnel, information, information technology, and supporting infrastructure; business function examples include accounting, sales, project management, and service delivery (e.g., actual performance of an outsourcing service like managed firewalls).

Term	Definition
Calculating business impact	The process to determine the effect on business operations and strategic viability from an incident. May express business impact in mathematical terms as Threat × Vulnerability = Impact.
Calculating risk	The process of determining potential effect on business from potential threats: Probability × Impact = Risk. This numerical value can help to prioritize risk mitigation.
Compliance	The act of complying with or adhering to applicable guidelines for appropriate business practice. Compliance requirements consist of regulatory and legal requirements as well as standards applicable to the organization, e.g., ISO 27001.
Confidentiality	Information is not disclosed to unauthorized personnel or automated entity.
Controls	The business and mechanistic safeguards to implement security policy with the general objective of preserving confidentiality, integrity, and availability.
Determining probability	The process of calculating the likelihood of a particular action occurring. For every vulnerability there is a probability of a threat occurring and for that threat exploiting that vulnerability.
Entity	A person or thing, where "thing" may include a device (PC, router, printer) or software (operating system, application, utility, background process).
Guidelines	A supplemental document to policy or standards that offers suggestions and recommendations on interpretation of threats, vulnerabilities, implementing safeguards, monitoring, responding, etc.
Information security management system	The International Standards Organization (ISO) defines ISMS to be "that part of an overall management system based on a business risk approach to establish, implement, operate, monitor, maintain, and improve information security."
Information security policy	A series of documents that express business perspective behind security. This may cover many of the key elements of the ISO 27002 standard.
Information security procedures	A series of documents expressing how to implement policy. Usually takes the form of a set of steps and instructions.
Information security standards	A series of documents that express recommendations on what to use to implement security policy.

Term	Definition
Integrity	Information remains unaltered from the creator's or owner's intended state.
ISMS policy	A specific policy advocating the need for an information security management system.
Key business functions	A key business function is one that represents the very reason for the existence of the organization. For example, a mortgage company provides loans; this is what it sells, how it generates revenue, and why it exists. Customers come to the mortgage company to obtain loans and pay a fee for loan processing. If 90 percent of the mortgage company's business is from its e-commerce site, that e-commerce site is a key business function.
Policy	A formal expression of appropriate business operations. Policies are supported by procedures and standards.
Residual risk	The portion of a risk remaining after implementing risk mitigation and arranging for appropriate risk sharing or transference. A 100 percent elimination of risk is not realistic; the goal is to optimize residual risk with investments in risk mitigation and sharing/transference.
Risk	The likelihood that a given threat will exploit a vulnerability, resulting in loss or damage of organization assets.
Risk acceptance	Decision to recognize threat and potential organizational vulnerability to that threat and do nothing about it based on degree of risk and return on investment (ROI) of any corrective or other action.
Risk analysis	Systematic analysis of organizational asset space, threat space to the organization, organizational business functions, and personnel to determine key aspects, potential loss of key aspects, and organization impact of loss.
Risk assessment	A process to determine organizational risk.
Risk ignoring	Decision not to address risk at all. This is significantly different from accepting risk as conscious: Risk acceptance is understanding that risk and potential impact to the organization. Ignoring risk is recognizing that the risk exists, but not understanding the risk well enough to make an intelligent choice to accept. The risk is ignored, not dealt with.

(continued)

Term	Definition
Risk management	The process of addressing organizational risk. Risk acceptance, sharing, transference, and mitigation are all part of risk management.
Risk mitigation	Reducing organizational risk by introducing safeguards, e.g., adding firewalls or intrusion detection, training employees on risk awareness, and many other options.
Risk sharing	Decision to reduce organizational risk by engaging another party to take on part of that risk, e.g., purchasing e-risk insurance to pick up costs of recovering from a security incident.
Risk transfer	Decision to reduce organizational risk by engaging another party to take on all of that risk, e.g., outsourcing operations and transferring risks associated with those operations to the outsourcer.
Security governance	The group or act of determining business risk and business drivers behind security; security governance produces policy that guides organizational behavior.
Security management framework	SMF; the authors' term for an outline that is organizational specific; finds foundation in an industry security standard (e.g., ISO 27002) and modifies this foundation to reflect relevant security compliance requirements.
Security management program	SMP; the authors' term for an overall effort to define and plan for the safeguard of information that includes personnel, organization, technology, and business processes and functions. The SMP is a document that defines the goals and practices of security, essentially the same as an ISMS.
Statement of applicability	SoA; ISO term for the document describing security controls and security control objectives relevant to the organization.
Threat	An entity or event that can inflict harm intentionally or unintentionally to organizational assets; entity may be a person, device, or other thing, and event may be natural, accidental, or one of intent.

Term	Definition
Threat identification (valuation)	The owner and others have been nominated to take part in analyzing threats. These threats are identified because they can affect specific assets and exploit or take advantage of the assets' vulnerabilities and create risks. All threats found with each assessment must be identified, and there are often several to assess. Be realistic when evaluating threats and only list threats that have a significant probability or are considered to have extreme impact. Threats can be from natural disaster, human error, or shortage of staff. Threats can be the result of a failure in technology. Furthermore, you have to calculate how often a threat can take place to still be considered acceptable.
Vulnerability	A flaw or weakness. A vulnerability may be organizational, procedural, systemic, or personnel.
Vulnerability identification	The process of discovering a flaw or weakness.

References

1. ISO/IEC 27001. *Information Technology—Security Techniques—Information Security Management Systems—Requirements*, first edition. October 15, 2005. Available from www.iso.org.
2. ISO/IEC 17799. *Information Technology—Security Techniques—Code of Practice for Information Security Management*, second edition. June 15, 2005. Available from www.iso.org.
3. FIPS PUB 199. *Federal Information Processing Standards Publication—Standard for Federal Information and Information Systems*. February 2004. Available from www.nist.gov.
4. Gamma. Available from http://www.gammassl.co.uk/bs7799/history.html.
5. Information gathered from ITSC Standards Technology Standard Committee. Standards news at RAISS forum. Available from http://www.itsc.org.sg/.
6. SP 800-18. *Guide for Developing Security Plans for Information Technology Systems*. Available from www.nist.gov. Guides the design and documentation of IT security controls.
7. *OECD Guidance for Security of Information System and Network—Toward a Culture of Security*. Available from www.oecd.org. Also, the new OECD guidance from 2002. Available from http://www.oecd.org/dataoecd/16/22/15582260.pdf.
8. Index of the ISO/IEC 17799, second edition. June 15, 2005. From pages III to VI.
9. Shewhart, Walter Andrew (1939). *Statistical Method for the Viewpoint of Quality Control*. New York: Dover. (1980) *Economic Control of quality of manufactured product/ 50th Anniversary Commemorative Issue*. American Society For Quality. For further information. http:en.wikipedia.org/wiki/Shewhart_cycle.
10. SP 800-60. *Guide to Mapping Types of Information Systems to Security Categories*. Available from www.nist.gov.
11. SP 800-30. *Risk Management Guide for Information Technology Systems from NIST* [National Institute of Standards and Technology]. Available from www.nist.gov.
12. ISO/IEC TR 13335-3. *Guidelines for the Management of IT Security: Techniques for the Management of IT Security from International Organization for Standardization*. Available from www.iso.org.
13. Peltier, T. (2005) *Information Security Risk Analysis*. Auerbach Publications.
14. Checklist for self-assessment for all controls for BS 7799-2:2002. Available from http://www.sans.org/score/checklists/ISO_17799_checklist.pdf. Also, self-assessment checklist from Netigy. Available from http://www.cccure.org/modules.php?name=Downloads&d_op=viewdownload&cid=67.

15. Here are some of the links to ISMS user groups: U.S. ISMS user group, http://www.us-isms.org/; international user group, http://www.xisec.com/; more information on ITU in Canada, http://www.ismsiug.ca; in Japan, www.j-isms.jp.

16. Accredited assessment schema based on common international standard—ISO 19011:2002, *Guideline on Quality and/or Environmental Management System Audit.* Available from www.iso.org.

17. Sarbanes–Oxley Act of 2002. Available from http://news.findlaw.com/hdocs/docs/gwbush/sarbanesoxley072302.pdf.

18. The URL where there is information on Base II from the European Commission: http://europa.eu.int/comm/enterprise/entrepreneurship/financing/basel_2.htm.

19. ISO 9001:2000. *Quality Management Systems.* Available from www.iso.org.

20. BS 7799-3:2006. *Guidelines for Information Security Risk Management.* Available from http://www.bsonline.bsi-global.com/server/index.jsp.

21. ISO TR 13335-4:2000 covers the selection of safeguards (meaning technical security controls). This standard is also currently under revision and will be inserted into ISO 27005. Available from www.iso.org.

22. SP 800-53A. *Guide for Assessing the Security Controls in Federal Information* (draft). Available from www.nist.gov.

23. SP 800-53. *Recommended Security Controls for Federal Information Systems.* Available from www.nist.gov. In effect another ISMS standard; contains a handy cross-reference table comparing its control coverage to that of standards such as ISO 17799:2005.

24. SP 800-55. *Security Metrics Guide for Information Technology Systems.* Available from www.nist.gov. Sounds more useful than it is (in my opinion), being little more than an enormous list of security things that could be measured.

25. FIPS 200. *Minimum Security Requirements for Federal Information and Information Systems.* Available from www.nist.gov.

26. SP 800-61. *Computer Security Incident Handling Guide.* Available from www.nist.gov.

27. SP 800-37. *Guide for the Security Certification and Accreditation of Federal Information Systems.* Available from www.nist.gov. Provides guidance on security certification, accreditation, and authorization of information systems.

28. SP800-26. *Government Audit Office Federal Information System Controls Audit Manual.* Available from www.nist.gov.

29. SP 800-37. *Guide for the Security Certification and Accreditation of Federal Information Systems.* Available from www.nist.gov. Provides guidance on security certification, accreditation, and authorization of information systems.

30. ISO 19011:2002. *Guidelines for Quality and/or Environmental Management Systems Auditing.* Available from www.nist.gov.

31. Control Objectives for Information and Related Technology (COBIT). Available from www.isaca.org.

32. Information Technology Infrastructure Library (ITIL). Available from www.itsmf.com.

Index